VISUAL QUICKSTART GUIDE

GOOGLE

AND OTHER SEARCH ENGINES

Diane Poremsky

Peachpit Press

APR 1 4   304219

Visual QuickStart Guide
Google and Other Search Engines
Diane Poremsky

Peachpit Press

1249 Eighth Street
Berkeley, CA 94710
510/524-2178
800/283-9444
510/524-2221 (fax)

Find us on the World Wide Web at: www.peachpit.com
To report errors, please send a note to errata@peachpit.com

Peachpit Press is a division of Pearson Education

Editor: Judy Ziajka
Project Editor: Becky Morgan
Production Coordinator: Myrna Vladic
Copyeditor: Judy Ziajka
Compositor: Kelli Kamel
Indexer: FireCrystal Communications
Cover design: The Visual Group
Cover production: George Mattingly / GMD

Notice of Rights

Notice of Liability

Trademarks

ISBN 0-321-24614-4

9 8 7 6 5 4 3 2

Printed and bound in the United States of America

Dedication

I'd like to dedicate this book to my husband, Phil. I love you.

Acknowledgments

Yes, Mom, the book is finally finished. Thanks, Judy, for helping to make this book the best. To Phil and Cece, thanks for all the dinners you cooked and dishes you washed when I was too busy to think about food.

Special thanks to Alfred and Emily Glossbrenner, authors of *Search Engines for the World Wide Web, 3rd Edition*, upon which this book is based.

About the Authors of the Previous Editions

The authors of over 60 books with combined sales of over one million copies, **Alfred** and **Emily Glossbrenner** have been alerting people to the power and possibilities of online information since 1982—long before Google and the World Wide Web even existed. Their uncanny knack for explaining complex subjects in a way that anyone can understand, combined with their conversational style, has earned them praise from publications as diverse as *MacWorld*, *Forbes*, and *The New York Times*. Recently, they put their search skills to work to write *How to Make Your Vacation Property Work for You!* (FireCrystal, 2004), a book/CD package designed to help vacation homeowners effectively advertise, rent, and make money from their second homes. For more information, visit www.fullybookedrentals.com.

TABLE OF CONTENTS

Part 3:   **Specialized Search Engines**

INTRODUCTION

Late in the year 2003, the Internet passed the 4 billion mark—4 billion Web pages, that is, all accessible via the World Wide Web. And with an estimated 7 million new pages being created every day, it's entirely possible that as you read this, the Net may be approaching 5, 6, or even 7 billion total pages.

So how in blazes does anyone *find* anything? That's the million-dollar question. If you're like us, the fascination of "browsing the Web"—clicking links to go aimlessly hither and yon—wore off years ago. We want to sign on, get the information we need, sign off, and go about our business and our lives.

Fortunately, some excellent tools are available on the Net to help you do just that—dozens of them, in fact. They're called *search engines*, and not surprisingly, the best of them consistently rank among the most popular sites on the Internet.

But the proliferation of search sites has created a new problem and a whole new set of questions. With so many search engines out there competing for our attention, how do we find out which are the really good ones? Does it make any difference which one we choose? Will a search for, say, `digital camera product reviews` or `Seinfeld episode guide` produce the same results whether we use AltaVista or Google or Yahoo?

How to Get the Most Out of This Book

This book will answer all of these questions and more. And like all the books in the *Visual QuickStart* series, it's designed to do so with a minimum of technical jargon and extraneous information. You'll find lots of step-by-step instructions and specific examples for using search engines in general and the very best ones in particular.

In writing the book, we've made just a few basic assumptions about you:

◆ You understand the fundamentals of working with a computer, such as how to use a mouse and how to choose menu commands.

◆ You have access to the Internet—either through an Internet service provider (ISP) like EarthLink or Comcast, or an online service like America Online (AOL), and you know how to sign onto the Net.

◆ You have some experience using a Web browser program like Microsoft Internet Explorer or Netscape Navigator to visit Web sites, and now you're ready to learn how to do more than just "surf the Net."

If you're not quite up to speed on one or more of these fronts, you may want to hold off on this book for the time being.

Instead, if you have a personal computer running Windows, check your favorite bookstore or local library for *The Little PC Book, XP Edition,* by Larry Magid. If you have a Macintosh, look for *The Little Mac Book* or *The Little iMac Book,* both by Robin Williams. Published by Peachpit Press, all three of these books include chapters specifically aimed at people who are venturing onto the Internet for the very first time.

For in-depth coverage of Internet Explorer, try Steve Schwartz's *Internet Explorer 5: Visual QuickStart Guide,* also published by Peachpit Press and available in both Windows and Macintosh versions.

Once you're comfortable using your computer and Web browser software—and you've spent some time exploring Web sites on your own—the information presented in *this* book will make a lot more sense.

How the Book Is Organized

The chapters in this book are organized into three parts, followed by three appendices. Here's what's covered in each one.

Part 1: Search Basics

In Part 1 of the book, we introduce you to the concept of search engines and how they work. You'll also learn about *keywords*—how to choose the right ones and the various methods of combining them for more effective searches. We round things out with some specific tips and techniques for using any search engine.

You should read the four chapters in this part of the book from start to finish, since each chapter builds on the information presented in the ones before. Also, you'll need this basic grounding in online searching to get the most out of the chapters on specific search engines in Parts 2 and 3.

Part 2: The Search Engines

In Part 2, you'll find chapters on the best and most powerful search engines available today. We've organized the chapters according to the popularity of the search engine, but you can read these chapters in any order. If you're somewhat familiar with one of the search engines covered here, you might start with that one and then branch out to learn about the others.

Even if you use one or more of these sites regularly, are you using the site's search features to maximum advantage? If you're not sure, read the relevant chapter in this part of the book and refer to the Quick Reference for search rules and examples.

By the time you're finished reading about a particular search engine, you'll know its strengths and weaknesses and how to use the major features to create effective queries. And whenever you need a refresher, you can consult the Quick Reference included in each chapter and in Appendix A.

Part 3: Specialized Search Engines

Part 3 presents some alternatives to the all-purpose "Swiss Army Knife" approach of the search engines covered in Part 2. Just as cooks and carpenters need special tools from time to time, so too do Web searchers: to find newsgroups, mailing lists, people, businesses, and other specialized content. This part of the book introduces you to some of the best of these special tools and helps you understand when to use them for faster, more efficient searches.

Appendices

The three appendices provide handy reference tools you can use as you search the Web.

Appendix A: Search Engines Quick Reference

This is a collection of all the Quick Reference guides and other summary tables from throughout the book, organized alphabetically by search engine. Our thought is that when you're online and need a quick reminder of, say, the HotBot or Yahoo search rules, you may find it more convenient to turn to this appendix instead of going back to the individual search engine chapter.

Appendix B: Internet Domains and Country Codes

The information presented here will help you take advantage of power-searching techniques like zeroing in on a specific *type* of organization (based on the Internet domain designation in its Web address) or locating sites that originate in a particular country.

Appendix C: Usenet Newsgroup Hierarchies

This appendix explains how newsgroups are named and gives you the information you need to limit your queries to specific newsgroups, a feature offered by some search engines.

PART 1

SEARCH BASICS

Search Basics

If you're new to online searching, we suggest that you read the four chapters in this part of the book from start to finish. With this information under your belt, you'll get a lot more out of the specific search engine chapters in Parts 2 and 3.

Chapter 1, "**Search Engines and How They Work**," brings you up to speed fast on what search engines are all about and how they accomplish the mammoth task of collecting information from Web sites around the world.

Chapter 2, "**Unique Keywords**," lays out specific steps for choosing the best search terms for your Web searches. Coming up with the right keywords is the essence of effective searching, and this chapter will show you how to do just that.

Chapter 3, "**Basic Search Tools**," builds on the keyword concept by showing you how to enter and combine search terms. Each search engine has its own way of doing things, but the basic concepts are similar from one search engine to the next. Once you know the basics, you'll be well equipped to deal with almost any search engine.

Chapter 4, "**Tips and Techniques**," lays out the "Seven Habits of Highly Effective Web Searchers," offers advice on customizing your Web browser, and presents some tried-and-true techniques for making your online sessions easier and more productive.

SEARCH ENGINES AND HOW THEY WORK

Listening to television news shows and reading the daily paper, you could easily get the impression that the Internet and the World Wide Web hold the answers to virtually any question you could possibly ask. Sign on to your favorite search engine, tap a few keys, and all the world's knowledge is there for the taking. It couldn't be simpler.

But ask anyone who has actually tried to use a search engine to answer a specific question or track down a particular fact or figure, and you're likely to hear a far different story: "I can't find *anything* on the Net." Or "The search engine I used turned up so *much* information, most of it totally useless, that I gave up."

The problem is at least twofold. First, the Internet is so vast and so lacking in organization that even longtime, experienced searchers express great frustration in using it to find information.

Second, most people who use search engines don't really understand what they are and don't bother to learn how to take full advantage of their unique information-finding features. Falling prey to the hype, perhaps, they simply type one or two words into a search form and are then unpleasantly surprised when they are presented with thousands (or even millions) of Web pages.

> *The current state of search engines can be compared to a phone book that is updated irregularly, is biased toward listing more popular information, and has most of the pages ripped out.*
>
> —Steve Lawrence and Lee Giles, authors of a widely publicized 1999 study of search engines for the NEC Research Institute

The Perils of Internet Searching

One of our favorite descriptions of what it's like to search the Internet is offered by Clifford Stoll, veteran searcher and author of *Silicon Snake Oil* and *The Cuckoo's Egg*. By way of background, and to help you appreciate Mr. Stoll's formidable research skills, we should mention that *The Cuckoo's Egg* recounts how he used the Net to track down the notorious "Hanover Hacker"—a trail that also led to a KGB-backed spy ring. That was in the late 1980s, before most of the world had even heard of the Internet.

But despite his considerable research background and demonstrated ability to find information, Mr. Stoll once described the Internet and his struggle to locate the answer to a specific question like this:

What the Internet hucksters won't tell you is that the Internet is an ocean of unedited data, without any pretense of completeness. Lacking editors, reviewers, or critics, the Internet has become a wasteland of unfiltered data. You don't know what to ignore and what's worth reading.

Logged onto the World Wide Web, I hunt for the date of the Battle of Trafalgar. Hundreds of files show up, and it takes 15 minutes to unravel them—one's a biography written by an eighth grader, the second is a computer game that doesn't work, and the third is an image of a London monument. None answers my question...

Figure 1.1 Google emphasizes *searching*—rather than browsing the Web by topic.

Search form

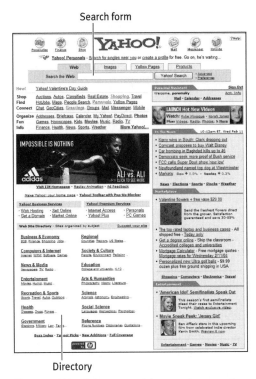

Directory

Figure 1.2 Yahoo's home page gives you two ways to look for information. You can type a query in the search form or click one of the subject areas and work your way through the site's comprehensive topic directory.

Figure 1.3 Most search engines, including Google, have a topic directory.

Search Engines to the Rescue

It's not likely that the Internet will become less chaotic any time soon. In fact, it's a virtual certainty that it won't. While the search engines are getting better at categorizing content, the number of pages included in a search is growing. Since no one is "in charge" of the Internet, it will always have a certain amount of disorganization. Once you understand and accept that, you'll be better able to deal with the chaos—and perhaps more forgiving when you can't find what you're looking for.

That said, let's move on to what you *can* do something about: developing a better understanding of search engines and how to use them to make sense out of the Internet's "ocean of unedited data."

Search engines defined

A *search engine* is a tool that lets you explore databases containing the text from hundreds of millions of Web pages. When the search engine software finds pages that match your search request (often referred to as *hits)*, it presents them to you with brief descriptions and clickable links to take you there.

Google (**Figure 1.1**) and other leading search engines focus primarily on providing a powerful search capability and offering the largest possible database of Web pages. But to compete with other popular search engines, such as Yahoo (**Figure 1.2**), they also give you the option of using a multilevel *topic directory* to browse a much smaller collection of Web pages for information on a given subject. (**Figure 1.3**).

continues on next page

Topic directories are prepared by human beings, who spend their days visiting, selecting, and classifying Web sites based on content. Yahoo maintains its own staff of "Yahoo Surfers" to perform this function and is widely considered to be the premier topic directory on the Net. Most of the other leading search engines rely on either LookSmart (`www.looksmart.com`) or the Open Directory Project (`dmoz.org`) for their topic directories.

As you browse the Internet, you'll notice that many sites have search engines displaying the "Powered by Google" or "Enhanced by Google" logos. In this situation, Google is a *search provider*, providing just the database used by the search, and the site is the search engine.

Search Engine, ISP, or Portal?

With the exception of Google, many of the popular search engines are more than just a search engine, providing portal services, subscriber-only online content, and Internet access, along with search capabilities.

MSN was founded as an online service, competing with AOL and CompuServe. MSN developed a search engine and later opened much of its subscriber-only network to all Internet users.

Yahoo, on the other hand, was built on a search engine and expanded to include portal services. Yahoo now provides ISP services in partnership with broadband providers. Its search engine is second only to Google in popularity only because many sites, including AOL, license the Google search engine and database for use on their own sites.

Here's the breakdown for the search engines covered in Part 2:

- **Google:** Search engine. Many sites use Google as a search provider to power their own searches.

- **Yahoo!:** Portal, search engine, and online content provider.

- **AOL:** Portal and search engine; for subscribers only.

- **MSN:** Portal, search engine, and online content provider.

- **Ask Jeeves:** Search engine; includes children's search engine.

- **AltaVista:** Search engine.

- **Excite:** Portal and search engine.

- **Lycos:** Search engine and portal.

- **HotBot:** Search engine; includes links to other search engines.

Search portals

In the early days of the Internet, there were a lot of upstart search engines vying for Internet users' attention and loyalty. Some, including Yahoo, felt the best way to keep people coming back was by offering everything an Internet user could want, all linked from one page. A *portal* draws users to the site with news, weather, links, and the search engine on the home page. Others, like MSN, decided that search engines were a means of drawing users and developed their own search engines.

As the Internet has matured and search engines consolidated, the portal sites are still very popular, with Yahoo's portal the most popular site on the Internet. According to the most recent figures, Yahoo is second only to Google in the number of searches preformed.

The Search Engines

Of all the search sites available today, Google is especially impressive, with over 4 billion pages in its database. Nearly 35 percent of all Internet searches are through Google. Several other search engines use Google's database to supplement their own, resulting in nearly 75 percent of all searches returning results from Google's database. While Google is the leader of the field, all of the search engines covered in this book have several things in common:

♦ They've been around for several years, and people keep coming back to their sites for searches.

♦ Their creators know the Net and the Web and have designed their sites and the underlying software with the primary goal of making searching as easy as possible.

♦ They all offer exceptionally large searchable databases, excellent help information, powerful search tools, and an overall "look and feel" that's conducive to searching.

Of course, like virtually all Web sites these days, they also carry advertising of one form or another (**Figure 1.4**). That's how they finance their operations and avoid having to charge subscription fees for the use of their services.

Many also offer *portal features* such as free e-mail, news, chat, stock quotes, and weather reports (**Figure 1.5**)—stuff that's completely unrelated to searching but presumably helps attract visitors (and thus advertisers). The idea is to get you to think of the site not just as a place to search but as your *portal to the Internet*—the first place you visit whenever you go online.

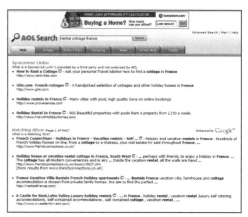

Figure 1.4 Advertising messages, such as the one at the top of this page, are common on search engine sites.

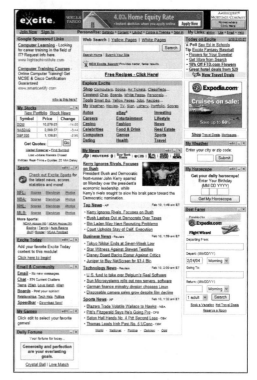

Figure 1.5 At many search engine sites, additional features such as news, weather, stock quotes, chat, and so forth get equal billing with searching.

Fortunately, the advertising and ancillary features interfere very little (if at all) with your ability to search effectively. Thus, we strongly recommend that you get to know at least a couple of these sites and choose one as your primary search engine.

If you already have a favorite Internet portal (AOL, Excite, MSN, or Yahoo all have large followings), consider making Google or one of the other search engines your *backup* search site—the place you go for a second opinion when you can't find exactly what you're looking for using your portal site's search feature.

✔ Tips

- One good way to quickly size up a search engine or portal is to look at its search tips and help information. Sites that are serious about searching will offer clear, detailed instructions for new and advanced users.

- Another way to judge how good a search engine is, is to search for something you are familiar with, such as a topic you know well or even your own name. Compare the results with those from other search engines.

THE SEARCH ENGINES

Where to find the search engines

We'll have much more to say about each of the popular search engines in Part 2 of this book, but if you'd like to visit them now, here's where to find them:

Google	www.google.com
Yahoo	search.yahoo.com
AOL	search.aol.com
MSN	search.msn.com
Ask Jeeves	www.ask.com
AltaVista	www.altavista.com
Excite	www.excite.com
Lycos	www.lycos.com
HotBot	www.hotbot.com

Figure 1.6 Google's official address is http://www.google.com. But you can just type Google in the address field in many browsers and press Ctrl+Enter (Windows) or Enter (Mac).

✔ Tips

- The official address, or URL (uniform resource locator) for any Web site always begins with http://. However, with the latest versions of Microsoft Internet Explorer (IE) and other Web browsers, you don't have to include this portion of the address.

- You can often even omit the www and com portions of a Web address (**Figure 1.6**). This approach doesn't work for multiple-word names separated by periods, but try it with any of the addresses in our search engine list. Just type the search engine name (altavista, google, yahoo, and so on) in your Web browser's Address or Location box and then press Ctrl+Enter (Windows) or Enter (Mac).

- For Web addresses ending in anything other than com (edu, gov, net, org, and so on), it's a good idea to type the complete address, like www.whitehouse.gov. IE currently makes the assumption that if you type, say, whitehouse, you're looking for www.whitehouse.com, which happens to be a pornography site instead of the official Web site for the home of U.S. presidents.

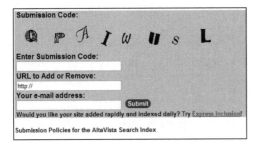

Figure 1.7 Here's a typical search engine submission form. The search engines try to make it as easy as possible for people to alert them to new sites.

How Search Engines Work

Search engines are designed to make it as easy as possible for you to find what you want on the Internet. But with hundreds of millions of Web pages stored on computers all over the world—and more being added all the time—how can search engines possibly collect them all? And what do they do with the information once they get it?

Spiders and indexes

Search engines do their data gathering by deploying robot programs called *spiders* or *crawlers*. Some even have names and personalities, like Scooter, the AltaVista spider. Scooter and other such programs are designed to track down Web pages, follow the links they contain, and add any new information they encounter to a master database, or *index*.

You don't really need to know the specifics. The key point to understand is that each search engine has its own way of doing things. Some have programmed their spiders or crawlers to search for only the *titles* of Web pages and the first few lines of text. Others snare every single word, ignoring only the graphics, video, sound, and other multimedia files.

The spiders' work is supplemented with information supplied directly to the search engines by professional and amateur Web developers. With millions of new Web pages being created every day, search engines make it easy for anyone to suggest a site for inclusion in a search engine index by completing a simple form (**Figure 1.7**).

continues on next page

How Search Engines Work

It may take weeks or even months for a form to be processed using these free submission services, however. So some search engines have begun offering express service to customers willing to pay a fee for having a Web site added to the database within a couple of days. Others are experimenting with charging customers to have their Web pages visited more frequently by the search engine's spider program.

These services go by different names, but they're often referred to generically as *paid-inclusion* or *pay-for-submission* services. Although there is some concern that paid-inclusion listings have the potential to skew search results, these services should help improve the freshness and comprehensiveness of search engine databases.

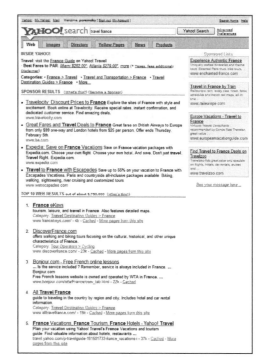

Figure 1.8 With Overture's pay-for-placement approach to presenting search results, these Web sites paid the most for the keyword *travel* and therefore get the top four slots with search engines that use Overture to provide sponsored results.

✔ Tips

- Yahoo currently charges $299 for adding a commercial Web site to its topic directory within seven days. (The free service can take as long as six months.)

- Inktomi, the search engine that powers MSN and a number of other leading search sites, charges $13 to $20 per page for a one-year subscription. (The more pages you submit, the lower the cost per page.) The service promises inclusion in the database within 72 hours and a return visit by the Inktomi spider every 48 hours.

- Don't confuse paid-inclusion and pay-for-submission services with the more controversial *pay-for-placement* services, which guarantee preferential treatment in search engine rankings. The GoTo search engine, now Overture (www.overture.com), pioneered the concept of pay-for-placement. Instead of charging a set fee for inclusion in its database, Overture allows Web site owners to bid on search terms that are relevant to their sites. The higher the bid, the higher that Web site appears in the list of search results (**Figure 1.8**). Yahoo, MSN, and AltaVista are among the search engines that use paid placements from Overture. They identify these sites as sponsored sites and separate them from other sites.

Relevancy formulas

Every search engine uses a different method for calculating *relevancy*—how well a particular Web page matches your search request. As mentioned, at Overture, the method is quite straightforward: the higher the bid, the higher a site's ranking.

For most search engines, however, the relevancy formulas are a closely guarded secret. And they are constantly being changed in an effort to stay one step ahead of crafty Web developers, some of whom engage in a practice called *spamdexing* or *spoofing*: doctoring a Web page to fool search engines into putting it high on the list of search results.

One of the most common tricks is to load a Web page with words—like *free* or *money* or *sex*—that may or may not have anything to do with the site (**Figure 1.9**). The Web page may even be designed so that the words are hidden from view when you look at the page with your browser.

A search engine can respond to tactics like this by rewriting its software, changing the relevancy formula to give a *lower* ranking to pages with a lot of repeated words.

Another popular method sites can use to receive higher ranking is encouraging other sites to link to them. Many search engines take into consideration the number of sites that link to a site when determining site ranking, and the more sites that link to a site, the higher the site appears in the list.

```
<META NAME="Keywords" content="web, Internet marketing, free money, web site, sex, adult,
video card, hardware, sound, bandwidth, offshore shared, virtual servers, host help, guides,
tutorials,xxx,interviews, webhosts, primer,articles, tutorials, promotion, promote,
guidelines, guide, advice, help,assistance, asistance">
```

Figure 1.9 One spamdexing or spoofing technique involves inserting a block of text like this in a Web page. The words may or may not have anything to do with the actual content of the page.

Google Bombing

Because many search engines rank sites based on the number of other sites that link to a site, Web site owners discovered they could have a little fun while making a statement by getting accomplices to link to sites and then using specific search keywords to find the site.

Soon, e-mails are circulating with instructions to search for the keywords, and the site reaches a top position in the search engine. In most cases, the amusement is the search results; a recent Google bomb for "weapons of mass destruction" also included a spoof of a "page not found" error (**Figure 1.10**).

Current events, Microsoft, and political figures are favorite targets of Google bombing, with search terms such as "miserable failure" bringing up Web sites for politicians.

Even though this type of activity is referred to as Google bombing, after the most popular search engine, this technique works with most search engines.

While search engine developers hope Google bombing is a fad that soon dies out, it's a relatively harmless activity. Since the search terms aren't ordinarily used in searches, it doesn't negatively affect search results.

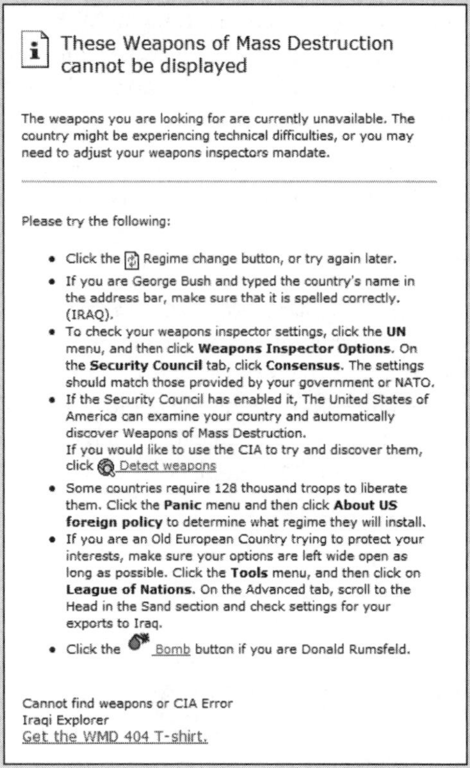

i These Weapons of Mass Destruction cannot be displayed

The weapons you are looking for are currently unavailable. The country might be experiencing technical difficulties, or you may need to adjust your weapons inspectors mandate.

Please try the following:

- Click the 🔁 Regime change button, or try again later.
- If you are George Bush and typed the country's name in the address bar, make sure that it is spelled correctly. (IRAQ).
- To check your weapons inspector settings, click the **UN** menu, and then click **Weapons Inspector Options**. On the **Security Council** tab, click **Consensus**. The settings should match those provided by your government or NATO.
- If the Security Council has enabled it, The United States of America can examine your country and automatically discover Weapons of Mass Destruction.
  If you would like to use the CIA to try and discover them, click 🔍 Detect weapons
- Some countries require 128 thousand troops to liberate them. Click the **Panic** menu and then click **About US foreign policy** to determine what regime they will install.
- If you are an Old European Country trying to protect your interests, make sure your options are left wide open as long as possible. Click the **Tools** menu, and then click on **League of Nations**. On the Advanced tab, scroll to the Head in the Sand section and check settings for your exports to Iraq.
- Click the 💣 _Bomb_ button if you are Donald Rumsfeld.

Cannot find weapons or CIA Error
Iraqi Explorer
Get the WMD 404 T-shirt.

Figure 1.10 Google bombing is an amusing but harmless way to bring attention to a cause. Searching for "weapons of mass destruction" finds this site.

Table 1.1

Search Engine Providers

SEARCH ENGINE	PROVIDER OF MAIN RESULTS	NUMBER OF PAGES INDEXED
AllTheWeb (Overture owned)	AllTheWeb	3.4 billion
AltaVista (Overture owned)	AltaVista	1 billion
AOL Search	Google	4.2 billion
Ask Jeeves (Ask owned)	Teoma	700 million
Google	Google	4.2 billion
HotBot (Yahoo owned)	Inktomi	3 billion
LookSmart	LookSmart/Zeal	2.5 billion
Lycos (Overature owned)	AllTheWeb	3.4 billion
MSN Search	Inktomi	3 billion
Netscape	Google	4.2 billion
Open Directory	Open Directory	6 million
Overture	Overture	2 million
Teoma	Teoma	1.5 billion
Yahoo	Yahoo	3.3 billion

How good are the spiders?

The beauty of spiders and crawlers is that they operate around the clock. But some take longer than others to make their rounds. Even the best of them have located and indexed only a fraction of the Web pages that are out there on the Internet. (See **Table 1.1** for a comparison of several of the leading engines.)

That's why you may successfully find a specific Web site using one search engine but not another. It's also a good reason to get into the habit of trying the same search on multiple engines.

At this writing, Google holds the record for the largest database: some 4.2 billion pages. AllTheWeb (the search engine that powers Lycos) is second, with 3.4 billion pages. And Inktomi's GEN3 database (the one used by MSN and HotBot) is a close third, with 3 billion pages.

But remember, even though Google has over 4 billion pages indexed, there are millions—and maybe billions—more Web pages that it hasn't indexed. But don't despair: a large percentage of those Web pages *have* been found by and included in the databases of one or more of the other leading search engines.

✔ Tips

- Keep in mind that when you use a search engine to "search the Web," what you are actually searching is that particular site's database of information, collected by a spider program and supplemented with entries submitted by site creators. Each search engine you use will produce a different set of results, because each creates and maintains its own database.

- When you explore a subject using a search engine's topic directory, you're likely to get far fewer hits, but the sites you find will all have been selected and classified by human beings.

More Information for Webmasters and Others

Many search engines provide basic information about how their spiders operate: what they search for, how many sites they visit in a day, how often the master database is updated, and so forth. You may have to dig a bit to find it, but it's probably there.

Start by checking the search engine's home page for an About link. Or try the search tips and help information, usually accessible via a Help link on or near the search form.

For even more detail, look for the site's instructions to Webmasters on how to submit a URL to the search engine. To learn more about the Google spider, database, and indexing methods, for example, go to the Google home page (www.google.com) and click Services & Tools and then All About Google.

Resources for Webmasters

If you're responsible for designing Web pages and making sure that people can find them on the Internet, you'll definitely want to track down the information provided by each of the major search engines on how their spiders operate and how their indexes are developed. You'll also want to pay a visit to one of the Net's premier resources for Webmasters: Search Engine Watch. This Web site (**Figure 1.11**) is hands down the best source of information we've encountered on how search engines work. Created several years ago by Internet consultant and journalist Danny Sullivan, Search Engine Watch is now owned by Internet.com (www.internet.com). But Mr. Sullivan continues to maintain the site, which is located at www.searchenginewatch.com.

Figure 1.11 The Search Engine Watch Web site at www.searchenginewatch.com is the definitive online source for information about search engines and how they operate.

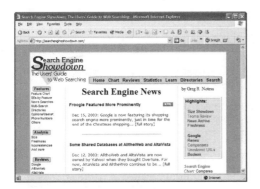

Figure 1.12 Search Engine Showdown at www.search-engineshowdown.com is aimed at *users* of search engines, rather than Webmasters.

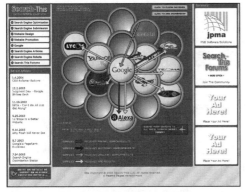

Figure 1.13 Search-This has information about search engine optimization (SEO). Use the decoder to learn what search engine a portal uses.

✔ Tips

- If you don't see what you want on the Search Engine Watch home page, try using the site's Search feature.

- Search Engine Watch publishes a twice-monthly newsletter issued via e-mail. You can sign up for free, but regular readers are encouraged to pay $99 for an annual subscription ($69 for six months), which helps support the site and entitles you to additional reports and information not available to the general public.

Among its many offerings is a section called Search Engine Submission Tips, with all the latest information on how to design a site for maximum visibility by all the search engines. For people who are simply curious about search engine technology, there's a wealth of interesting information—facts and figures about search engine sizes, comparative reviews and ratings, tutorials, a glossary, and more.

Other great resources

Search Engine Watch is aimed largely, though not exclusively, at Webmasters. If you're primarily interested in learning about search engines so that you can become a more effective *searcher*, we recommend these sites:

Search Engine Showdown: Created and maintained by researcher and writer Greg R. Notess, this award-winning site (**Figure 1.12**) compares and evaluates search engines from a user's perspective. Check here for regularly updated feature lists, detailed reviews, and performance reports. The site is located at www.searchengineshowdown.com.

Search-This: Created to provide information on search engine optimization (SEO) along with Web site design, development, promotion, and marketing strategies, Search-This has a graphic Search Engine Decoder (**Figure 1.13**), which shows the links between search engine databases and search portals. The site is located at www.search-this.com.

continues on next page

Web Search: This site (**Figure 1.14**), hosted by Web consultant Chris Sherman, is a good source of search tips, tutorials, and feature articles. One of the About.com subject guides, it's located at websearch.about.com.

Pandia Search Central: Named after a Greek goddess of light and enlightenment, the Pandia Web site (www.pandia.com) is beautifully designed and full of great information (**Figure 1.15**). Its creators, Per and Susanne Koch, who live in Norway, are dedicated to helping Internet users become more effective searchers. They have produced a truly remarkable resource for doing just that.

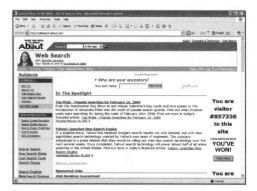

Figure 1.14 The Web Search site at websearch.about.com is a good place to look for beginner's guides and tutorials on search engines.

Figure 1.15 Pandia (www.pandia.com) is another excellent source of beginner's guides, tutorials, and search tools.

2

UNIQUE KEYWORDS

The biggest challenge with any type of online searching is choosing the right search terms, or *keywords*. This goes double for Web searching because, when you use search engines like Google and AltaVista, what you are typically searching is the *full text* of Web pages collected automatically by spider or crawler programs.

That sounds great in theory. But ask any librarian or professional searcher—anyone who makes a living using high-powered, high-cost databases like Dialog, Dow Jones/News Retrieval, and Lexis-Nexis—about full-text searching. What they'll tell you is that it's actually the most difficult type of searching in the online world.

To help you understand why, we'll take a look in this chapter at searching another type of database that most people are familiar with: the electronic card catalog at the local library. Then, with that as background, we'll explore how to meet the challenge of full-text searching by choosing the right keywords for your Web searches.

The Challenge of Full-Text Searching

Traditional databases like the electronic card catalog at your local library use *field searches*. If you're interested in the writer Kurt Vonnegut, for example, you would search for Vonnegut in the database's Author field to produce a list of his books. Click a title, and all the relevant information about that book will be presented in familiar, card-catalog format (**Figure 2.1**).

If, on the other hand, you're looking for Kurt Vonnegut's biography or other information *about* him, you would search for his name in the Subject field. Or maybe what you really want is a recent magazine article that features Kurt Vonnegut, in which case you'd use the periodicals database instead of the one for the library's collection of books.

Web search engine databases don't distinguish between various record fields like other databases do. So when you search on Kurt Vonnegut's name, you'll get a hodge-podge of Web sites, many of them personal home pages created by Vonnegut fans (**Figure 2.2**).

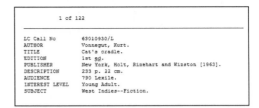

Figure 2.1 Search for author Kurt Vonnegut at your local library, and you'll get information like this for each of his books.

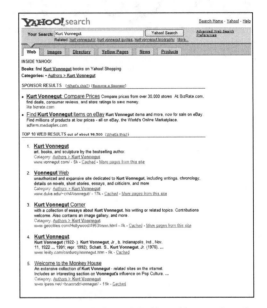

Figure 2.2 Search the Web for Kurt Vonnegut, and there's no telling what you'll come up with, as these results show.

Web page field searches

Field searching with Web search engines, if it's available at all, is limited to fields having to do with the Web page itself—its title, its Web address or URL (uniform resource locator), the date the page was created, and so forth—not the information *on* the page.

Searching these Web page fields can be useful, but you are limited to the keywords the Web page author used. As a result, this type of searching doesn't come close to matching the capabilities of traditional database field searching. For this reason, you need to get quite good at coming up with the *right* keywords to conduct efficient searches. For example, to more easily find a list of titles written by Kurt Vonnegut, you might use `"kurt vonnegut book titles"`. To find information about a specific book, you would use the title of the book as a keyword.

Choosing the Right Keywords

Learning to come up with the most effective keywords for your Web searches will take time and practice. Don't be surprised or disappointed if you're not successful every time. After all, even the best online searchers find Web searching to be quite a challenge.

We don't pretend to have all the answers ourselves, but here are some points to keep in mind that can help you improve your Web searching success rate.

To get the best search results:

1. **Use the most specific keyword you can think of.** Take the time to think about the words that will almost certainly appear on the kind of Web page you have in mind. Then pick the most specific or unusual word from that list.

    If you're looking for information about efforts to save tiger populations in Asia, for example, don't use `tigers` as your search term. You'll be swamped with Web pages about the Detroit Tigers, the Princeton Tigers, and every other sports team that uses the word *tigers* in its name.

    Instead, try searching for a particular tiger species that you know to be on the endangered list—`Bengal tiger` or `Sumatran tiger` or `Siberian tiger`. (With some search engines, you'll need to enclose the words in quotation marks to let the engine know you want a *phrase search*: `"Bengal tiger"`)—that is, you want to search for that exact sequence of words. Chances are, you'll find sites like the one in **Figure 2.3** near the top of the list.

Figure 2.3 Searching for a unique phrase like Bengal tigers is more likely to produce a site like this near the top of your search results list than would a search for the far more common tigers. (Source: www.bengal-tigers.org.)

Figure 2.4 Set searching is easy with AltaVista. Once you've located sites offering information about Bengal tigers, for example, you can look for images of Bengal tigers by selecting the Images tab.

Figure 2.5 When you have too many results to be useful, refine your original search by searching within the results.

2. Make it a multistep process. Don't assume that you'll find what you want on the first try. Take your best shot. Then review the first couple of pages of results, paying particular attention to the sites that contain the *kind* of information you want. What unique words appear on those pages? Make a few notes and then do another search using those words.

You might even try changing the *order* in which you type your keywords in the search form's text box. Some search engines give more weight to the first word in your query than to those that appear second or third, on the assumption that you will typically put your most important search word first.

Consequently, a search for endangered tiger species might very well produce different results than a search for tiger endangered species.

3. Narrow the field by searching just your previous results. If your chosen keyword returns relatively good information but too much to review comfortably, try a second search of just those results. This is sometimes referred to as *set searching*.

Most of the leading search engines make set searching quite easy by providing tabs on the search results page that allow you to search specific content, including images, audio or video clips, and current news stories (**Figure 2.4**). Search Within Results allows you to refine the original search and reduce the number of hits (**Figure 2.5**). For example, searching for cubs within the results at Google reduces the hits from some 21,000 to 3,500.

continues on next page

But even if the search engine doesn't provide this option, you can accomplish essentially the same thing by simply adding another keyword to your search request and submitting it again. For example, AltaVista doesn't offer an option to search within results, but adding another keyword and rerunning the search gives you the same result (**Figure 2.6**).

4. **Look for your keyword in the Web page title.** Often the best search strategy is to look first for your unique keyword in the *titles* of Web pages. All the search engines allow you to search Web page titles, but the rules for doing so vary slightly depending on which search engine you're using.

   With AltaVista, HotBot, and Lycos, you can put a Title field-search term right in your query. For example, if you're looking for information about marriage customs in the Middle Ages, start with a search of Web pages that have the words *Middle Ages* in the title, like this: `title:"Middle Ages"` (**Figure 2.7**). Then do a second search of just those results, looking for `"marriage customs"`.

   With Google, follow the same steps, but instead of `title:`, use the search term `allintitle:"Middle Ages"`.

   With Yahoo, use `t:"Middle Ages"` to find the phrase *Middle Ages* in topic categories and Web page titles.

   Notice that in each of these examples, there is no space between the colon and the phrase being searched for.

5. **Find out if case counts.** It's important to know whether the search engine you're using pays attention to uppercase and lowercase letters in your keywords. Will a search for *Java*, the Sun Microsystems program, also find sites that refer to the program as *JAVA*?

Figure 2.6 If your favorite search engine doesn't offer searching within results, add keywords to the original search keywords and search again.

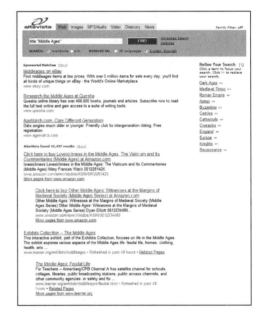

Figure 2.7 Notice that the phrase *Middle Ages* appears in all the Web page titles shown here. That's because we specified that we wanted to search for `title:"Middle Ages"`. Note that sponsored results ignore the title tag.

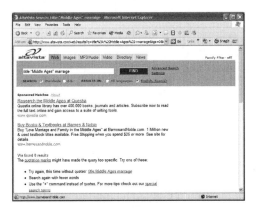

Figure 2.8 Spelling errors—typing `marraige` instead of `marriage`, for example—often stump the search engine and produce a "no results found" message.

Figure 2.9 Search engines often detect misspelled words and suggest corrections.

✔ Tips

- The Quick Reference guides in Parts 2 and 3 of this book (and repeated in Appendix A) are a good place to look for specifics on field searching and case-sensitive searching with different search engines.

- Pluralized keywords often return different results than singular ones. A search for `Bengal tigers` includes some pages not found in a search for `Bengal tiger`.

Some search engines ignore case completely. But with others (AltaVista and HotBot, for example), if you use *any* uppercase letters, the search engine will assume that you want to look for only that combination of uppercase and lowercase characters.

Consequently, for the broadest possible search, the best approach usually is to use all lowercase letters for your queries.

6. **Use initial caps to search for proper names.** As we've said, it's usually a good idea to enter your queries in lowercase letters because that gives you the broadest possible search. The keyword `java` will find references to *java, Java, JAVA,* and even *jaVa.*

   But when you're looking for a person's name, a geographical location, a book or movie title, or anything else that you might reasonably expect to be presented with an initial capital letter, by all means type your query that way. Doing so will greatly reduce the number of *false drops*: pages that contain the words in your query but are completely off the mark.

7. **Check your spelling.** If you've used the best keyword you can think of and the search engine comes back with the message "No results found" or fewer results than you expected, check your spelling before you do anything else.

   Nine times out of 10, the reason a search engine comes up empty-handed is because of a spelling or typing error (**Figure 2.8**).

   While searches for commonly misspelled words often have limited success, many search engines will suggest corrections for misspelled words, as long as you aren't using advanced search options (**Figure 2.9**).

BASIC SEARCH TOOLS

As we've said before, choosing the right keywords is the essence of effective searching. It's especially important for *Web* searching, because there's so much information out there—some of it worthwhile, much of it totally useless—and there's no single company or organization responsible for organizing and making sense of it.

But coming up with good, unique keywords is actually just half the battle. You also need to know how to *enter and combine* keywords, taking advantage of the basic search tools offered by the major search engines. Your success rate will improve dramatically once you learn what these tools are and when and how to use them.

Search Tools at a Glance

Here are the basic search tools you'll read about in this chapter:

- Plain-English searches
- AND searches
- OR searches
- NOT searches
- NEAR searches
- Nested searches
- Wildcards
- Stopwords

Specific procedures vary from one search engine to the next, of course. In fact, some search engines have a different set of instructions depending on whether you're using their simple or advanced versions. But certain general concepts apply across the board. That's what we'll cover here.

Once you have this basic understanding of the tools that are available, you'll be better equipped to deal with just about any search engine you encounter on the Web. The chapters in Parts 2 and 3 will fill in the details for some of the best of them.

Searching in Plain English

For new Web searchers, one of the best tools going is *plain-English* or *natural-language* searching. Most of the leading search engines have developed techniques that are amazingly good at finding what you want based on a simple question—especially if the question includes at least one unique keyword or phrase.

One problem with plain-English searches like the one shown in **Figure 3.1** is that they typically produce a very large number of hits. But as long as the information you're looking for shows up at or near the top of the list, it doesn't really matter.

Another problem you're likely to encounter when you type your first plain-English search is fitting it into the small search box that's provided by many search engines. Don't be misled into thinking that you're limited to typing a very short question. The box in Figure 3.1 may look small, but at most search sites, you can type a question containing at least 10 words. The first part will simply scroll out of view on the left side of the box.

Figure 3.1 Plain-English searches like this often produce excellent results. Many search engines encourage you to simply "ask a question." While the search returns 21,000 hits, the hits on the first page will probably answer your question.

Figure 3.2 The Ask Jeeves Web site at www.ask.com specializes in providing high-quality answers to plain-English questions.

✔ Tips

■ All of the search engines do a pretty good job of handling plain-English searches. But if you really like this method of looking for information on the Web, be sure to try Ask Jeeves (`www.ask.com`) (**Figure 3.2**).

■ Word order and phrasing can make a big difference in plain-English searches. If you don't find what you're looking for with a direct question, try rephrasing your query, putting the most unusual or specific word or phrase first:

Query 1: `What companies offer "parental control software"?`

Query 2: `"parental control software" companies`

Think of this type of search as a two-step process. The direct-question approach of Query 1 may not work. But it will help you clarify your search request and zero in on the most specific term, which you can place first in Query 2. And remember that how you phrase a question can change the results: "What is a stalactite?" and "What are stalactites?" return different results.

■ You can use a question mark at the end of your question when entering a natural-language query, but you don't need to. The search engine knows that your entry is a question and returns the same results either way.

Searching for Multiple Words and Phrases

The most important search strategies to learn for any search engine are the techniques the site provides to look for *multiple* words and phrases. Plain-English queries are great, and they can probably handle many of your search requirements. But when you need more precision than you can get from a plain-English search, here are the features to look for:

- **AND search.** How do you tell the search engine that you want to find Web sites that include references to Keyword A *and* Keyword B?

- **OR search.** How do you specify that it's not necessary for *both* keywords to appear in the results, as long as one *or* the other is present?

- **NOT search.** How do you look for one keyword while specifically *excluding* another?

- **NEAR search.** How do you find two words or phrases in close *proximity* to one another?

The technical term for this type of searching is *Boolean* searching, and AND, OR, NOT, and NEAR are among the traditional *Boolean operators*.

Over the next few pages, you'll learn how to perform AND, OR, NOT, and NEAR searches with the leading search engines. You'll also find out how to use parentheses to combine words and phrases to create more complex queries.

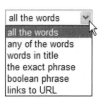

Figure 3.3 You can sometimes perform AND searches simply by choosing All the Words from a menu like this one.

Figure 3.4 Some search engines have an All of These Words field that you can use for an AND search.

Common Methods for Doing AND Searches

- Search for Monet AND Renoir.

- Search for +Monet +Renoir.

- Search for Monet Renoir and select the All the Words option.

AND Searches

Searching for two or more keywords—both of which *must* appear in the results—is an excellent strategy for performing precise searches and greatly reducing the number of search results you have to consider. Some search engines offer more than one method for performing AND searches, so you can choose the one you like best.

The most common way to tell a search engine that you want an AND search is to put a plus sign in front of each word or phrase that *must* appear in the results: +Renaissance +sculpture.

Other search engines require that you actually use the Boolean operator AND to combine words or phrases: needlepoint AND supplies, for example, to look for references to both terms. You may even be required to use full caps for AND. To avoid having to remember whether or not full caps are necessary, you should get into the habit of using full caps all the time for AND.

Some search engines make AND searching extremely easy by offering it as a menu option. You simply type two or more unique keywords or phrases and then choose All the Words from a drop-down menu (**Figure 3.3**) or enter your search words in a field with a similar label (**Figure 3.4**).

✔ Tips

- Some search engines default to an AND search, and others default to an OR search. HotBot, for example, assumes that you want an AND search unless you tell it differently. AltaVista, on the other hand, defaults to OR searching.

- Whenever you perform an AND search, you should put the most specific search term first, because some search engines pay attention to word order and factor it into their relevancy rankings.

OR Searches

OR searches cast a much broader net than AND searches and may result in a very large number of hits for you to consider. They make good sense, though, when there's more than one way that the person, object, or thing you're looking for might be referred to within a Web page or other document. If you're researching the Clinton presidency, for example, you'd want to look for references to *President Clinton* or *Bill Clinton* or *William Jefferson Clinton*.

Some search engines perform an OR search by default. In other words, if you type several words or phrases, leaving a space between each one, the search engine assumes that you want to find references to *any one* of them: `"President Clinton" "Bill Clinton" "William Jefferson Clinton"`.

Other search engines require you to actually type the word OR between the words or phrases: `Greenspan OR "Federal Reserve Chairman"`. Full caps may or may not be required for the word OR, but using them is a good habit to get into.

Finally, some search engines offer OR searching as a menu option or radio button. You type your search words and phrases and then choose the option labeled Any of the Words or some such (as opposed to All the Words). See **Figures 3.5** and **3.6** for examples.

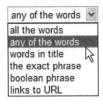

Figure 3.5 Choosing Any of the Words from a menu like this is the way you tell some search engines to perform an OR search.

Figure 3.6 Here's another approach to OR searching. Type the words in the Any of These Words field to indicate that the search engine should look for any of the words you've typed in the search form.

> ## Common Methods for Doing OR Searches
>
> ◆ Search for UPS U.P.S.
>
> ◆ Search for UPS OR U.P.S.
>
> ◆ Search for UPS U.P.S. and select the Any of the Words option.

```
TOP 10 WEB RESULTS out of about 6,350,000  (What's this?)

 1.  Python Language
     www.python.org at CNRI
     Category: Programming Languages > Python
     www.python.org/ - 11k - Cached - More pages from this site

 2.  PythOnline
     official Monty Python site. Includes spam, of course.
     Category: United Kingdom > Comedy Groups > Monty Python
     www.pythonline.com/ - 2k - Cached - More pages from this site

 3.  Daily Python-URL
     Daily Python-URL. Daily news from the Python universe, presented by your friends
     at PythonWare. ... It says it's an online supplement to the Python 2.1 Bible. ...
     www.pythonware.com/daily/ - 62k - Cached - More pages from this site

 4.  Dive Into Python
     Dive Into Python. Python from novice to pro. Find: ... It is also available in multiple
     languages. Read Dive Into Python. This book is still being written ...
     diveintopython.org/ - 16k - Cached - More pages from this site

 5.  Numerical Python
     SourceForge Home. Purpose. Numerical Python adds a fast, compact,
     multidimensional array language facility to Python. Availability. ...
     pfdubois.com/numpy/ - 19k - Cached

 6.  The Vaults of Parnassus: Python Resources
     The Vaults of Parnassus contain large database of Python scripts, modules, and
     resources. Python is an object oriented interpreted programming language. ...
     www.vex.net/parnassus/ - 19k - Cached

 7.  Why Python?
     ... Issue 73: Why Python? Posted on Monday ... My first look at Python was an accident,
     and I didn't much like what I saw at the time. It was early ...
     www.linuxjournal.com/article.php?sid=3882 - More pages from this site

 8.  Starship Python -- Python Programming Community
     This is a site for the Python community, hosted by crew.self. As Python
     is free, so too is the Python Starship. If you want to join ...
     starship.python.net/ - 7k - Cached - More pages from this site

 9.  ActiveState O'Reilly Python cookbook code samples ratings review
     Python Cookbook. Welcome to the Python Cookbook! This is a collaborative
     collection of techniques which hosts your contributions to Python lore. ...
     aspn.activestate.com/ASPN/Python/Cookbook/ - 41k - Cached - More pages from this site

10.  It's Monty Python's Flying Circus
     includes episode guide, images, and sounds from the television series.
     Category: United Kingdom > Comedy Groups > Monty Python
     bau2.uibk.ac.at/sg/python/monty.html - 6k - Cached - More pages from this site
```

Figure 3.7 A NOT search like python -monty or python NOT monty can help you avoid some of the sites that might otherwise be listed and find snakes instead.

NOT Searches

Here's the example you'll come across again and again to illustrate when to use a NOT search: You're looking for information on snakes and key in a search for *python*. Much to your dismay, your search results are full of Web pages aimed at devoted Monty Python fans (**Figure 3.7**). What to do?

The answer, of course, is to *exclude* Monty Python pages with a NOT search. Usually that means putting a minus sign in front of the word you want to avoid: python -monty. (Notice that there's no space between the minus sign and the word that's being excluded.)

Some search engines allow (or require) the use of the word NOT (or AND NOT) to exclude a word: python NOT monty or python AND NOT monty.

✔ Tip

- NOT can be a very powerful operator. But when you use it, you can unwittingly throw out the baby with the bath water. Suppose the definitive Web site on pythons—"The Master Python Page"— happens to have been created by someone named Monty Shields. The NOT search in our example could prevent you from ever finding it. Learn to use NOT searches, but be aware of the potential for inadvertently excluding good material.

Common Methods for Doing NOT Searches

- ◆ Search for python -monty.
- ◆ Search for python NOT monty.
- ◆ Search for python AND NOT monty.

NEAR Searches

Sometimes you're not just interested in finding multiple keywords that are *mentioned* in the same document. You want to be able to specify that they appear in *close proximity* to one another. That's what NEAR searching is all about.

AltaVista is one of the few search engines that offers NEAR searching. And it's available only as part of the Advanced and Power Search capabilities, not on the main AltaVista search form. The format is `Constitution NEAR "Electoral College"` (**Figure 3.8**).

✔ Tip

- Just how near is NEAR? AltaVista defines it to mean that the terms must appear within 10 words of each other.

Figure 3.8 With AltaVista, you can perform a NEAR search like this to find references to the word *Constitution* within 10 words of the phrase *Electoral College*.

Common Methods for Doing NEAR Searches

- ◆ Use AltaVista (Advanced Search and Power Search only).

- ◆ Search for `Japan NEAR climate` to find the two terms within 10 words of each other.

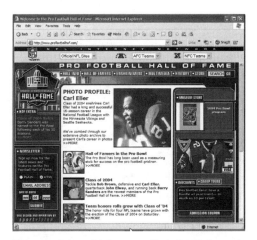

Figure 3.9 It doesn't take a complicated nested search to find the Web site for the Pro Football Hall of Fame in Canton, Ohio.

Parentheses and Nested Searches

Some search engines allow you to create more complex queries by grouping AND, OR, NOT, and NEAR statements using parentheses. For example, you could use a search like `Canton NEAR (Ohio OR OH)` to find any reference to Canton, Ohio, whether the state name is spelled out in full or abbreviated.

You can even create what are called *nested searches,* which can get quite complex, with one search statement nested within another: `Canton NEAR ((Ohio OR OH) AND ("Pro Football" NEAR "Hall of Fame"))`.

Our advice is to use parentheses in your searches sparingly, and only when you really need them. Complex nested searches are fine for the professionals. But for most search tasks, and especially for new online searchers, they're not worth the `mental NEAR ((energy OR effort) AND aggravation)`!

You'll be far better off concentrating on coming up with good, unique keywords and sticking to simple combinations using AND, OR, NOT, and (possibly) NEAR searches. The entry `Canton AND "Pro Football" AND "Hall of Fame"`, for example, is much more straightforward (and less error prone) than the complex nested search presented earlier and will very likely lead you to a page like the one shown in **Figure 3.9**, which is probably just what you hoped to find.

Tips for Using Parentheses and Nested Searches

◆ Use parentheses sparingly, if at all.

◆ Unique keywords combined with AND, OR, NOT, and NEAR often work just as well and are less error prone.

◆ Complex nested searches are best left to the professionals.

Using Wildcards

Searching with *wildcards*—sometimes referred to as *truncation*—means using a special character, typically an asterisk, to indicate that you want to look for variations on a particular word: for instance, you might enter medic* to find references to *medical, medicine, medicinal*, and *medication*.

Rules differ from one search engine to the next, but most require that you use at least three other characters along with the asterisk. And it's usually a good idea to also include at least one specific keyword in your query (**Figure 3.10**). Otherwise, your search may take painfully long and return too many hits to be truly useful.

✔ Tips

- Some search engines allow you to place wildcard characters in the middle (or even at the beginning) of a word.

- You may be given a choice between two different wildcard symbols, depending on whether you want to search for *multiple* characters or a *single* character.

- For specifics on using wildcards with a particular search engine, see the Quick Reference guides in Parts 2 and 3 of this book.

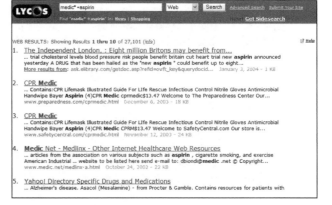

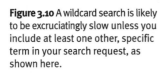

Figure 3.10 A wildcard search is likely to be excruciatingly slow unless you include at least one other, specific term in your search request, as shown here.

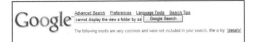

Figure 3.11 The Google search engine tells you exactly what words have been ignored from your query: in this case, *the*, *a*, and *by*.

```
WEB RESULTS: Showing Results 1 thru 10 of 249,559 (xfx)
1. To Be or Not To Be (1983) Comprehensive Movie Review
   To Be or Not To Be (1983)Movie Review ... cents per review! To Be or Not To Be (1983) Starring: Mel ...
   job also. --Samantha , Resident To Be or Not To Be (1983) Scholar ...
   www.allwatchers.com/Topics/Info_4290.asp   February 3, 2004 - 31 KB

2. Shakespeare and the Globe theater
   Hamlet
   shakespeare.eb.com   December 15, 2002 - £11 B

3. The Jakarta Post - Online Special: East Timor: To be or not to be a ...
   ... Everest Expeditions East Timor: To be or not to be a member of ASEAN? Some ... presidential election
   East Timor: To be or not to be a X(B)anana Republic Indonesia ... East Timor: To be or ...
   www.thejakartapost.com/special/oa_24.asp   February 4, 2004 - 15 KB

4. RhymeZone Shakespeare Search
   A fast full-text search engine of all of Shakespeare's works, including the unique ability to browse his 150
   000 lines incrementally.
   www.rhymezone.com/shakespeare/   October 1, 2003 - 9 KB

5. TTooLs Movie-Archiv
   ... Sein oder Nichtsein (To Be or Not To Be ... Sein oder Nichtsein (To Be Or Not To Be ... angereichert,
   und Brooks' Maxi-Single "To Be or Not to Be-The Hitler Rap" hielt sich ...
   www.ttool.de/tmovies/index.php?show=Sein%20oder%20Nic...   February 3, 2004 - 8 KB

6. artechock film : FILMINFO : Sein oder Nichtsein (To Be or Not to Be)
   ... Sein oder Nichtsein (To Be or Not to Be).
   www.artechock.de/film/text/filminfo/s/se/snodni.htm   January 9, 2003 - 8 KB

7. Inga's World: To be or not to be...
   www.ingawusa.tk   January 17, 2004 - 533 B
```

Figure 3.12 A Lycos search for "to be or not to be" finds Hamlet's soliloquy, even though the phrase is composed entirely of common stopwords. The secret is to enclose the words in quotation marks.

Tips for Using Stopwords

◆ Every search engine ignores certain very common words (*stopwords*) such as *the*, *to*, *with*, and the Boolean operators.

◆ To look for words that might be confused with Boolean operators, put them in double quotation marks: `Portland NEAR "OR"`.

◆ Some search engines recognize stopwords that are included in phrases enclosed in double quotation marks: `"to be or not to be"`.

Dealing with Stopwords

You may come across the term *stopwords* at search engine sites, often in the help information or search tips. Stopwords are words that search engines ignore because they are too common, or because they are reserved for some special purpose.

The list varies from one search engine to the next, but it typically includes words like *a, an, any, the, to, with, from, for, of, that, who,* and the Boolean operators AND, OR, NOT, and NEAR. We're not aware of any major search engine that publishes its complete list. But Google does the next best thing—it tells you if it has ignored one or more of the words in your query (**Figure 3.11**).

Should you need to use a stopword as part of a search, you can sometimes signal the search engine *not* to ignore it by setting it off in double quotation marks: `Portland NEAR "OR"`.

Some (though not all) search engines also pay attention to stopwords that are included as part of a phrase: `"The Man Who Came to Dinner"` or `"to be or not to be"` (**Figure 3.12**). Most of the search engines do a pretty good job of recognizing and acting on stopwords that are included in phrases.

✔ Tips

■ Most major search engines offer all of the basic tools described in this chapter. But keep in mind that the specifics vary from one to the next. In some cases, a search engine may even have a different set of rules depending on whether you're using its simple or advanced search form.

■ Parts 2 and 3 of this book introduce you to many of the specifics for particular search engines. Be sure also to check the search tips and help sections for any search engine you use regularly to learn about new features that may have been added.

TIPS AND TECHNIQUES

4

So far, we've covered search engines and how they work, the importance of choosing unique keywords, and the basic search tools offered by most search engines on the World Wide Web. We'll wrap up this part of the book with some specific tips and techniques that will help you get the most out of the time you spend online—no matter what search engine you decide to use on a regular basis.

We'll start with Alfred and Emily Glossbrenner's "The Seven Habits of Effective Web Searchers." Then we'll offer suggestions for customizing your Web browser so that you can access your favorite search tools automatically. We'll conclude with some advice on keyboard shortcuts and other timesavers.

The Seven Habits at a Glance

1. Develop the Internet habit.

2. Use the best tool for the job.

3. Read the instructions.

4. Choose unique keywords.

5. Use multiple search engines.

6. Consider the source.

7. Know when to look elsewhere.

The Seven Habits of Effective Web Searchers

We're not professional searchers, but we've logged a lot of hours over the years searching the Internet and other online systems. We have a pretty good idea of what works and what doesn't. Here are our recommendations for effective Web searching, organized into seven steps, or habits, that can make you a better searcher.

1. Develop the Internet habit.

When you have a question about anything—and we mean *anything*—your first step in nearly every case should be to check the Net. The answer may lie deep within a company-sponsored Web site, or in a newsgroup posting from two years ago, or among the millions of listings in a white or yellow pages directory, or somewhere else. But with the right search tool and search strategy, chances are you can find it.

2. Use the best tool for the job.

For day-to-day searching, you can't go too far wrong with any of the popular search engines (Google, Yahoo, AltaVista, and so on). Don't forget, though, that each has its strong points—summarized in the sidebar "The Popular Search Engines and What They Do Best" later in this chapter and covered in more detail in Part 2 of this book—that you'll want to consider when choosing the one to use for a particular job.

Keep in mind, too, that as good as these search engines are, they're not the best tools for every job. For example, some search engines include results from Usenet newsgroups as well as the Web. But to take full advantage of newsgroups, you'll want to use Google Groups (`groups.google.com`). Google archives nearly every newsgroup and over 800 million posts and is optimized for newsgroup searches (**Figure 4.1**).

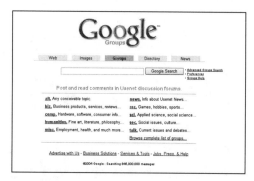

Figure 4.1 Google Groups (`groups.google.com`) is the ideal tool for searching newsgroups. No other site even comes close.

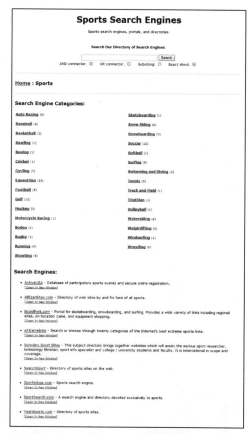

Figure 4.2 Search Engine Guide (`searchengineguide.com`) is a great place to look for special-purpose search engines. Browse by category or use the search feature, as we've done here to look for sports-related search engines.

✔ Tip

- Usenet newsgroups (or *newsgroups* for short) are freewheeling global conversations on virtually every subject imaginable. They've been around far longer than the World Wide Web and are an excellent source of advice, personal opinions, and commentary. Think of them as a means of expanding your circle of acquaintances when you're looking for things like recipes, travel tips, software fixes and work-arounds—you name it.

Part 2 of this book will introduce you to Google groups, while some of our other favorite special-purpose search engines, like Yahoo Groups (`groups.yahoo.com`) for locating Internet mailing lists and InfoSpace (`www.infospace.com`) for finding people are in Part 3.

To track down other special-purpose engines using a searchable directory, visit Search Engine Guide at `searchengineguide.com` (**Figure 4.2**).

The Popular Search Engines and What They Do Best

- **AltaVista** is a good choice for finding obscure facts and figures. It's one of the few search engines to offer full Boolean and case-sensitive searching, as well as a variety of field-search options to help target a search.

- **AOL Search** uses Google's database to provide search services for AOL subscribers. Nonsubscribers can use AOL Search at `search.aol.com`.

- **Ask Jeeves** is a popular search engine for natural-language questions. Part of the Ask Jeeves family, Ask Jeeves for Kids provides kid-friendly content safe for children.

- **Excite** uses the Infospace database and is a good general-purpose search engine and includes people and business searches on its home page.

- **Google** covers more of the Net than any other search engine. When thoroughness counts, be sure to check Google. Its method of ranking Web sites based on *link popularity* (the more links to a particular site, the higher its ranking) works especially well for general searches.

- **HotBot** makes searching for multimedia files and locating Web sites by geography exceptionally easy. If you want the power of AltaVista with a much simpler interface, go with HotBot.

- **Lycos** is another good choice for multimedia searches. Use it as well for finding phrases containing common stopwords (for example, `"to be or not to be"`). Unlike some search engines, Lycos won't ignore stopwords in phrases.

- **MSN Search** is the fourth most popular search engine, partly because it's on the default start page in Internet Explorer. Its database is not as thorough as Google's or Yahoo's.

- **Yahoo** has the most-detailed Web directory, making it an excellent choice for exploring a subject to find out what's available on the Net.

THE SEVEN HABITS OF EFFECTIVE WEB SEARCHERS

3. Read the instructions.

No two search engines work exactly the same way, so it pays to read the online help and search tips provided at the site. For example, some search engines default to an AND search—type several words in the search box, and the engine will assume that you want to find *all* of them in your search results. Other search engines take the same request and by default perform an OR search—returning pages that contain *any* one of the words but not necessarily all of them.

At the minimum, you need to learn how to perform AND, OR, and phrase searches at any site you use on a regular basis. Another important point to zero in on is *case-sensitivity*—whether the search engine recognizes and acts upon uppercase and lowercase letters in your search request. Some search engines offer case-sensitive searching; others ignore case completely.

4. Choose unique keywords.

Before launching a search, take the time to think about what unique words or phrases are likely to appear in the information you want to find and try them first. To locate sites devoted to Impressionist painters, for example, you might try `Monet AND Renoir AND Degas`. That's sure to produce better results than a search for `impressionists` or `painters`.

What about the complete text of a famous quotation or literary work or even a joke you heard at the office? Try a phrase search on some small portion that you remember: `"tiger tiger burning bright"` to locate the William Blake poem (**Figure 4.3**), or `"man walks into a bar"` for that joke you'd like to add to your repertoire.

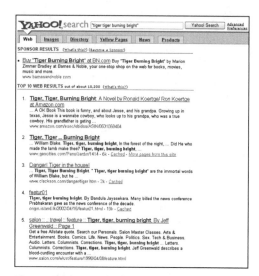

Figure 4.3 A few words of a poem enclosed in double quotation marks are often all it takes to locate the complete work, as shown here.

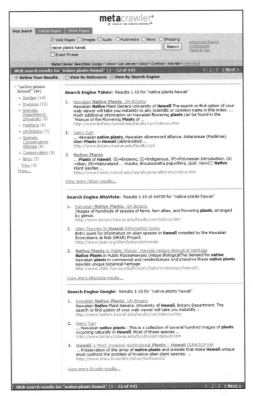

Figure 4.4 With MetaCrawler and other metasearch services, you can direct your query to multiple search engines—in this case, Yahoo, AltaVista, and Google.

5. Use multiple search engines.

Every search engine has its own way of doing things, and none of them covers everything. In fact, as you may recall from our discussion of spiders in Chapter 1, even Google—which currently holds bragging rights to the largest database of Web pages—has yet to find and index much of the Web. So when thoroughness counts, you should plan on using several search engines.

✔ Tips

■ You can automatically submit a query to multiple search engines using what are called *metasearch* services. MetaCrawler (`www.metacrawler.com`) is one of the oldest and most popular (**Figure 4.4**). Others with large followings include Dogpile (`www.dogpile.com`), ProFusion (`www.profusion.com`), and CNET Search.com (`www.search.com`). These services have caught on with many professional and casual searchers, who find that they can be real timesavers.

continues on next page

Multiple Search vs. Metasearch

It might take a bit more time to visit two or three search engines and enter separate queries at each one. But you're likely to get better results in the long run.

Metasearch engines and the Mac's Sherlock feature have several major limitations:

◆ Phrase and Boolean searching are generally not available.

◆ Most return only 10 to 50 hits from any given search engine.

◆ They are highly susceptible to timeouts.

- Macintosh users running Mac OS 8.5 and later versions have a *built-in* metasearch capability. Part of the operating system's Sherlock application, the Internet Search tab lets you specify a word or phrase as well as the sites you want to search (**Figure 4.5**).

- The major drawback to using a metasearch service (or the Mac's Sherlock metasearch feature) is that it takes your query and reduces it to its *simplest* form—stripping out quotation marks, for example, and any other punctuation and search terms that can't be handled by *all* the engines on the metasearch service's list. That may or may not be a problem, depending on the nature of your search. But the search won't produce the same results as going yourself to, say, three different search engines and crafting a query for each one that follows the prescribed format and takes advantage of each engine's unique search features.

- We've also found metasearch engines to be more prone to timeouts than regular search engines. And they typically return only a small number of results (10 to 50) from any given search engine.

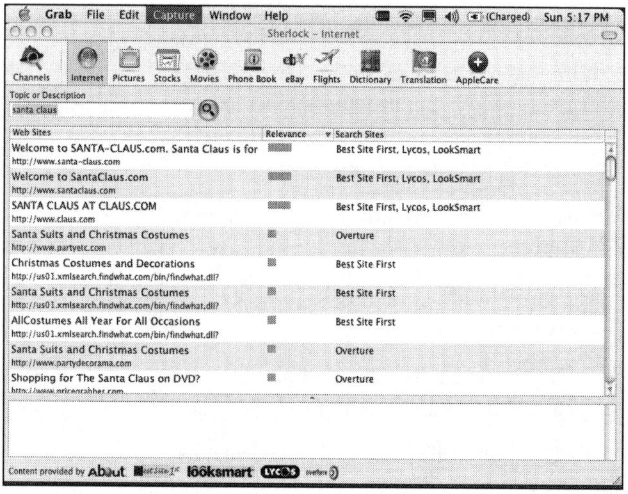

Figure 4.5 Mac users have a built-in metasearch capability called Sherlock. Type a word or phrase in the Topic or Description text box as shown here, select the engines you want to query, and click the search icon.

✔ Tip

- Many Web sites include an About Us or Company Info link that you can click to get more information about the company behind the site.

Avoiding Search Rage

Based on the results of a survey reported in a recent issue of Danny Sullivan's newsletter *Search Engine Report*, it takes about 12 minutes for the average person to start feeling anger and frustration at not finding what he or she is looking for on the Net. Consequently, Sullivan recommends that you follow the "10-minute rule."

If you haven't found what you're looking for in 10 minutes, says Sullivan, it's time to try more traditional alternatives—like contacting your local librarian or picking up the telephone and calling directory assistance to get the phone number of a company that might be able to help you.

6. Consider the source.

Just because it's on the Net doesn't mean the information is either accurate or true. After all, virtually anyone can publish anything on the Internet and the World Wide Web. So be skeptical at all times.

If the information is on a Web site, try to determine the following:

- What person or organization created the information?

- What's the motivation behind it?

- When was the material last updated?

The same goes for newsgroup postings, where unscrupulous marketers sometimes plant positive comments about their own products and negative ones about their competitors'—making it appear as though the comments were made by actual users of the products.

7. Know when to look elsewhere.

Don't assume that the Internet contains the sum total of human knowledge. The Net will always surprise you, both with the information that it does contain and with its lack of information on some specific topic.

Part of being a good online searcher is knowing when to stop. The information you want may or may not be available online. And if it *is* online, it may be buried so deep that it's not worth the time and trouble to locate it.

Your efforts may be better spent getting the information, fact, figure, or whatever you need using conventional printed reference works: almanacs, dictionaries, encyclopedias, and so forth. Start with the reference section at your local library, or ask the reference librarian for help.

continues on next page

THE SEVEN HABITS OF EFFECTIVE WEB SEARCHERS

✔ Tips

■ For really tough search assignments, your best bet may be to find a recognized expert on the subject. Start by consulting the "Sources and Experts" list compiled by news researcher Kitty Bennett of the *St. Petersburg Times*. It's available at www.ibiblio.org/slanews/internet/experts.html.

■ You might also consider hiring a professional searcher (or *information broker,* as they are known in the trade). For recommendations, contact the Association of Independent Information Professionals. The organization's Web site at www.aiip.org (**Figure 4.6**) includes information about its member-referral program.

■ To learn more about becoming a professional searcher yourself, check your local library or favorite out-of-print book source for *The Information Broker's Handbook: Third Edition* by Sue Rugge and Alfred Glossbrenner. Although it's no longer in print, this book is still considered by information professionals to be the definitive work on the subject.

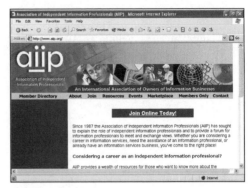

Figure 4.6 To hire a professional searcher, visit the AIIP Web site (www.aiip.org) and look for information about the organization's member referral program.

Customizing Your Web Browser

By default, Microsoft Internet Explorer (IE), is set up so that whenever you go online, you'll be taken automatically to the MSN home page at www.msn.com (**Figure 4.7**).

While MSN Search does a good job, you may prefer to use a different search engine for most of your searches. If this is the case, you have several options.

First, you can customize your Web browser so that the search engine you use most often comes up automatically when you sign on. Use this method if your favorite search engine is also a portal site. This way, you can get to it quickly at any time by clicking your browser's Home button (**Figure 4.8**).

continues on next page

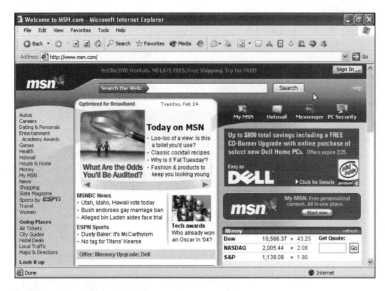

Figure 4.7 This is the MSN home page, the place that Microsoft hopes Internet Explorer users will begin all their online sessions.

Figure 4.8 Once you've customized your Web browser with your preferred home page location, clicking the Home button will take you there instantly.

However, there are better, faster ways to reach your favorite search engines. Most search engines have small applications you can install that add a new toolbar to Internet Explorer (**Figure 4.9**). This makes your favorite search engine easy to reach from any Web page. Most search bars also include other useful tools, including links to popular features provided by the sites.

Or you may prefer to use Internet Explorer's Search Explorer bar.

To customize the default settings for IE searches:

1. Connect to the Internet, if you are not already connected.

   Open the IE Search Explorer bar by clicking the Search button on the Standard toolbar (**Figure 4.10**).

   The Search Explorer bar opens (**Figure 4.11**). The default search engine for the Search Explorer bar is MSN Search.

Figure 4.10 Use Internet Explorer's Search Explorer bar. Select the type of search you need and enter the keywords.

Figure 4.9 Install a search toolbar for your favorite search engine.

CUSTOMIZING YOUR WEB BROWSER

Clear search   Customize

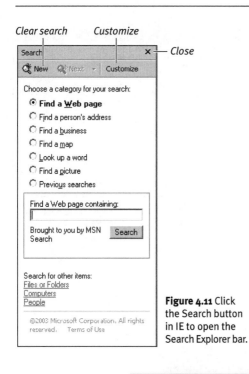

Close

Figure 4.11 Click the Search button in IE to open the Search Explorer bar.

2. Choose Customize to open the Customize Search Settings dialog box (**Figure 4.12**). *Then do one of the following:*

▲ To set a different search engine for each search type listed in the dialog box, select Use Search Assistant; then select the search engine you want to use for each type of search.

continues on next page

Use Search Assistant

Use one search service

Use Search Companion

Autosearch settings (address bar search)

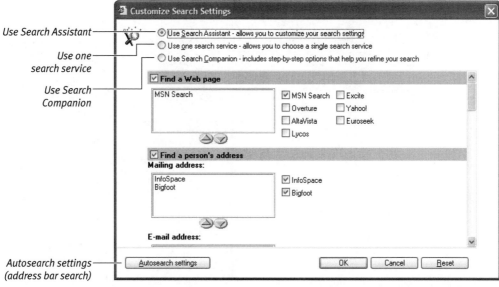

Figure 4.12 Use the Customize Search Settings dialog box to choose the default engine to use for your searches.

CUSTOMIZING YOUR WEB BROWSER

▲ To set the same search engine as the default for all searches, select Use One Search Service (**Figure 4.13**); the Search Explorer bar displays the search engine of your choice (**Figure 4.14**).

▲ To use the animated Search Companion, select Use Search Companion (**Figure 4.15**).

Figure 4.13 Select your favorite search engine if you prefer to use one search engine as the default.

Figure 4.14 When one search engine is selected, the site's search page appears in the Search Explorer bar.

Figure 4.15 An animated search companion can help you with your search.

Figure 4.16 Search from IE's address bar using your default search engine settings.

Figure 4.17 Select from several search engines or disable address bar searching using the Customize Autosearch Settings dialog box.

Using IE's address bar search

Fast and easy access to your favorite search engine doesn't require you to set your home page to a search engine or use toolbars or the Search Explorer bar. Just enter your keywords in the browser's address bar. Enter a question mark (?) or type go or find and then type your keywords and press Enter (**Figure 4.16**).

To change the search engine IE uses for address bar searches:

1. Connect to the Internet; open the IE Search Explorer bar by clicking the Search button on the Standard toolbar (Figure 4.10).

2. Choose Customize (Figure 4.11) to open the Customize Search Settings dialog box (Figure 4.12).

3. Click the Autosearch Settings button to open the Customize Autosearch Settings dialog box (**Figure 4.17**). Then choose the search provider you want to use.

4. In the When Searching field, *do one of the following:*

   ▲ To disable address bar searching, choose Do Not Search from the Address Bar.

   ▲ To use the address bar search and display results in the browser window, choose Just Display Results in Main Window.

   continues on next page

CUSTOMIZING YOUR WEB BROWSER

When you choose MSN as your search engine, you have two additional options in the When Searching field:

▲ To display previews of the top sites, choose Just Go to the Most Likely Site.

▲ To display the results in the Search Explorer bar and preview the most likely sites in the browser window, choose Display Results, and Go to the Most Likely Site.

✔ Tips

■ You can also change Autosearch settings using the Internet Options dialog box. On the IE toolbar, choose Tools > Internet Options and click the Advanced tab. Scroll down until you find the address bar options near the bottom of the tab (**Figure 4.18**). Make selections to control the way results are displayed or to disable address bar searching.

■ Windows power users can create custom address bar searches, triggered by typing a search prefix and then your keywords. You can use any search engine that returns the URL in the address bar. You'll need to use the TweakUI power toy to create the search—use an address bar search for tweakui power toy to find it. After installing it, navigate to Internet Explorer and select Search (**Figure 4.19**); then click Create to open the Search Prefix dialog box. Enter a search prefix and paste the search URL in the fields, replacing the search keyword with %s (**Figure 4.20**). Now you can perform your custom searches by typing just the prefix plus your keywords in the address bar.

Figure 4.18 Customize additional search settings in the Internet Options dialog box.

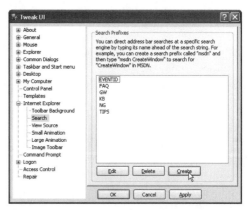

Figure 4.19 Use TweakUI to create address bar searches for many of your favorite sites.

Figure 4.20 Enter a prefix and the search URL, replacing the search string with %s.

Changing your start page to your favorite search engine

If you'd like to customize your Web browser so that the home page is your favorite search engine, here are the steps to follow.

To make your favorite search engine your start page:

◆ **Internet Explorer 5 and up (Windows users):** Choose Tools and then choose Internet Options. In the home page Address box, type the complete Web address (including http://) of your favorite search engine. Then click OK.

Note: If you are running an older version of IE for Windows, choose View (instead of Tools) to change your default home page.

◆ **Internet Explorer 5 (Mac users):** Choose Edit and then choose Preferences. Then click Browser Display in the list on the left side of the screen. In the home page Address box, type the complete Web address (including http://) of your favorite search engine and click OK.

Note: If you're running IE 4.5 for Mac, the link to choose from the list on the Preferences page is Home/Search (instead of Browser Display).

◆ **Netscape 4 and up (Windows and Mac users):** Click Edit and then choose Preferences. On the Navigator page, make sure the Home Page radio button is selected. In the Location box, type the complete Web address (including http://) of your favorite search engine. Then click OK.

Once you've set your browser's default home page location as described here, that's the site that will greet you whenever you sign on. It's also the one you'll be taken to when you click your browser's Home button or select the menu option that tells the browser you want to "Go Home."

Complete Web Addresses for Popular Search Engines

◆ AltaVista:
http://www.altavista.com

◆ AOL Search:
http://search.aol.com

◆ Ask Jeeves:
http://www.ask.com

◆ Excite:
http://www.excite.com

◆ Google:
http://www.google.com

◆ HotBot:
http://www.hotbot.com

◆ Lycos:
http://www.lycos.com

◆ MSN Search:
http://search.msn.com

◆ Yahoo:
http://search.yahoo.com

CUSTOMIZING YOUR WEB BROWSER

To add other search engines to your Favorites or Bookmarks:

◆ With Internet Explorer, go to the search engine site, click Favorites, and then choose the option for adding a page to your Favorites.

Or use the keyboard shortcut Ctrl+D (Windows) or Command+D (Mac).

◆ With Netscape Navigator, go to the search engine site, click Bookmarks, and then choose Add Bookmark (if you're using Netscape 4) or Add Current Page (for Netscape 6).

Or use the keyboard shortcut Ctrl+D (Windows) or Command+D (Mac).

Figure 4.21 Type just the domain name and the browser will add `www.` and `.com` for you.

Keyboard Shortcuts and Other Timesavers

Customizing your Web browser so that it starts automatically with your favorite search engine is one way to save time and get the ball rolling faster when you need to search for information on the Net. Now let's take a look at some other techniques for making your online sessions easier and more productive.

Keyboard shortcuts

Searching for menu commands can be a nuisance with any application, Web browsers included. We find that it's often faster and easier to perform common tasks with a couple of keystrokes. These keyboard shortcuts (**Table 4.1**) for Windows and Macintosh systems work with both Microsoft Internet Explorer and Netscape Navigator.

Making short work of Web addresses

We've mentioned this shortcut before but it bears repeating here: With the latest versions of Microsoft Internet Explorer (IE) and Netscape Navigator, you don't have to type `http://` in your browser's Address or Location box to get to a Web site. You can even leave out `www` and `com` to access your favorite search engine—or any site that begins and ends with those letters.

For example, to go to the Google Web site (`http://www.google.com`), just type `google` in your browser's Address or Location box (**Figure 4.21**) and press Ctrl+Enter (Windows) or Enter (Mac).

Table 4.1

Keyboard Shortcuts

TASK	WINDOWS	MACINTOSH
Go to the next Web page.	Alt+A	Command+[
Go to the previous Web page.	Alt+S	Command+]
Add current Web page to Bookmarks/Favorites.	Ctrl+D	Command+D
Organize Bookmarks/Favorites.	Ctrl+B	Command+B
Copy highlighted text from a Web page.	Ctrl+C	Command+C
Paste highlighted text	Ctrl+V	Command+V
Find text on a Web page.	Ctrl+F	Command+F
Print current Web page.	Ctrl+P	Command+P
Open History folder.	Ctrl+H	Command+H
Open new Web page.	Ctrl+L	Command+L
Open new Browser window.	Ctrl+N	Command+N

Searching for text in Web pages

Search engines often return pages that are loaded with text, and it's not immediately clear that the information you want is there. To avoid the time and trouble of scrolling and reading through page after page, let your Web browser's Find feature do the work for you.

With IE and older versions of Netscape (prior to Version 6), the Find feature is located on the Edit menu. With Netscape 6, it's on the Search menu. Alternatively, with both IE and Netscape, you can access the Find feature by using the keyboard shortcut Ctrl+F (Windows) or Command+F (Mac).

When the Find dialog box appears (**Figure 4.22**), simply enter the word or phrase you want to locate on the Web page and then click your browser's Find (or Find Next) button.

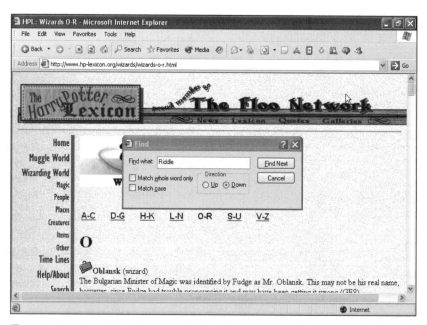

Figure 4.22 Locating the word *riddle* on this Harry Potter Web page is a snap (or a click!) with your browser's Find feature.

New	▶
Open...	Ctrl+O
Edit with Microsoft Office FrontPage	
Save	Ctrl+S
Save As...	
Page Setup...	
Print...	Ctrl+P
Print Preview...	
Send	▶
Import and Export...	
Properties	
Work Offline	
Close	

Figure 4.23 If your browser offers a Print Preview feature, it will be on the File menu. You can save time and paper by using Print Preview to selectively print just the pages you need from a multipage Web page.

Avoiding long print jobs

Imagine clicking your Print button and then discovering that the Web "page" you're printing is actually 28 pages long—and all you wanted was a couple of telephone and fax numbers that appear about two-thirds of the way through the document.

The secret to avoiding a problem like this is to activate your browser's Print Preview feature *before* clicking the Print button.

If you're using IE 5 (Windows or Mac) or Netscape 4 for Windows, you'll find the Print Preview link (**Figure 4.23**) on the File menu. (Unfortunately, Netscape 4 for Macintosh and Netscape 6 for Windows and Mac don't offer Print Preview.) Using Print Preview, find the page that contains the information you're after. (You'll probably have to zoom in to read the text and the page numbers that appear in the footer.) Then print just the page (or pages) you need.

Alternatively, with both IE and Netscape, you can highlight the text you're interested in and then copy and paste it to another application, such as Word or Notepad, using the keyboard shortcuts Ctrl+C to copy and Ctrl+V to paste (in Windows) or Command+C and Command+V (on the Mac). Then print your text from there.

✔ Tip

- From time to time, you'll encounter a Web page that won't appear properly in the Print Preview window. The header and footer may be there, for example, but the main text—the portion you're most interested in printing—will be blank. When that happens, try sending the page to yourself as an e-mail message using the Send (or Send Page) link on the File menu.

Opening a second Web browser

Sometimes the Web is painfully slow, and a complicated search can seem to take forever to finish. When that happens, consider opening a *second* browser window so that you can go about your business and check back in a couple of minutes.

In IE, the command sequence is File > New > Window (**Figure 4.24**). In Netscape, choose File > New Navigator Window (in Windows) or File > New Navigator (on the Mac).

Alternatively, in both IE and Netscape, you can use the keyboard shortcut Ctrl+N (Windows) or Command+N (Mac).

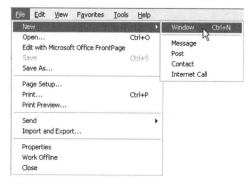

Figure 4.24 You can open a second Web browser window from the Internet Explorer File menu, as shown here. Netscape Navigator works much the same way.

Viewing search results in a new window

How many times has this happened to you: You've initiated a search and produced a list of results that looks quite promising. You begin clicking individual items and the links on those pages to see if they contain the information you're after. Eventually, you want to get back to your original results list. But it's buried so far down in the Back button's list that you can't easily find it. Or it may have even disappeared completely.

You can avoid this problem by keeping your search results on the screen and viewing individual results in a *new* window. Here's the technique: Instead of clicking a link, right-click (Windows) or Control-click (Mac) and then choose the menu option for opening the page in a new window (**Figure 4.25**).

Figure 4.25 Right-clicking The Muggle World brings up the menu that includes an option for opening the link in a new browser window.

Dealing with broken links and "Page Not Found" messages

Some percentage of your searches are bound to lead you to Web pages that no longer exist. When that happens, try deleting everything after the last slash in the URL that appears in your browser's Address or Location box. Then press Enter. The Web site you're after may indeed still exist, but the particular file you specified may have been eliminated or renamed.

PART 2

THE SEARCH ENGINES

The Search Engines

Once you have a basic understanding of search engines and searching (either through direct experience or by reading Part 1), you'll be ready for these chapters on the search engines.

We'll start with the very best—the six most popular search engines:

◆ **Google**

◆ **Yahoo!**

◆ **AOL Search**

◆ **MSN Search**

◆ **Ask Jeeves**

◆ **AltaVista**

We'll discuss the search engines in the order of their popularity; Google and Yahoo handle nearly 60 percent of all Internet searches.

Then we'll discuss the best of the rest—search engines you may find useful for their simple interfaces or advanced search capabilities:

◆ **Excite**

◆ **Lycos**

◆ **HotBot**

Feel free to skip around this part, perhaps starting with a search engine you've used before or heard about and want to try.

And remember: You don't need to master all of these search engines. Use the information presented in this part to learn about the particular strengths of each tool. Work through the step-by-step examples and try some sample searches of your own with the book opened to the appropriate Quick Reference guide.

✔ Tip

■ Once you've identified the search engine you like best, consider making it the default starting location for your Web browser, as suggested in Chapter 4. Add other search engines to your browser's Bookmarks or Favorites list so that you can get to them quickly when you need to consult a second (or third) search engine.

GOOGLE

Google™

Good to Know

◆ Created at Stanford in 1998, Google is one of the top-rated search sites, earning high praise for its simple interface, spot-on search results, and ad-free home page.

◆ Google's database is the largest of all the leading search engines, with more than 4 billion Web pages.

◆ Search results include matches from Google's gigantic database as well as the human-compiled Web directory created by the Open Directory Project.

◆ Google is currently the only search engine that indexes the full text of PDF files and includes them in search results.

◆ Boolean operators and other "power search" capabilities are fairly limited, but Google does such a good job of producing relevant results that this limitation doesn't matter for most searches.

Google is the most popular search engine used today. Google handles more than 200 million requests a day and has a 34.9 percent share of online searches in the United States. The nearest rival is Yahoo, with 27.7 percent. The company made headlines in June 2000 with the announcement that its Googlebot spider had indexed more than a billion Web pages—the first search engine to reach that milestone. It made headlines again in February 2004 as the first search engine to index over 4 billion pages.

More important, Google gets high marks for the *relevancy* of its search results. Using a patent-pending technology, Google not only searches for keywords and phrases—it also employs sophisticated *link analysis* and *data mining* techniques to determine how search results are ranked and presented.

continues on next page

Contact Information

Google, Inc.
Mountain View, CA
Phone: 650-623-4000
Fax: 650-618-1499
www.google.com/contact

The underlying theory is that the best Web sites on a particular topic will have been discovered by other Web users, who will then include links to those pages in their own Web sites. So the more popular a site—based on the number of other sites that link to it—the higher it appears in your search results.

Google doesn't give you nearly as much control over your queries as AltaVista or HotBot. You can't use Boolean operators other than OR, for example, nor can you perform case-sensitive or wildcard searches. Phrase searches are problematic: if the phrase you're searching for includes a common word like *about* or *with*, Google will ignore the word unless the phrase is enclosed in quotation marks.

But frankly, these limitations aren't really a problem for most day-to-day search tasks. As long as you give Google two or three unique keywords to work with, there's a good chance you'll find what you're looking for within the first few listings in your search results.

✔ Tips

- Google was created in 1998 by Stanford doctoral students Larry Page and Sergey Brin, who dropped out of the school's computer science program, got venture-capital funding, and launched the service as a privately held company in 1999.

- Several sites, including AOL Search (`search.aol.com`), have licensed the Google technology, so when you search at those sites, your results are coming (at least in part) from the Google database. As a result, Google handles close to 75 percent of all searches.

- Prepare to be amazed the first time you conduct a Google search. Because the search engine's work is spread out over a network of some 6,000 PCs, most searches take less than half a second.

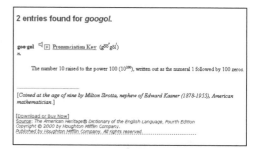

2 entries found for *googol.*

goo·gol [P] Pronunciation Key (gōō'gôl')
n.

The number 10 raised to the power 100 (10¹⁰⁰), written out as the numeral 1 followed by 100 zeros.

[*Coined at the age of nine by Milton Sirotta, nephew of Edward Kasner (1878-1955), American mathematician.*]

[Download or Buy Now]
Source: *The American Heritage® Dictionary of the English Language, Fourth Edition*
Copyright © 2000 by Houghton Mifflin Company.
Published by Houghton Mifflin Company. All rights reserved.

Figure 5.1 The word *google* is based on a mathematical term coined in 1938 by a young boy named Milton Sirotta. This definition is from `dictionary.reference.com`.

- *Google* is a play on the word *googol* (**Figure 5.1**), coined in 1938 by an American mathematician's nine-year-old nephew. The boy had been asked by his uncle what word he would use for a truly gigantic number, represented by 1 followed by 100 zeros. Google's founders chose the name to convey their commitment to organizing the immense body of information available on the Web. Today, a billion pages; tomorrow, a googol!

- For more information about Google—press releases, corporate history, job openings, products from the company store—click Jobs, Press, & Help on the search engine's home page.

Figure 5.2 The Google home page is the least cluttered among all the leading search engines. The search form gets exclusive billing, and there are no banner ads.

Figure 5.3 Google gives you two choices for submitting a query: Google Search to display a list of results and I'm Feeling Lucky to go directly to the first site on the list.

The Google Home Page

If you prefer to do your Web searches in a clutter-free environment, you'll *love* the Google home page (**Figure 5.2**). Talk about a search engine that's focused on searching! No Web directory to browse. No portal features such as news headlines, weather reports, and stock quotes to procrastinate with. No banner ads or annoying animated graphics to distract you.

The Google home page is devoted *exclusively* to its search form. The Web directory and advanced features like field searching and language options are all relegated to underlying pages.

Search form

The Google search form (**Figure 5.3**) consists of a box for entering queries, plus your choice of two buttons to send the queries off for processing:

◆ **Google Search**. This is the button you'll use most of the time. It works just like you'd expect—processing your query and producing a list of results.

◆ **I'm Feeling Lucky**. This button automatically takes you to the first Web page in your search results, instead of displaying the list—an interesting idea, but not all that necessary. Google returns search results with such blinding speed (usually a half second or less) that skipping the results list doesn't save much time.

Google defaults to an AND search, looking for *all* the words that you type in the search box, so plus signs (+) aren't necessary. The only Boolean operator that Google recognizes is OR, which must be typed in full caps: `genetics OR genome`.

Advanced Search option

The Advanced Search link (**Figure 5.4**) on the Google home page takes you to a fill-in-the-blanks form that you can use for somewhat more sophisticated queries (**Figure 5.5**). You can limit your search to specific Web page fields (titles, URLs, domains, and links) or to pages written in a particular language.

The Advanced Search form also allows you to display more search results per page (up to 100) and gives you access to several topic-specific search tools: Apple Macintosh, BSD Unix, Linux, U.S. government, and universities.

Google Directory option

To reach the Google directory, you need to click the More link (shown in Figure 5.2) and then the Directory link (**Figure 5.6**) takes you to a hierarchical guide to the Web, organized into 16 major topic categories and dozens of subcategories (**Figure 5.7**). Like a number of leading search engines, Google gets its Web directory from the Open Directory Project (`dmoz.org`), a volunteer effort to identify and catalog the best Web sites, based on the judgments of human beings rather than automated spider programs.

When you enter a query using the Google search form, your results automatically include matching categories and sites from the Web directory. But on occasion, you may want to browse the directory or search its contents, instead of searching the entire Web. That's what the Google Directory link is for.

Figure 5.4 Google's Advanced Search option gives you access to some additional features not available on the home page.

Figure 5.5 Using this form on the Advanced Search page, you can create more complex queries and exercise some control over how your results are presented.

Figure 5.6 Google doesn't display its Web directory on the home page. You have to click the More link and then select Directory to display it.

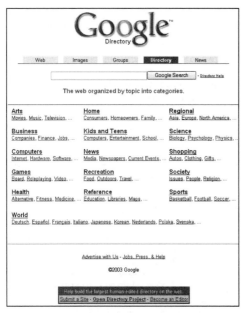

Figure 5.7 Once you're on the Google Directory page, you can search the directory or drill down through its many categories and subcategories.

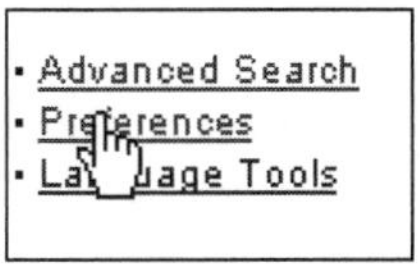

Figure 5.8 You can customize a handful of Google search options using the Preferences link.

Figure 5.9 To get back to the Google home page from anywhere within the site, click the company logo.

✔ Tips

■ The Preferences link (**Figure 5.8**) on the Google home page gives you access to several useful customization options. You can set language preferences, increase the number of results per page from 10 to 100, specify that your results be displayed in a new browser window, and turn on content filtering. For more on Google preferences, see "Customizing Google" later in this chapter.

■ To make Google your default home page, follow the instructions in "Customizing Your Web Browser" in Chapter 4.

■ You can get back to the Google home page at any time by clicking the Google logo (**Figure 5.9**) at the top of every page within the site.

Searching with Google

Doing a search from the Google home page is pretty straightforward. There are no drop-down menus or radio buttons to consider. Just type several unique words or phrases in the search box and click Google Search to submit your query. Chances are you'll get pretty good results most of the time.

If you decide to make Google your primary search engine, however, you should know a few basic details about entering and combining keywords so you can search with more precision. To refine your queries even further, you can include field-search terms to zero in on Web page titles, URLs, domain names, and links.

To enter a query:

1. Go to the Google home page (www.google.com) and type several descriptive words or a phrase in quotation marks in the search box (**Figure 5.10**). Google allows you to use up to 10 words in your search.

   By default, Google performs an AND search, looking for *all* the words, so there's no need to put plus signs (+) in front of required words. In fact, if you do use plus signs, Google typically ignores them.

   The only time you need to use a plus sign is when you are searching for a very common word (or *stopword*), like *about* or *for* or *with* (**Figure 5.11**). In that case, the plus sign signals Google that the word should *not* be treated as a stopword: +about guides, for example, to search for information on the company that creates the About guides to the Internet (www.about.com).

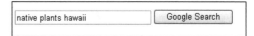

Figure 5.10 When you type multiple words in the search box, Google assumes that you want to find *all* the words. You don't need to link them with AND or put plus signs (+) in front of them.

Figure 5.11 Plus signs are required only for very common words, which Google typically ignores. A search like this tells Google not to ignore the word *about*.

Figure 5.12 Use the Boolean operator OR in full caps to tell Google that you want to look for one word *or* the other.

2. To tell Google that you want to perform an OR search, type your search words separated by OR in full caps: hilary OR hillary, for example, to look for either spelling of the name (**Figure 5.12**). You *must* use full caps for OR so that Google knows to treat it as a Boolean operator.

3. To exclude a certain word or phrase from your search results, type a minus sign (–) directly in front of it: Portobello –mushrooms, for example, if you're looking for information about Portobello Road rather than the fungus.

4. To include synonyms in your search, use a tilde (~) in front of the word. For example, a synonym search for ~food includes pages about nutrition and recipes in the results (**Figure 5.13**)

continues on next page

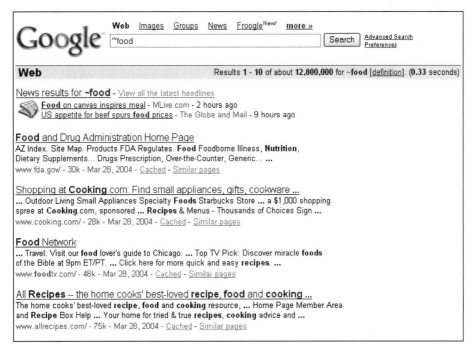

Figure 5.13 Use a tilde (~) to perform a synonym search. Searching for ~food finds pages about nutrition and recipes as well as food.

✔ Tips

- Except for the OR operator, Google isn't sensitive to case. You can type search words and phrases in uppercase, lowercase, or a combination, and you'll get the same results.

- As with most of the leading search engines, you can search for a phrase—even one that's composed almost entirely of stopwords—by enclosing the phrase in double quotation marks. If you find that Google ignores your phrase because it contains stopwords, you can redo your Google search, putting plus signs in front of the words that were ignored the first time around. (Don't put plus signs in front of all the words, though, or you'll be back to square one.) Alternatively, try another search engine. Lycos (www.lycos.com) is an especially good choice, because it will *not* ignore common words that are part of a phrase enclosed in double quotation marks.

- Results include links to news stories, when available, and a definition of the search items.

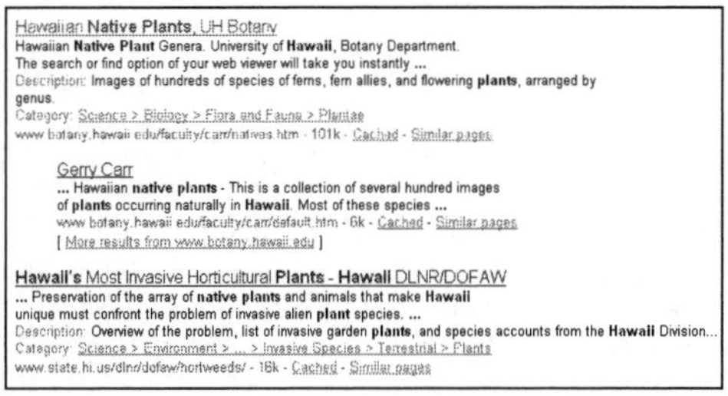

Figure 5.14 Google puts your search terms in bold to make them easy to spot and presents only two Web pages from any given site, one indented below the other.

Figure 5.15 To uncluster your results and view more Web pages from a given site, click the More Results From link.

Figure 5.16 If you have trouble connecting to a Web site listed in your search results, click Cached to display a copy of the page as it looked when last visited by the Google spider.

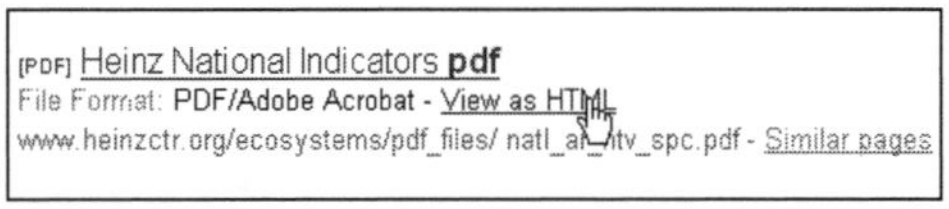

Figure 5.17 You have two options with PDF files: click the link following the [PDF] label to view the file with the Adobe Acrobat Reader, or click View as HTML to view it in HTML format.

To view your search results:

1. Click Google Search (or press Enter) to display your results, 10 to a page, with your search terms highlighted in bold and presented with a few words of surrounding text from the Web page.

   Google clusters the results and presents only two Web pages from any given site—one indented below the other—to give you more variety in your search results (**Figure 5.14**).

2. To uncluster the results and view additional pages from a particular Web site, click the More Results From link (**Figure 5.15**).

3. In some cases, Google also gives you the option of clicking a Cached link (**Figure 5.16**) to display a copy of the Web page at the time it was indexed by the Google spider. If you have a problem linking to the current version of the Web page (because the site is down, for example), try retrieving the cached version.

4. Your search results may include items that begin with a [PDF] label. Google is in the process of indexing the full text of Adobe PDF (Portable Document Format) files that are available on the Web. If you have the free Adobe Acrobat Reader installed, you can download and view these items by clicking the link next to the [PDF] label. Otherwise, click View as HTML (**Figure 5.17**) to view the document in HTML format .

continues on next page

✔ Tips

- Each item on the Google search results page includes a Similar Pages link that's intended to help you find other sites that might be of interest. Sometimes it works, and sometimes it doesn't. A more consistently effective way to find related sites is to click the Category link (**Figure 5.18**), if there is one. That will take you to the appropriate spot in the Google Web directory, where you will find related sites that have been chosen by human beings, not an automated scout program.

- The statistics bar (**Figure 5.19**) at the top of the search results page displays your query and tells you how many results were found and how long the search took. If one of your search terms is underlined, you can click it for an instant definition.

Hawaiian **Native Plants**, UH Botany
Hawaiian **Native Plant** Genera. University of **Hawaii**, Botany Department.
The search or find option of your web viewer will take you instantly ...
Description: Images of hundreds of species of ferns, fern allies, and flowering **plants**, arranged by genus.
Category: Science > Biology > Flora and Fauna > Plantae
www.botany.hawaii.edu/faculty/carr/natives.htm - 101 Cached - Similar pages

Figure 5.18 Category links, labeled as such and easily recognized by the greater-than (>) symbols separating the various subtopics, can help you find Web pages with related content.

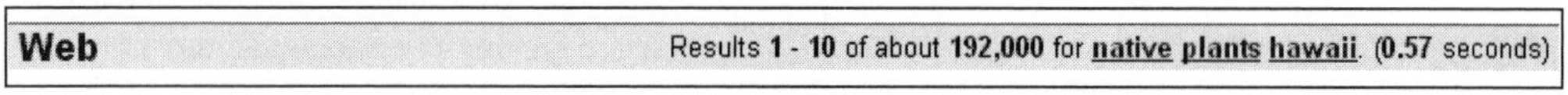

| Web | Results **1 - 10** of about **192,000** for **native plants hawaii**. (0.57 seconds) |

Figure 5.19 In addition to finding out how many search results Google located (and how quickly), you can use the statistics bar to get a definition for any search word or phrase that's underlined.

Figure 5.20 You can refine a Google search by simply adding another word to your query and running the search again.

To refine a Google query:

1. Try adding another unique word to the search box at the top of the search results page (**Figure 5.20**) and submitting your query again.

   Since Google looks for *all* the words in your query, this has the effect of searching *within* your original results (also known as *set searching*). It's faster than scrolling to the bottom of the page and using the Search within Results option.

2. As you may recall from the discussion of keywords in Chapter 2, one of the best ways to narrow the focus of a search is to zero in on Web page *titles*.

   ▲ Enter `allintitle:` followed directly (no space after the colon) by a phrase in quotation marks or by multiple words that you want to find in Web page titles: `allintitle:human genome project history` (**Figure 5.21**).

   ▲ To perform an OR search of words in titles, enter `intitle:` followed directly by two or more words separated by spaces: `intitle:genome DNA mapping`.

   continues on next page

Figure 5.21 To produce these results, we searched for `allintitle:human genome project history`. Note that all of the search terms appear in bold in the Web page titles.

✔ Tips

- You can also use URL, domain, and link field-search terms in your Google queries. For examples, see the Google Quick Reference (**Table 5.1**).

- For even easier field searching, click Advanced Search and use the fill-in-the-blanks form and drop-down menus to focus on Web page titles, URLs, domain names, or links.

- Google's search tips and help information are splendid—written in plain English and covering just about any question you might have about how to construct a query and interpret the results. You'll find a Search Tips link on every search results page or by clicking All About Google.

Table 5.1

Google Quick Reference		
FOR THIS TYPE OF SEARCH:	**DO THIS:**	**EXAMPLES:**
Plain-English Question	Simply type a phrase or question that expresses the concept, using as many words as necessary.	`Who invented the steam idea or engine?`
Phrase Search	Type the phrase surrounded by double quotation marks (common words will be ignored, even with quotation marks.	`"industrial revolution"`

AND Search (multiple words and phrases, each of which must be present)	Type the words (or phrases in quotation marks) separated by a space, without any special punctuation. Use a plus sign (+) only if one of the words in your query is a very common word (or *stopword*).	`Edison "light bulb"`
		
		`+about guides history`

OR Search (multiple words and phrases, any one of which may be present)	Type words or phrases (no quotation marks allowed) separated by OR (full caps required).	`phonograph OR speaking machine`
NOT Search (to exclude a word or phrase)	Use a minus sign (–) directly in front of the word or phrase you want to exclude.	`Lincoln -"town car"`
Synonym Search	Use a tilde (~) in front of the search word to include synonyms in the search.	`~food returns recipes and nutrition information.`
Case-Sensitive Search	Not available.	
Date Search	Advanced search option; choose from within the last three months, six months, or year.	
Field Search	Type the field-search term followed by a colon and the search word or phrase. Note that there is no space after the colon. (For fill-in-the-blanks field searching, use Advanced Search.)	
	Titles. Use `allintitle:` or `intitle:` with one or more search words. The first example would look for *both* words in page titles; the second would look for *either* word.	`allintitle:inventions inventors` `intitle:inventions inventors`
	URLs. Use `allinurl:` or `inurl:` with one or more words you want to find in the URL. The first example would look for *both* words; the second would look up *either* word.	`allinurl:pdf 1099` `inurl:patents trademarks`
	Domains. Use `site:` followed by a domain name or type (com, edu, gov, and so on) along with the search word or phrase you want to find at that site or domain type.	`site:nationalgeographic.com inventions` `site:gov patents`
	The first example would find pages at the National Geographic Web site that include the word *inventions*. The second would find government (gov) Web sites that include the word *patents*.	
	Links. Use `link:` with a specific Web address to find all pages that link to that address. The example would find pages that link to the U.S. Patent and Trademark Office. You *cannot* combine a `link:` search term with another search word or phrase.	`link:www.uspto.gov`
Numeric Range	Type the lower number followed by three periods and then the higher number. Don't use spaces between the numbers or periods. Leave off either number to do an open-ended search.	`20...30  ...100  1000...`
Nested Search	Not available.	
Proximity Search	Not available.	
Wildcard Search	Not available.	

Using Advanced Search

Many diehard Google fans never avail themselves of the offerings on the Advanced
Search page (**Figure 5.22**). In most cases,
that's because searching from the Google
home page produces such consistently good
results. Why bother mastering advanced
techniques when typing a few unique words
and phrases gets the job done so effectively?

Advanced Search form

Page-Specific Search form

Links to specialized search forms

Figure 5.22 Google's Advanced Search page lets you create more complicated queries using fill-in-the-blanks forms and drop-down menus.

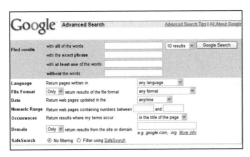

Figure 5.23 Creating an advanced search couldn't be easier. Fill in the blanks and select from the menu options.

Figure 5.24 You can type words in one or more of these four search boxes to tell Google whether you want to perform an AND, OR, phrase, or NOT search.

Figure 5.25 If you like being able to scroll quickly through 20 or more search results, you can boost the number of results presented on each page to a maximum of 100.

Well, the fact is, *advanced search* is actually a bit of a misnomer for this page. *Power-assisted search* comes closer to describing what you'll find here. For certain types of queries, you can save keystrokes and avoid having to remember (and correctly type) special search terms and punctuation. Just fill in the blanks and choose options from the appropriate drop-down menus, and away you go!

The Advanced Search page also lets you control certain aspects of the presentation of your search results, with options for increasing the number of results per page, choosing your preferred language, and filtering out content that you may find offensive.

To enter an Advanced Search query:

1. Click Advanced Search on the Google home page and use the fill-in-the-blanks form at the top of the page (**Figure 5.23**) to construct your query. Start by entering your search words or phrases in the appropriate search boxes according to whether you want to look for *any* of the words, *all* the words, the *exact phrase*, pages *without* a certain word, or a combination (**Figure 5.24**).

   You don't need to use any punctuation, as long as you enter your search terms in the correct boxes. To look for a phrase, for example, type it, without quotation marks, in the With the Exact Phrase box. To perform a NOT search, type *only* the word you want to exclude (no minus sign) in the Without the Words box.

   Searches are *not* case sensitive, so you'll get the same results using uppercase, lowercase, or a mix of the two.

2. To see more than the standard 10 results per page (so that you can scroll through them more quickly), use the drop-down menu (**Figure 5.25**) to boost the number as high as 100.

continues on next page

USING ADVANCED SEARCH

3. To limit your search to Web page titles or URLs, make a selection from the Occurrences menu (**Figure 5.26**).

This procedure has the same effect as using one of Google's field-search terms (`allintitle:`, `intitle:`, `allinurl:`, `inurl:`) in your query.

Figure 5.26 The Occurrences menu lets you focus your search on Web page titles or URLs.

4. To restrict your search to Web pages written in English or some other language, use the Language menu (**Figure 5.27**).

Google's default setting is Any Language.

5. Use the Numeric Range field to restrict results. Use it to search for a CD player priced between $50 and $100, to find tips above tip number 100, or to find a page containing a number below 20. To enter a range in a query on the home page, use the format 50...100, separating the numbers with three periods. Leave off either number for open-ended searches: `100...` or `...20`.

6. To limit your search to a specific domain name or type (`com`, `edu`, `gov`, `org`, `net`, and so on), use the Domain option. Using this option is similar to using Google's `site:` field-search term.

For example, type `npr.org` in the Domain search box to tell Google to look for your search words only at the NPR Web site (**Figure 5.28**). Or type `org` to focus on all sites that are classified as nonprofit organizations.

To specifically avoid the NPR site, instead of Only, choose Don't from the Return Results from the Site or Domain dropdown menu in the Domain section.

Figure 5.27 Most Web pages are written in English, but if you want to make sure that you see *only* English-language pages, change the Language menu option from Any Language to English.

Figure 5.28 The Domain section makes it easy to limit your search to a specific Web site, in this case, `npr.org`.

Figure 5.29 The Date section allows you to limit your search to pages updated recently.

7. To restrict the search to recently updated sites, choose the Date option (**Figure 5.29**) and from the drop-down menu select Past 3 Months, Past 6 Months, or Past Year. The default selection is Anytime; it often returns results from pages indexed in the late 1990s that haven't been updated since.

8. When you're ready to submit your query, click Google Search or press Enter.

✔ Tips

■ Google presents search results the same way, regardless of whether you search from the Google home page or the Advanced Search page. For details, see "Searching with Google" earlier in this chapter.

■ You can permanently change your settings for language, number of search results per page, and content filtering using Google's Preferences feature. For details, see "Customizing Google" later in this chapter.

To search for similar pages or links:

1. Scroll down to the Page-Specific Search area of the Advanced Search page and enter a Web address in either the Similar or Links box (**Figure 5.30**).

2. *Do one of the following:*

   ▲ Type a Web address in the Similar box to find other Web pages with content that is similar or related, based on information collected and analyzed by Google's automated scout program. Then click Search to submit your query.

   ▲ Type a Web address in the Links box and click Search to find pages that link to that site. (This produces the same results as using a `link:` field-search term in a Google query.)

✔ Tips

- Of the two Page-Specific Search options, you'll probably find Links to be the most useful. Webmasters and Web site creators often use link searches to get a handle on a site's popularity—the more links, the more popular the site.

- Link searches can also be quite effective in tracking down similar or related Web sites. If you're a fan of Burt's Bees, for example, a link search for www.burtsbees.com could help you locate other Web sites that offer beeswax products.

Figure 5.30 Instead of looking for Web pages that are similar to www.burtsbees.com, we've specified that we want to locate all the pages that link to it.

Figure 5.31 Each of these links leads to a special Google search page.

Figure 5.32 Search for free image editors on the Apple Macintosh search form, and Google will know that you don't want to see PC or Windows tools.

To perform specialized searches:

◆ Scroll down to the Topic-Specific Searches area of the Advanced Search page (**Figure 5.31**) and click one of the links for Google's specialized search tools. Options include Apple Macintosh, BSD Unix, Linux, U.S. Government, and Universities.

Choose Apple Macintosh, for example, and you'll be presented with a special Google search form (**Figure 5.32**) that you can use to search for all things Mac—without including the words *apple* or *macintosh* in your queries.

✔ Tip

■ Just for fun, we tried searching for *pie* using the Apple Macintosh search form, expecting that we might get a "No results found" message. Instead, the first two pages of search results were dominated by Web pages offering apple pie recipes! Clearly, these specialized tools are works in progress.

Customizing Google

Google doesn't currently offer much in the way of customization features. You can't change the content and layout of the home page, for example, nor can you save Google searches so you can run them again.

What you *can* do is control the language that Google uses to communicate with you as you search. You can also make a couple of adjustments in the way your results are presented, and you can turn on Google's SafeSearch content filter if you wish.

The customization process takes only a minute—there's no sign-up requirement or membership form to fill out and only a few options to consider. It's certainly worth doing if you decide to make Google your primary search engine.

To customize Google:

1. Go to the Google home page (www.google.com) and click Preferences to access the page that allows you to customize your search settings (**Figure 5.33**).

2. The first two settings have to do with language preferences.

    ▲ If English isn't your native tongue, you can use the Interface Language menu (**Figure 5.34**) to change Google's tips and messages to another language (**Figure 5.35**), overriding the browser language settings.

    ▲ If you want make sure that your Google results never include Web pages written in languages you don't understand, use the Search Language area to limit your results to specific languages (**Figure 5.36**). (You can click as many boxes as you wish.)

Figure 5.33 The Preferences page lets you change Google's default language settings and control certain aspects of the results display.

Figure 5.34 Google "speaks" more than a dozen languages, which you can choose from the Interface Language menu.

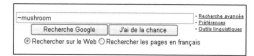

Figure 5.35 With the Interface Language menu set to French, Google's buttons and menus are in French.

Figure 5.36 The Search Language area of the Preferences page lets you limit your Google searches to Web pages written in one or more languages.

Number of Results	Google's default (10 results) provides the fastest results Display [10 ▾] results per page.
Results Window	☐ Open search results in a new browser window.

Figure 5.37 These settings let you increase the number of items displayed on each page of your Google results and specify that you want to open search results in a new browser window.

SafeSearch Filtering	Google's SafeSearch blocks web pages containing explicit sexual content from appearing in search results. ○ Use strict filtering (Filter both explicit text and explicit images) ◉ Use moderate filtering (Filter explicit images only - default behavior) ○ Do not filter my search results.

Figure 5.38 By default, Google's SafeSearch content filter filters out explicit images.

3. In the SafeSearch Filtering area, you can adjust SafeSearch content filtering (**Figure 5.37**). The default setting is moderate filtering, which blocks most Web pages containing pornography and explicit sexual content from your search results. You can also turn filtering off or enable extreme filtering if young children use your computer.

4. The next two settings give you a small measure of control over how your search results are presented (**Figure 5.38**).

▲ Many Web searchers prefer to boost the Number of Results setting from the default of 10 results per page to as many as 50 or 100. (Displaying more results per page makes scrolling through a large number of results, or searching them with your browser's Find feature, faster and easier.)

▲ If you select the Results Window option, whenever you click an item on your Google search results page, a new browser window will open to display it. As with the number of results per page, this is a personal preference that may or may not be important to you.

5. When you're finished customizing Google, click Save Preferences (**Figure 5.39**). Note that Preferences are saved in a cookie, so you'll need to enable cookies if you disabled them.

continues on next page

CUSTOMIZING GOOGLE

Save your preferences when finished and **return to search**.	[Save Preferences]

Figure 5.39 Be sure to save your settings before leaving the Preferences page.

✔ Tips

- Your Google Preferences settings apply to searches from both the Google home page and the Advanced Search page.

- If you decide to make Google your primary search engine, you may want to customize your Web browser so that it takes you to Google automatically whenever you go online and whenever you click your browser's Home button. You can tell your browser to use either the Google home page or the Advanced Search page as its default home-page location, using these addresses: http://www.google.com (Google home page) http://www.google.com/advanced_search (Advanced Search page). If you're not sure how to set your Web browser's home-page location, see "Customizing Your Web Browser" in Chapter 4.

Google and Practical Jokes

If you're a practical joker, you've probably already annoyed friends, family, and co-workers by changing their keyboard or Internet Explorer language.

Google's language options give you one more chance to annoy your loved ones. The Interface Language menu includes such unconventional languages as Elmer Fudd, Hacker, Klingon, and Pig Latin.

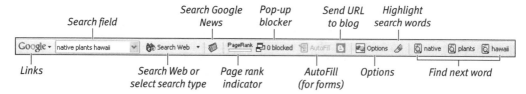

Figure 5.40 Install the Google toolbar and you'll have many of Google's tools at your fingertips even when you're not at the Google site.

Figure 5.41 You can search any Google site from the toolbar.

Using Google's Tools

In the past, you needed to set Google as your home page if you wanted its search tools at your fingertips. This is no longer necessary. Instead of setting your browser home page to Google, you can install the Google toolbar, for Internet Explorer, or the Google deskbar, which works with any browser and adds a search field to your Windows taskbar.

Google toolbar for Internet Explorer

In addition to a search field, the Google tool-bar (**Figure 5.40**) includes helpful features such as a menu for selecting a specific area of the Google site to search (**Figure 5.41**), a button to highlight the search terms on a Web page, buttons to find the next instance of a keyword on a page, and an indicator that shows the current page's ranking in the search results.

continues on next page

USING GOOGLE'S TOOLS

The Google button offers links to Google's home page, Advanced Search, Google Groups, and other Google sites (**Figure 5.42**) as well as to the Toolbar Options dialog box and help and an option to clear the search history.

In addition, the toolbar has buttons you can use to block pop-ups, add the current URL to a blog (or Web log) at Google's blogger.com site, or visit Google's news site at news.google.com.

Click Options to open the Toolbar Options dialog box.

◆ Use the Options tab to remove accessories you don't want or need (**Figure 5.43**).

Figure 5.42 You can easily go to a Google site using the toolbar's links to Google Web pages.

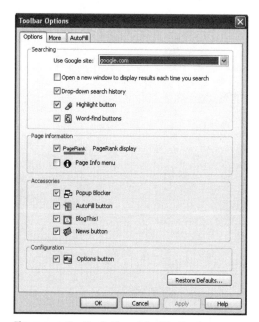

Figure 5.43 Use the Options tab of the Toolbar Options dialog box to hide or show features and accessories.

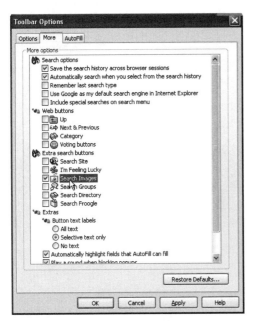

Figure 5.44 Use the More tab to add buttons to the toolbar for your favorite searches.

◆ Use the More tab to add buttons or features to the toolbar (**Figure 5.44**). For example, if you search Google Groups often, add a button for Search Groups to the toolbar, rather than choosing Google Groups from the Search menu.

◆ The AutoFill tab holds personal information, such as your name and address, that's used to fill in online forms automatically. It can also hold your credit card information. If your computer is used by others, don't use AutoFill.

Google deskbar

The deskbar is a toolbar added to your Windows taskbar, not unlike the Address toolbar, and it returns the search results in a mini-viewer window (**Figure 5.45**). The mini-viewer is resizable and has the basic browser options: browse forward and backward, open the search in a normal browser window, or close the search window.

Using the deskbar is simple: type your keywords in the taskbar field and click the Search button (**Figure 5.46**). The mini-viewer opens with the results of your search.

In addition to the standard Google searches, including I'm Feeling Lucky, Google Groups, and Search News, you can add URLs to your favorite search engines or sites, provided the site includes the search string in a URL in the address bar, like this search for campaign at the New York Times:

http://query.nytimes.com/search/query?
query=campaign&date=site1week

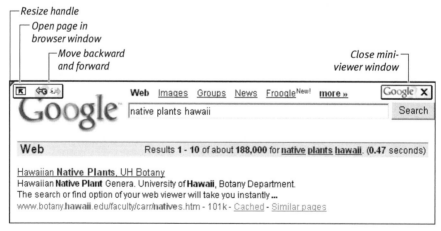

Figure 5.45 The Google deskbar places a toolbar on the Windows taskbar, opening a mini-viewer when you execute a search.

To create a custom search in the deskbar:

1. Search for something at your favorite Web site and copy the URL.

   For example, you can create a search at the *New York Times* Web site.

2. Click the arrow beside the Begin Search button in the taskbar (Figure 5.46) and select Options from the menu.

3. In the Options dialog box, select Customized Searches.

4. Click Add to open the Custom Search Description dialog box.

5. Enter a name for your search and paste the URL in the URL field (**Figure 5.47**). Enter a shortcut key if desired.

continues on next page

Type search
words   Begin search

Figure 5.46 The taskbar toolbar contains only the search field and button.

Select search type
and options

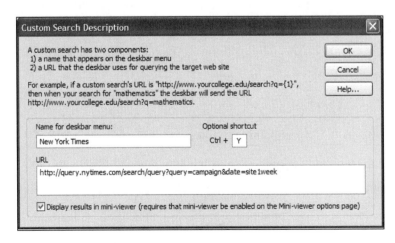

Figure 5.47 Add searches for your favorite sites to the deskbar. Any site that shows the search string in the URL can be added. In this example, we're creating a search for the *New York Times* Web site.

6. Locate your search string in the URL and replace it with {1} and click OK (**Figure 5.48**).

Now you can use the deskbar to search at your favorite sites. Enter a search string and your shortcut key or choose the search by name from the Begin Search menu (**Figure 5.49**).

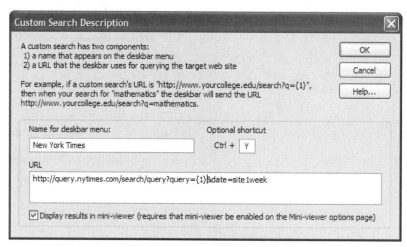

Figure 5.48 Copy the search URL from IE's address bar, paste it in the URL field, and replace the search words (*campaign* in this example) with {1}.

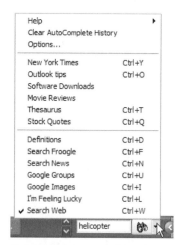

Figure 5.49 Enter a search word or phrase in the search field and select *New York Times* from the menu to begin your search.

GOOGLE SPECIALTY SEARCHES

Google™

Google supports a number of specialty searches, making finding things on the Web easier than ever. You can use it to look up tracking information and phone numbers, map addresses, and check the status of airline flights. While in each of these cases, your Google search returns a link to another site containing the specific information you seek, you need fewer mouse clicks compared to when you use the sites directly.

For example, to look up UPS tracking information directly through the UPS Web site, you need to go to UPS.com, select your country, enter your tracking number, and agree to the terms and conditions before you get the online tracking information. When you use Google, you just enter the tracking number in the search field and click the link, and you go directly to UPS's tracking information. The process is even more convenient when you use the Google toolbar or use Google as your browser home page.

You also can use Google to comparison shop. Use Google's Froogle to research products and compare prices or browse the mail-order catalog collection at Google.

Good to Know

◆ Google is always looking for innovative ways to present the contents of the Google search engine database.

◆ For the newest types of Google searches, go to www.google.com/options.

Contact Information

Google, Inc.
Mountain View, CA
Phone: 650-623-4000
Fax: 650-618-1499
www.google.com/contact/

Number Searches

As already mentioned, you can use Google to track packages. That's because Google now supports number searches—just enter your number, and Google returns a link to relevant information. You can use Google's number search capability to search on a wide variety of numbers, including the following:

◆ UPS, FedEx, and USPS tracking numbers

◆ Airline flight numbers, to check flight status, including gate, departure, and arrival times

◆ Area codes, to find where the area code is located

◆ Phone numbers, for reverse phone number lookups

◆ Vehicle ID numbers (VINs)

◆ UPC codes

◆ FAA airplane registration codes (typically found on the airplane's tail)

◆ FCC equipment ID numbers

◆ Patents

Except for patent searches, you need to enter just the number and click Search. A patent search requires the format **patent 123456**.

In addition to returning a link to the appropriate Web site, Google reports whether it finds any matches for your number in its search database. If it does, it includes these results as well. You'll most often see such additional results when you enter short numbers such as telephone area codes or zip codes. For longer numbers, such as package tracking numbers, Google most likely will tell you that it couldn't find any matches in its database.

✔ Tip

■ Click the Tools & Services link on the Google home page to see the most up-to-date search offerings from Google.

Figure 6.1 Use a package tracking number as your search keyword.

Figure 6.2 Google recognizes that you've entered a package tracking number and provides a link to the carrier's Web site—in this case, ups.com—so you can quickly learn where the package is. Google also tells you whether it found any sites in its database that contain your tracking number.

Figure 6.3 Google links to the flight status pages at travelocity.com and fboweb.com.

To track packages:

1. Enter the package's tracking number, including any spaces, in Google's search field (**Figure 6.1**).

2. Click Search.

   Google recognizes that the number is a tracking number and provides a link to the shipper's Web site (**Figure 6.2**).

3. Click the link to view your information.

To check flight status:

1. Type the flight number in the Google search field, using the format either ua11 or usair 782.

2. Click Search.

3. Select the link to travelocity.com or fboweb.com to view the results (**Figure 6.3**).

✔ Tip

■ Look up weather conditions and general information about possible delays at any airport by entering the airport code, followed by the word *airport*. For instance, lax airport returns information on Los Angeles International Airport. Results are returned from the FAA database, located at www.fly.faa.gov.

NUMBER SEARCHES

To find the location of an area code:

1. Enter an area code in the search field. For example, to learn where the 570 area code is, type **570** in the search field.

2. Click Enter.

The first result identifies the region and includes a link to `mapquest.com` (**Figure 6.4**).

To do a reverse phone number search:

1. Enter a telephone number in the format 4235551212.

2. Click Search.

Google displays the name and address and includes links to Yahoo! Maps and MapQuest (**Figure 6.5**).

Note that the phone number needs to be listed for Google (or any directory) to find it.

Figure 6.4 Enter a telephone area code to learn what region of the country it is in and to view a map of the area, if desired.

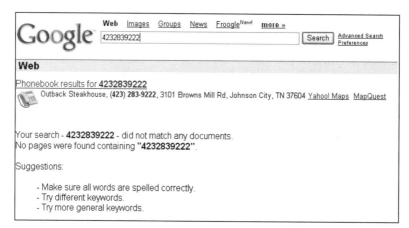

Figure 6.5 Do a reverse phone number lookup to discover the number's owner and address and, if you want, obtain a map of the location.

✔ Tips

- Traditional phone number formats (423) 555-1212 or 423-555-1212 will also work, but 423.555.1212 will not.

- If the owner of a phone number has published it at a Web site, Google will find the number, as it would any other keyword, if you use the same format that the Web site uses for the phone number, even if that format is 423.555.1212.

- If Google can't find the phone number, try searching for just the last seven digits, without the area code. You may discover that although the number is not listed in a directory service, it is listed in other documents on the Internet.

Calculating with Google

You don't need a calculator when you have access to Google. Just type the equation or natural-language query in the search field and click Search.

Use the Google calculator to find the answer to math problems (**Figure 6.6**):

5*5+2-10

Do you need to know how many teaspoons are in a cup? Enter this:

A cup in teaspoons

Use it to convert U.S. measurements to metric ones:

3.6 miles in km

To learn more about the expressions the Google calculator uses and to view sample expressions, visit http://www.google.com/help/calculator.html.

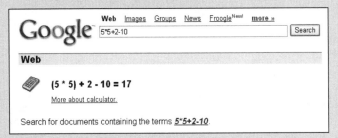

Figure 6.6 Use Google as a calculator. The search field accepts equations and natural-language queries.

NUMBER SEARCHES

Other Specialty Searches

You can also use the Google search box to find and map addresses, locate businesses, find information about stocks, and perform an ever-growing host of other specialty searches.

To look up an address:

◆ In the search box, enter a last name and a city and state (or zip code). Then click Enter. Google performs an address lookup.

To map an address:

1. Enter an address in the search field (**Figure 6.7**) and click Enter.

   The first result links to Yahoo Maps and MapQuest. If other matches are found, they are listed next.

2. Click one of the map links to map the address or click one of the links from the Google database to go to that site.

To find local businesses:

◆ In the search box, enter a business type and city, in this format: `pizza cleveland`. Then click Search.

   The state abbreviation is not required, but if you include it, you are more likely to get results from the correct city: `pizza cleveland tn` (**Figure 6.8**).

Figure 6.7 Enter a street address and a city and state or zip code to find a link to a map of the area. If the address is on Web pages contained in the Google database, search results are listed as well.

Figure 6.8 Find local businesses by entering the business type and city. Include the state for smaller cities to be sure Google knows the right location.

Figure 6.9 Enter up to 10 stock symbols to look up information about stocks.

To look up stock market information:

1. Enter stock symbols in the search box.

   You can enter up to 10 symbols, separating symbols with a space (**Figure 6.9**).

2. Click Search.

   Stock market results are provided by leading financial sites and presented in a tabbed interface (**Figure 6.10**).

continues on next page

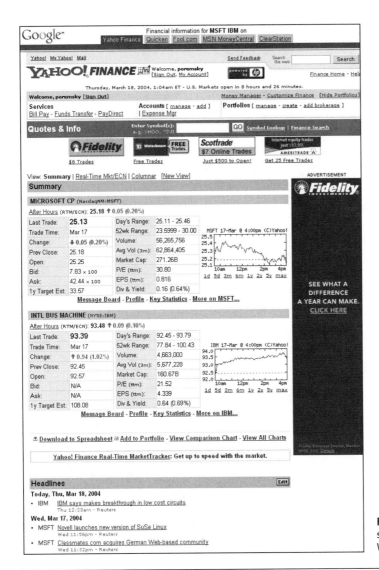

Figure 6.10 Get results from several leading stock market Web sites.

✔ Tips

- Using Google for these specialty searches is especially convenient if you are using the Google toolbar or deskbar (discussed in Chapter 5) or set Google as your home page.

- Google Labs (`labs.google.com`) showcases the concepts that it is experimenting with. Some of the concepts, such as keyboard shortcuts, are used across the Google site, while other projects are destined to never leave the laboratory. Other items, such as Google Sets, are just for fun.

- Many search engines have followed Google's lead and also provide address and number searches from the search fields on their home pages. See each search engine's Help for more information on the types of searches that the home page search field supports.

- **Table 6.1** summarizes some of the popular specialty searches that you can perform from the Google search field.

Google Fights

If you have a few minutes to kill, visit Google Fight (`www.googlefight.com`) for a frivolous view of Google results. Enter two keywords, and in a few seconds you'll know which word is found in Google's database more often. You can draw any conclusion you want as to why the one keyword appears more often than the other.

Table 6.1

Google Specialty Search Formats and Keywords		
FOR THIS TYPE OF SEARCH:	USE THIS FORMAT:	EXAMPLES:
Address Lookup	Enter the last name and the city and state or zip code. Punctuation and case are ignored.	smith jackson tn
Airline Flight Information	Enter the flight number.	ua11 or usair 782
Airport Weather and Delays	Enter the airport code followed by the word *airport*.	jfk airport
Business Search	Enter the business type and the city. The state is optional but should be used for smaller cities.	pizza cleveland
Calculator	Enter an equation or natural-language query.	3.6 miles in km or 5*5+23
FAA Airplane Registration Numbers	Enter the plane's number, usually found on a plane's tail.	n199ua
FCC Equipment IDs	Put the word *fcc* before the equipment ID and include spaces or dashes. Not case sensitive.	fcc B4Z-34009-PIR
FedEx Tracking Numbers	Enter the tracking number.	999999999999
Map Addresses	Enter the street and the city and state or zip code. Punctuation and case are ignored.	124 main johnson city tn
Patent Numbers	Put the word *patent* before the patent number.	patent 5123123
Telephone Area Codes	Enter the three-digit area code.	650
Telephone Numbers (reverse lookup)	Enter the 10-digit number. You can also use the traditional format, with parentheses or hyphens, but the format with periods will not work.	4235551212 or (423) 555-1212 or 423-555-1212 are acceptable; 423.555.1212 won't work.
UPC Codes	Enter the number without spaces or dashes; be sure to include the first and last numbers.	073333531084
UPS Tracking Numbers	Enter the tracking number.	1Z9999W999999999
USPS Tracking Numbers	Enter the number as received from USPS, including spaces.	1234 1234 1234 1234 1234 1234 12
Vehicle ID Numbers (VINs)	Enter the number as written.	1AAAAA999A9AA99999

OTHER SPECIALTY SEARCHES

Product Searches at Froogle

When you want to buy a product, you can search Google for it as you would for anything else, using keywords, the UPC, and the part number to come up with an assortment of product reviews and sites that sell the item. Or you can use another Google-owned site created just for locating products and the sites that sell them. It's called Froogle and is located at froogle.google.com (**Figure 6.11**).

You can search Froogle in two ways: by entering model, part, or UPC numbers or keywords in the search field, or by browsing the directory on Froogle's home page. Froogle also offers advanced search capabilities.

Figure 6.11 Use Froogle to comparison shop or browse merchandise.

Figure 6.12 Enter the product you're looking for and then click Search Froogle.

As in a regular Google search, you enter your search terms in the search field and click Search Froogle or press Enter (**Figure 6.12**). The Froogle search algorithm weighs the words and brings up the most likely matches first (**Figure 6.13**). For example, a search for `tablet pc viewsonic acer` returns Viewsonic and Acer Tablet PCs on the first page of results. Subsequent pages list other brands of Tablet PCs, but not writing tablets or desktop PCs.

continues on next page

Figure 6.13 Froogle lists the most likely matches.

PRODUCT SEARCHES AT FROOGLE

The only Boolean operator that Froogle recognizes is the minus sign (–) for NOT searches. Prefix the minus sign (–) to words to exclude them; for instance, `tablet pc -viewsonic -acer` would find all brands of Tablet PCs except Viewsonic and Acer. Remember not to put a space between the minus sign and the keyword. In addition, you can use double quotation marks to identify phrases or words you want kept together, but in many cases, it's not necessary.

The results page lists an assortment of items that match your keywords. Use the menu on the left to refine your search (**Figure 6.14**).

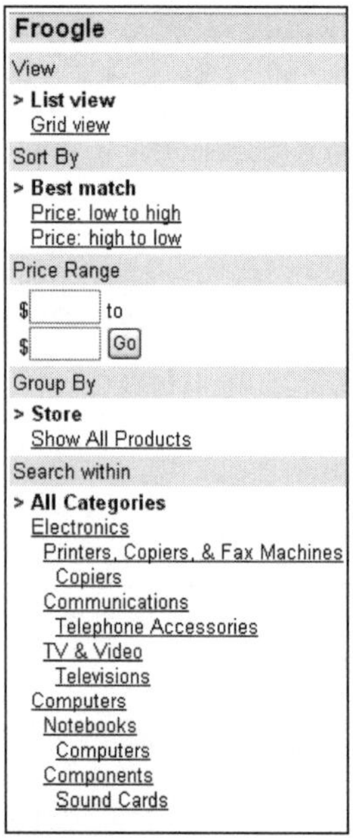

To refine your results:

◆ In the menu on the left, *do any of the following:*

▲ Choose Grid View (**Figure 6.15**) to see only the product names and images.

▲ Change the sort order to view results from low price to high or from high price to low.

Figure 6.14 Use this menu to refine the search or to sort by price or best match, group by store, or search within categories.

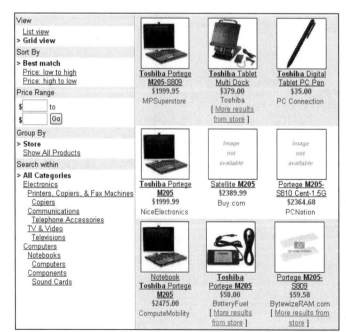

Figure 6.15 Switch to Grid view to see only the product picture, name, and price.

Figure 6.16 To learn how to include merchandise in the Froogle database, click Information for Merchants at the bottom of the page.

▲ Restrict the results by price; for example, if you know the approximate price that you want to pay, you can remove items you aren't interested in by including a price range.

▲ Group items by the store that sells them or show all items.

▲ Restrict your search to a specific category.

✔ Tip

■ Online merchants can include their store contents in the Froogle database. For more information and instructions, click the Information for Merchants link found at the bottom of each page (**Figure 6.16**).

Performing advanced Froogle searches

Froogle supports advanced search options. The page looks a lot like the standard Google Advanced Search page, but the options are tuned to comparison shopping.

To use Advanced Froogle Search:

1. Click the Advanced Froogle Search link to open the Froogle Advanced Search page (**Figure 6.17**).

continues on next page

Figure 6.17 Use the Froogle Advanced Search page to control the results of your search.

2. *Select any of the following search options:*

▲ Search based on the specified search criteria. Like Google, Froogle supports searching for results that contain all of the words in a search phrase, the exact phrase, or at least one of the words, as well as results that don't include specified words. You can enter words in more than one field.

▲ Show up to 100 results per page.

▲ Sort by best match or by price (high to low or low to high) (**Figure 6.18**).

▲ Set a price range for the product. Enter numbers in either or both fields. If you know that the product you want costs over $2000, enter 2000 in the low amount field but leave the high amount field empty. If you want only products costing between $35 and $50, enter 35 and 50 in the fields.

▲ Search for your keywords in the product name or description, in the product name only, or in the product description only (**Figure 6.19**).

▲ Select a specific category to search (**Figure 6.20**).

▲ Group the results by store or show all products.

▲ Choose List view, which includes descriptions, or Grid view, for pictures and product names only.

▲ To reduce the chances of getting results from adult sites, choose Filter Using SafeSearch.

3. Click the Search Froogle button when you are finished entering the criteria for your search.

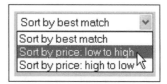

Figure 6.18 Change the sort order from best match to price, choosing from low to high or high to low.

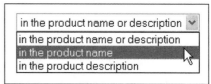

Figure 6.19 Select where Froogle should look for your search words: in the product name, in the description, or in both.

Figure 6.20 Restrict your search to the selected category.

✔ Tips

■ The preferences you set on the Froogle Advanced Search page apply to the entire Google site, not just Froogle.

■ Froogle is currently in beta version. This means it's a work in progress.

Browsing Google Catalogs

If you prefer to browse mail-order catalogs, visit Google Catalogs (`catalogs.google.com`). The catalog collection contains scanned pages from the merchants' catalogs, and you can search for items in all catalogs or browse individual catalogs. When you find something you want to purchase, click a link to the merchant's online store or place an order by phone. Although it's not as nice as thumbing through pages of a printed catalog, when someone says "it's item B on page 32," you can quickly find the correct product (**Figure 6.21**).

Figure 6.21 Browse mail-order catalogs at `catalog.google.com`.

PRODUCT SEARCHES AT FROOGLE

More Comparison Shopping Sites

When you're researching a product online or looking for a good deal, also check out the sites on the following list. Most offer comparison shopping, product reviews, and merchant ratings.

- **Amazon** (www.amazon.com): Use Amazon to check prices and availability in any of Amazon's partner stores. Limited product reviews available.

- **AOL** (shopping.search.aol.com): Available to both AOL subscribers and nonsubscribers, AOL supports browsing by departments or searching by keyword.

- **BizRate** (www.bizrate.com): Best known for its merchant ratings and merchant reviews, BizRate offers comparison shopping at over 40,000 online merchants.

- **DealTime** (www.dealtime.com): Part of the Shopping.com network, DealTime offers comparison shopping and directory browsing.

- **eBay** (www.ebay.com): Although eBay is best known as an online auction house, many merchants sell goods at fixed prices through eBay stores.

- **Epinions** (www.epinions.com): Best known for its unbiased opinions, product reviews, and product ratings.

- **MSN** (shopping.msn.com): A product search and directory service; merchants selling in MSN's eShops rank high in the results.

- **mySimon** (www.mysimon.com): Browse departments or search for a specific item.

- **NexTag** (www.nextag.com): Another product comparison site; search for goods or browse NexTag's shopping directory.

- **PriceGrabber** (www.pricegrabber.com): One of the oldest comparison shopping sites on the Internet. Browse the directory or search for a specific item.

- **Yahoo** (shopping.yahoo.com): A comparison shopping and directory service. Although Yahoo provides shopping cart services to small merchants, its shopping search includes many other online stores as well.

Figure 6.22 Zeitgeist is a mirror on our culture, with the popular events of each week preserved for all time.

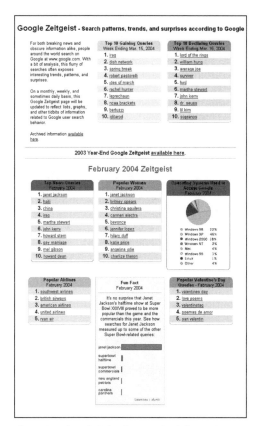

Figure 6.23 Google Zeitgeist contains information about search patterns, trends, and other data collected in Google's server logs.

Google Zeitgeist

If you're interested in search patterns and trends, then Zeitgeist is for you.

Zeitgeist is a German word that means the general intellectual, moral, and cultural climate of an era, and the queries we make at Google have much to say about what current events are important enough to search for (**Figure 6.22**).

Zeitgeist is best known for its weekly lists of search keywords that are gaining and declining in popularity. It also presents information on the browsers, languages, and operating systems that people use to search Google (**Figure 6.23**).

The site also provides a window on the past with archives of data, beginning with 2001.

You'll find Zeitgeist at `www.google.com/press/zeitgeist.html`.

YAHOO!

YAHOO!®

Founded in 1995, Yahoo has survived many changes. Starting out as a directory service, Yahoo maintained a staff to build and categorize its database. As the Internet grew, Yahoo used Google's database to supplement results from its own directory and developed an improved search engine, Yahoo! Search Technology, that rivals Google's and indexes some 3 billion pages.

During the early years, Yahoo added services such as free e-mail and created a portal site, drawing enough users to place it a close second behind Google in the number of searches initiated.

continues on next page

Good to Know

◆ Yahoo is the Web's second-most-popular search site.

◆ Created at Stanford University in 1994, Yahoo was the first major attempt at organizing and classifying the information available on the Internet.

◆ Yahoo is a good place to start when you need general information on a topic, or when you are not quite sure what you're looking for but have a sense that you'll know it when you see it.

Contact Information

Yahoo!, Inc.
Sunnyvale, CA
Phone: 408-349-3300
Fax: 408-349-3301
www.yahoo.com (Yahoo portal)
search.yahoo.com (Yahoo Search)

YAHOO!

✔ Tips

- Yahoo was developed in 1994 at Stanford University by David Filo and Jerry Yang, graduate students in electrical engineering. At the time, they were simply interested in keeping track of their personal favorite sites on the Internet. But before long, word got out, and they began getting hundreds of messages a day alerting them to wonderful sites that should be added to the Yahoo directory. Eventually the workload started interfering with their studies, so the pair dropped out of school, raised a million dollars in venture capital, and turned their dorm-room project into one of the Internet's most popular (and successful) businesses.

- Today, most search engines include a human-compiled directory on their home pages—often Open Directory (www.dmoz.org) or LookSmart (www.looksmart.com). But Yahoo develops its own subject directory and continues to set the standard. Its classification system is so detailed that the *San Jose Mercury News* has called Yahoo "the closest in spirit to the work of Linnaeus, the 18th-century botanist whose classification system organized the natural world."

The Yahoo Home Page

One of the things you'll come to appreciate about Yahoo is that once you've learned your way around the home page (**Figure 7.1**), chances are good that you won't have to relearn where things are any time soon. Unlike most of the other major search sites, Yahoo settled on the overall organization and "look and feel" of its home page early on and seldom fiddles with it.

continues on next page

Search form —
Reference tools —
Web directory —
Specialty Yahoos —

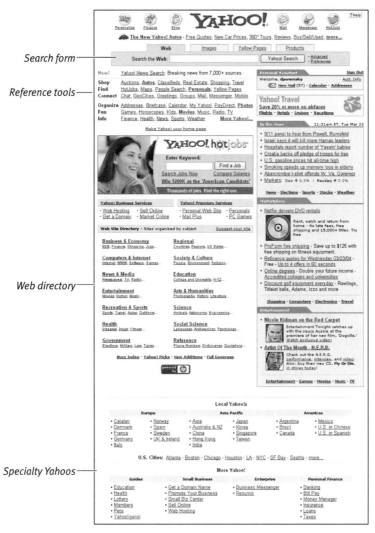

Figure 7.1 The Yahoo home page.

The Yahoo home page is designed not just for searching but as a portal page as well, offering news headlines, e-mail services, stock quotes, and so forth. From a searcher's perspective, the most important features to zero in on are the search form and the Web directory.

Here's a quick look at how to use those features, as well as a couple of other search-related tools.

Search form

To search Yahoo, type a word or phrase in the Yahoo search form (**Figure 7.2**) and click the Search button. Within seconds, you'll be presented with the top 10 Web sites that match your request.

Web directory

When you simply want to explore what the Web has to offer on a rather broad topic, use the Web directory (**Figure 7.3**). Click one of the 14 major topic categories and then work your way through the subcategories, moving from general to more specific information.

When you find a category that looks promising, you can either continue to drill down further into the directory or do another keyword search of just that particular category.

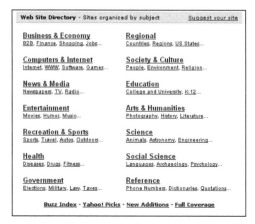

Figure 7.3 Yahoo's Web directory categorizes sites into the 14 broad subject areas shown here.

Figure 7.2 The Yahoo search form.

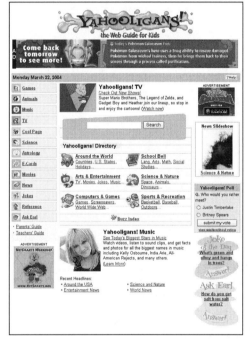

New!	The New Yahoo! Autos - powerful engine, new interior.
Shop	Auctions, **Autos**, Classifieds, Real Estate, Shopping, Travel
Find	HotJobs, Maps, People Search, **Personals**, Yellow Pages
Connect	Chat, GeoCities, Greetings, Groups, Mail, Messenger, Mobile
Organize	Addresses, Briefcase, Calendar, My Yahoo!, PayDirect, **Photos**
Fun	Games, Horoscopes, Kids, **Movies**, Music, Radio, TV
Info	Finance, Health, News, Sports, Weather **More Yahoo!...**

Make Yahoo! your home page - **Yahoo! Toolbar with Pop-Up Blocker**

Figure 7.4 These reference tools on the Yahoo home page can help you find the answers to many common search questions.

Figure 7.5 Yahooligans Web Guide for Kids is one of many specialized versions of the Yahoo search service, all accessible from links on the home page.

Figure 7.6 Click the Personalize link in the Yahoo navigation bar to create your own customized version of the Yahoo home page.

Other search-related tools

If you decide to use Yahoo on a regular basis, you'll want to explore and become familiar with two other search-related features on the home page:

♦ **Reference tools:** Sometimes the fastest way to find a particular type of information is to use a specialized tool. Yahoo offers a collection of them (**Figure 7.4**) right below the search form. You'll find a shopping directory, business yellow pages, people-finding tools, maps and driving directions, classifieds and personals, daily news headlines, stock quotes, local weather and TV listings, sports scores, and more.

♦ **Specialty Yahoos:** The Yahoo home page also offers links for country-specific versions of its search service, regional directories for U.S. cities, and special Yahoo guides on subjects such as autos, careers, personal finance, and real estate. There's also a link for Yahooligans, a version of the Yahoo search service designed just for kids (**Figure 7.5**); click the Kids link to open this page.

✔ Tips

■ You can tailor Yahoo to your personal interests and information needs by clicking the Personalize link (**Figure 7.6**) at the top of the Yahoo home page. For more on this feature, see "Customizing Yahoo" later in this chapter.

■ To make Yahoo your default home page, follow the instructions in "Customizing Your Web Browser" in Chapter 4.

■ To get back to the Yahoo home page at any time, click the Yahoo logo that appears at the top of most pages, or look for and click the Yahoo! link.

Searching with Yahoo

Now let's try an actual Yahoo search to see how it works and how the search results are presented. Start by going to the Yahoo home page (www.yahoo.com).

To search with Yahoo:

1. Type a word or phrase in the Yahoo search form (**Figure 7.7**) and click the Search button to submit it.

   ▲ Yahoo ignores the words AND, OR, and NOT. Therefore, to do an AND search, put a plus sign (+) directly in front of each word or phrase that you want included in your search results.

   ▲ For OR searches, type each word or phrase separated by a space.

   ▲ For NOT searches, put a minus sign (–) in front of the word or phrase you want to exclude.

   ▲ Enclose phrases in double quotation marks.

Figure 7.7 To do an AND search, put a plus sign (+) in front of each word or phrase.

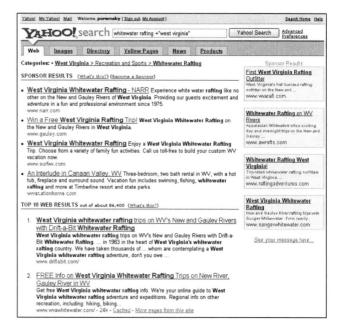

Figure 7.8 Here's how Yahoo presents search results. Category matches come first, followed by sponsored results and then Web results.

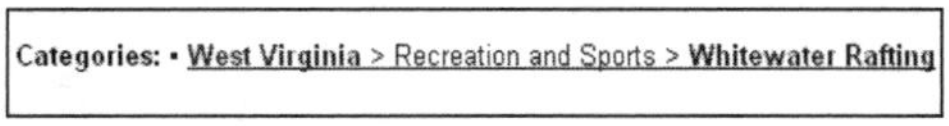

Categories: • West Virginia > Recreation and Sports > **Whitewater Rafting**

Figure 7.9 Use the Categories links at the top of the results page to browse by category.

Yahoo will search its database for Web sites that match your query. Categories, if any are found, are listed just below the search form, followed by Sponsored Results (if any) and Web Results (**Figure 7.8**). Your search terms will be displayed in bold to make them easier to spot.

2. To explore any Web site on the results page, simply click it. Web site links, of course, take you directly to the site. If category links appear at the top of the results page (**Figure 7.9**), you can click these links to browse a category in the Yahoo Web directory; you'll have the opportunity to do another search or explore more links on the category page (**Figure 7.10**).

continues on next page

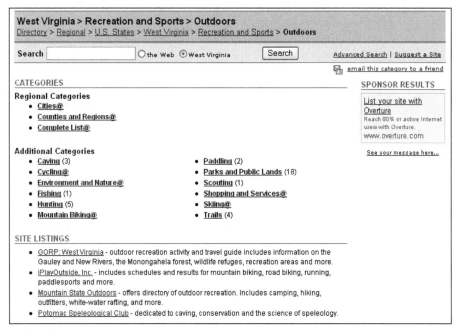

Figure 7.10 The category page includes a search form, sponsored results, and category results.

SEARCHING WITH YAHOO

3. If you choose to do another search while you're on a category page, you have the option of limiting it to the category you're currently exploring. Simply enter one or more search terms and click the radio button labeled Just This Category (**Figure 7.11**). In some cases, you'll see the category name in place of Just This Category.

4. To search or browse a broader category, click one of the upper-level category names (**Figure 7.12**).

5. To look for news articles or Internet events that match your search request, go back to the results page and click News in the menu bar (**Figure 7.13**).

Figure 7.11 Yahoo gives you the option of limiting your directory search to the category you're currently exploring—a neat feature that comes in handy for refining a query.

Figure 7.12 Choose a category link to see the categories for any topic.

Figure 7.13 The menu bar on the results page allows you to direct your search to Yahoo's database of news articles and Internet events.

✔ Tips

- Plain-English queries aren't recommended in Yahoo. You'll likely find more results if you limit your Yahoo queries to a couple of words or phrases rather than a complete question.

- Case doesn't count in Yahoo, so you can use uppercase, lowercase, or a combination when you type your queries in the Yahoo search form, and you'll get the same results.

- To search the Yahoo directory for recently added categories and Web sites, click the Advanced Search link on the Yahoo home page, enter your query, and use the drop-down menu to select a time frame ranging from one day to four years.

- If you create a search that you expect to use again, you might want to save it using Yahoo's Saved Searches feature. For more on this feature, see "Customizing Yahoo" later in this chapter.

- For a summary of Yahoo search commands and syntax, see the Yahoo Quick Reference (**Table 7.1**).

continues on next page

SEARCHING WITH YAHOO

Table 7.1

Yahoo Quick Reference		
FOR THIS TYPE OF SEARCH:	DO THIS:	EXAMPLES:
Plain-English Question	Not recommended.	
Phrase Search	Type the phrase as a sequence of words surrounded by double quotation marks.	`"Russian lacquer boxes"`
AND Search (multiple words and phrases, each of which must be present)	Use a plus sign (+) in front of a word or phrase that *must* appear in the results.	`+antiques +Victorian`
OR Search (multiple words and phrases, *any* one of which may be present)	Type words or phrases separated by a space, without any special notation.	`eggs "Carl Faberge"`
NOT Search (to exclude a word or phrase)	Use a minus sign (–) in front of a word or phrase you want to exclude from your results. To find software Easter eggs, for example, you might want to exclude the word *Fabergé*.	`"Easter eggs" -Faberge`
Case-Sensitive Search	Not available.	
Date Search	Not available. However, you *can* search for categories and Web sites that have been added to the Yahoo directory within a certain time frame.	
	To do that, click Advanced Search on the Yahoo home page and use the drop-down menu to select a time frame.	
Field Search	To search titles of Web page documents, enter `intitle:` directly in front of a word or phrase.	`intitle:"oriental rugs"`
	To search Web page URLs, enter `inurl:` directly in front of the word you want to find.	`inurl:carpeting`
	To search within a domain, enter `site:` directly in front of the domain you want to search.	`site:microsoft.com`
	To limit a search to a particular host, enter `hostname:` in front of the domain.	`hostname:office.microsoft.com`
	To search for multiple words in fields, use multiple search terms with plus signs (+)	`.+inurl:oriental +inurl:rug`
	To not include a keyword in the results, use a minus sign (–).before the field name.	`intitle:oriental -intitle:rugs` or `Xbox -site:microsoft.com`
	To search for documents or other sites that are linked to a site, use `link:`	`link:http://www.microsoft.com`
Nested Search	Not available.	
Proximity Search	Not available.	

Yahoo Field Searches

Yahoo allows a variety of field searches.

- **Title searches:** To limit your search to the titles of Web pages, enter `intitle:` followed by a word or phrase—for example, `intitle:"Victorian furniture"` to find Web pages with the phrase *Victorian furniture* in the title.

- **URL searches:** The entry `inurl:antiques` would find sites with the word *antiques* in the URL.

- **Domain searches:** Enter `site:` before your search term to find all documents within a particular domain and its subdomains: for example, `site:microsoft.com` to search only Microsoft sites.

- **Host searches:** To limit a search to a particular host, use the `hostname:` keyword. For example, `hostname: office.microsoft.com` searches only the `office` site at Microsoft.

- **Link searches:** Use `link:` to find documents that link to a particular URL: for example, `link:http://www.poremsky.com/`.

The use of multiple field names is supported in Yahoo. Use plus (+) and minus (–) signs to include or restrict keywords in the `intitle:` and `inurl:` fields.

To find URLs such as `www.oriental-rugs.com` and `rugs.com/oriental.html`, use this search format:

`+inurl:oriental +inurl:rug`

To find pages with Outlook in the title but not Outlook Express, and that also have Outlook somewhere in the URL, use this format:

`intitle:outlook -intitle:express inurl:outlook`

At first glance, `site:` and `hostname:` appear to do the same thing: return pages in a specific domain. Many times, they will return the same results. However, `hostname` forces an exact match. For example, both `site: microsoft.com` and `hostname: office.microsoft.com` find office.microsoft.com, but `hostname:` will find only this site whereas `site:` will find any other microsoft.com site as well.

Using Yahoo's search shortcuts

Like Google, Yahoo now supports a number of specialized searches, including package, weather, and airline tracking. Yahoo refers to the specialized search keywords used in many of these searches as *shortcuts*.

When you use these simple keywords in your search, Yahoo displays the specific information you're looking for at the top of your Web results.

To find the local weather forecast, enter the city name followed by the weather keyword: Seattle weather (**Figure 7.14**).

To find an address on a map, enter, for example, map 59 E Broadway New York.

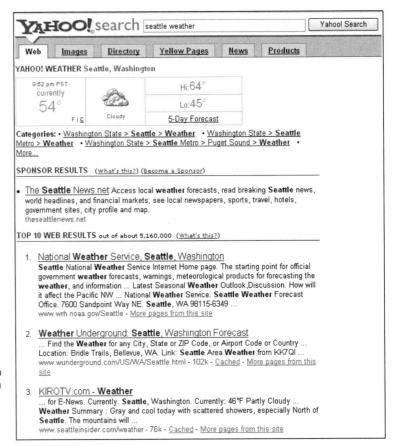

Figure 7.14 Use Yahoo's special search keywords to quickly find information. In this search, we used the weather keyword to find the current weather conditions in Seattle.

120

To find a local business listing, enter the zip code and a business name or category: 37601 restaurants.

Using any of these keywords brings up the relevant information as the first listing on the results page, followed by sponsored listings and Web results. **Table 7.2** contains a complete list of current keywords.

To go directly to a Yahoo page with more information instead of the search results page, type the keyword followed by an exclamation mark (!) For instance, type dallas weather! and you'll get a Web page with detailed information about the weather in Dallas (**Figure 7.15**).

Yahoo uses the exclamation point as a shortcut to go directly to other Yahoo pages: type sports! in the search form to go to the Yahoo! Sports page.

✔ Tips

■ For best results, use the state abbreviation for smaller cities and towns.

■ Install the Yahoo Companion toolbar to make searching Yahoo shortcuts easier. See Customizing Yahoo later in this chapter.

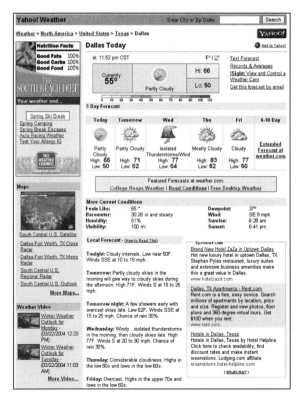

Figure 7.15 When you use the exclamation point with the special keywords, the appropriate Yahoo site opens.

Table 7.2

Yahoo Special Search Shortcuts

To find:	Do this:	Examples:
Airport Information (with links to the latest conditions, links to maps, directions, local weather, and airport terminal maps where available)	Enter an airport name or airport code.	`hartsfield airport` or `atl airport`
Book Search	Enter the book's ISBN.	`032122373X`
Definitions (from the American Heritage® Dictionary and a link to additional meanings and related information, including pronunciation and etymology)	Enter `define` followed by any English word.	`define rampage`
FAA Registration Numbers.	Enter the aircraft registration number, usually found on the tail of an airplane.	`n3601p`
FedEx Tracking	Enter `fedex` plus the tracking number.	`fedex 12345678`
Flight Tracker	Enter an airline name or code and flight number.	`American airlines 22` or `aa 22`
Hotel Search (location and links to a detailed description of the property, including a map showing the property's location in relation to various points of interest, and a calendar to check availability)	Enter the type of accommodation and location desired.	`dallas hotels` or `Asheville bed and breakfast`
Maps and Driving Directions	Enter a street address, city, and state or the keyword `map` and a location.	`55 e broadway new york` or `map chicago`
News	Enter the keyword `news` and any topic currently in the news.	`news election`
Patents	Enter `patent` and any U.S. patent number.	`patent 1234567`
Sports: College (scores and information about games in progress)	Enter a college or team name, the name of the sport, and the keyword `scores`.	`duke basketball scores`
Sports: Professional (scores and information about games in progress)	Enter a team name and the keyword `scores`.	`dodger scores`
Stock Quotes (including latest price, intraday chart, news headlines, and links to additional financial information)	Enter `Quote` and the ticker symbol.	`quote msft`
Traffic Reports	Enter the location followed by the keyword `traffic`.	`Chicago traffic`
UPC Bar Codes (with links to product information)	Enter the UPC bar code.	`01795106435`
UPS Tracking	Enter the tracking code.	`1Z40EW620354504737`
USPS Tracking	Enter `usps` and the tracking number.	`usps 1234 1234 1234 1234`
Vehicle Identification Number (VIN)	Enter the 17-character VIN.	`ZFFYT53A510122721`
Weather (current conditions)	Enter `weather` and a location.	`weather houston`
Yellow Pages Search	Enter a business category and a city or a business name in a city.	`starbucks omaha` or `restaurants in denver`

USING ADVANCED SEARCH

Using Advanced Search

Yahoo offers a second search form on what it calls the Advanced Web Search page (**Figure 7.16**). This form gives you advanced search capabilities not available on the Yahoo home page:

continues on next page

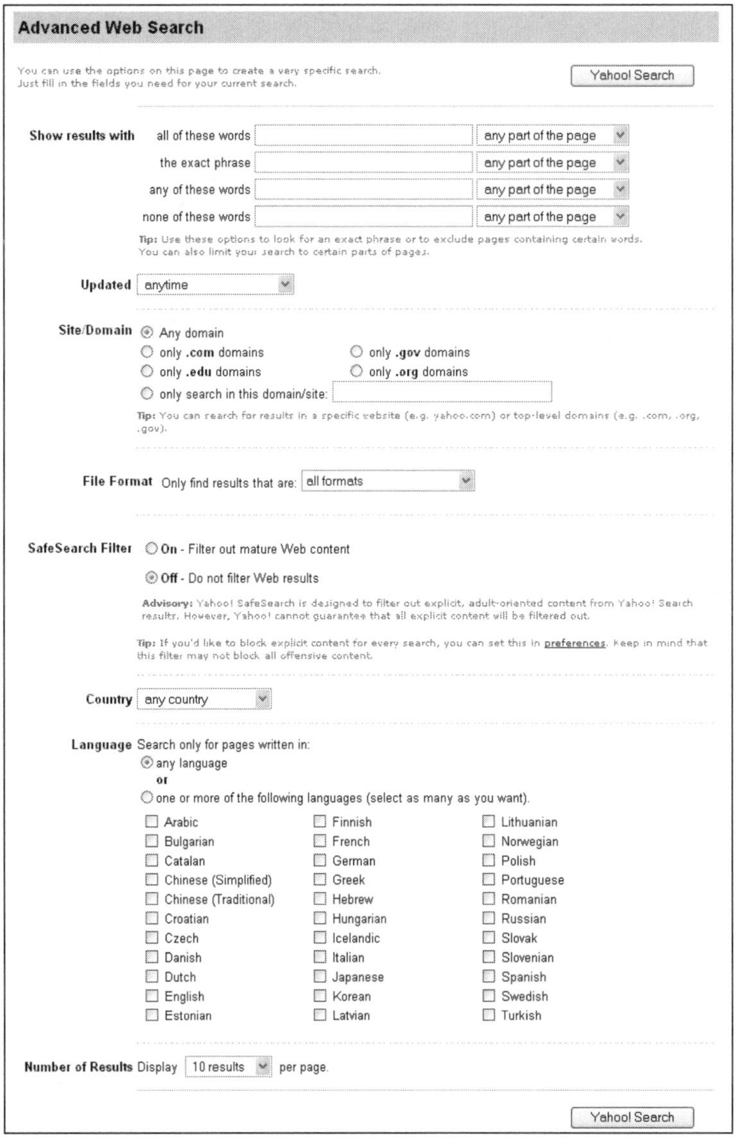

Figure 7.16 Yahoo's Advanced Web Search page offers several advanced search features not available on the home page.

◆ Search for all of the words, the exact phrase, any of the words, or none of the words. You can search for the keywords anywhere in the page, in the URL, or in the page title (**Figure 7.17**).

◆ Limit your search of the Yahoo directory to categories or Web sites added within a specified time frame ranging from any time to the past three months, six months, or year.

◆ Restrict your search to specific domains.

◆ Return results that are in a specific file format (**Figure 7.18**).

◆ Enable the filter to reduce the chances that the results will include "adult" content.

◆ Restrict the search to pages found at sites in a specific country.

◆ Search for pages written in a specific language.

◆ Change the number of matches displayed on each page of your search results from 10 to 100 per page.

✔ Tip

■ For a summary of Yahoo search commands and syntax, see the Yahoo Quick Reference (Table 7.1) presented earlier in this chapter. The same rules apply to the search forms on both the Yahoo home page and the Advanced Web Search page.

Figure 7.17 Search options include looking for the keywords in any part of the page, only in the title, or only in the URL.

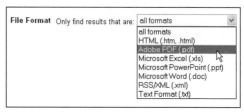

Figure 7.18 You can restrict the search to a specific file type.

Using Yahoo's Web Directory

As we've said before, when it comes to organizing the Web by topic, Yahoo has set the standard. All the major search engines offer Web directories of some sort, often provided by third parties like Open Directory or LookSmart. But Yahoo offers three advantages over most of its competitors:

◆ You can simultaneously search both its human-compiled Web directory and a gigantic database of more than 3 billion Web pages, and Yahoo will present the combined results to you in a well-organized and readable format.

◆ You can easily avoid (or zero in on) business and shopping Web sites and sites that are of only regional interest because Yahoo makes a distinction in its directory between commercial and noncommercial sites, and between sites that are of global interest and those that are relevant to only a specific geographic region.

◆ If you find a category in the Yahoo directory that looks promising, you can search again within just that category to find the exact information that you're after.

Think of Yahoo's directory as an incredibly detailed outline of what's available on the Web. And the outline itself, as well as a 25-word description of each site, can be searched. So you can usually zero in on just the information you need, without having to wade through descriptions of hundreds, if not thousands, of irrelevant sites.

continues on next page

The best way to understand what we're talking about is to simply go to the Yahoo home page (www.yahoo.com) and choose a category from the Web directory (**Figure 7.19**). Then explore (or drill down) through the resulting pages that offer subtopics and sub-subtopics of greater and greater specificity.

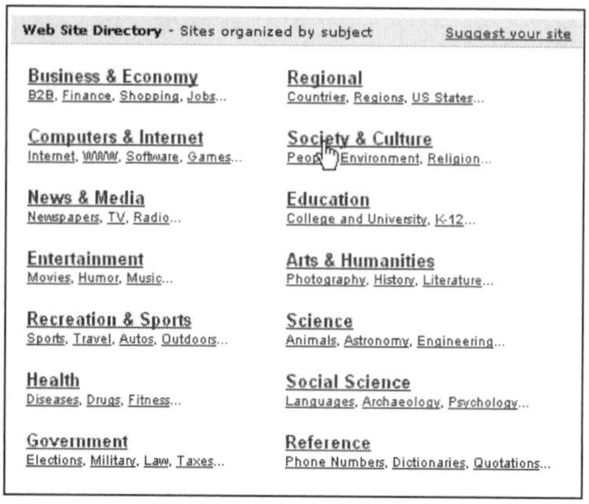

To browse the Web by topic:

1. Click one of the 14 topic categories on the Yahoo home page (www.yahoo.com) to display the subtopics for that category (**Figure 7.20**), along with some helpful information about each one:

   ▲ The numbers in parentheses tell you how many entries are categorized under a particular subtopic.

Figure 7.19 Yahoo's Web directory is organized into 14 major topic categories.

Figure 7.20 Here's what you see when you click on Society & Culture in the Yahoo Web directory—almost two dozen subtopics, presented alphabetically.

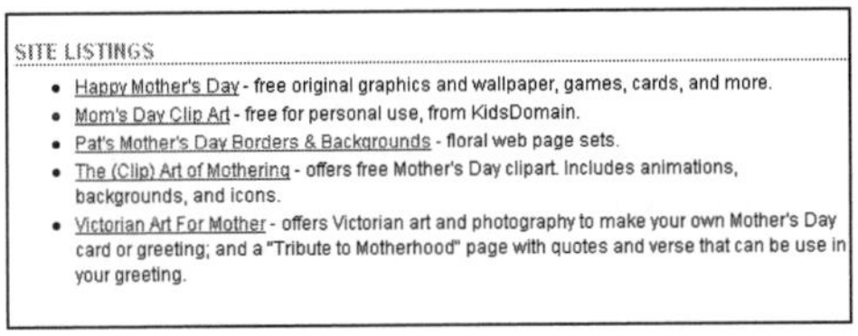

SITE LISTINGS

- Happy Mother's Day - free original graphics and wallpaper, games, cards, and more.
- Mom's Day Clip Art - free for personal use, from KidsDomain.
- Pat's Mother's Day Borders & Backgrounds - floral web page sets.
- The (Clip) Art of Mothering - offers free Mother's Day clipart. Includes animations, backgrounds, and icons.
- Victorian Art For Mother - offers Victorian art and photography to make your own Mother's Day card or greeting; and a "Tribute to Motherhood" page with quotes and verse that can be used in your greeting.

Figure 7.21 The Web site descriptions in the Yahoo directory are brief but informative.

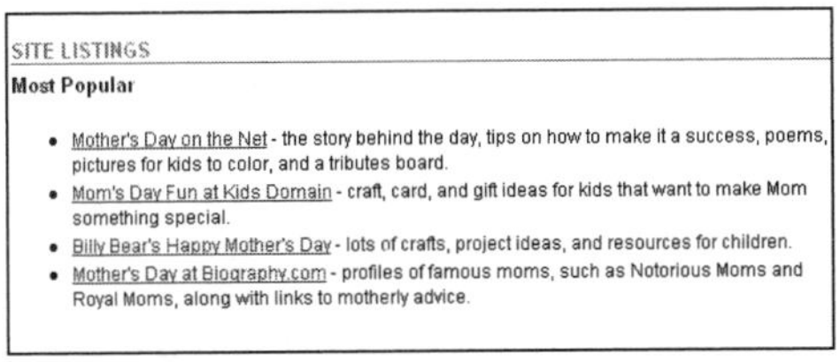

SITE LISTINGS

Most Popular

- Mother's Day on the Net - the story behind the day, tips on how to make it a success, poems, pictures for kids to color, and a tributes board.
- Mom's Day Fun at Kids Domain - craft, card, and gift ideas for kids that want to make Mom something special.
- Billy Bear's Happy Mother's Day - lots of crafts, project ideas, and resources for children.
- Mother's Day at Biography.com - profiles of famous moms, such as Notorious Moms and Royal Moms, along with links to motherly advice.

Figure 7.22 For categories with a large number of Web sites, Yahoo often provides guidance on the ones that are most popular.

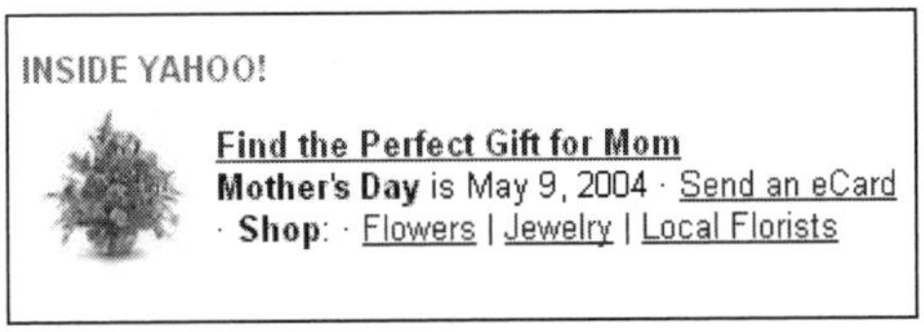

INSIDE YAHOO!

Find the Perfect Gift for Mom
Mother's Day is May 9, 2004 · Send an eCard
· **Shop**: · Flowers | Jewelry | Local Florists

Figure 7.23 Topic-related features created by Yahoo are presented in a section of the results page called "Inside Yahoo!"

▲ The @ symbol means that the topic's primary location is elsewhere in the Yahoo directory. (Clicking one of these links takes you to the topic's primary location.)

▲ The word *NEW!* (highlighted in yellow) identifies topic categories that have been added recently to the Yahoo Web directory. Yahoo's 14 main topics haven't changed in some time, but new subtopics and sub-subtopics are being added all the time.

2. Work your way down through the Yahoo directory. You'll eventually reach a page that includes a set of links for specific Web sites, presented alphabetically, along with a brief description of each one (**Figure 7.21**). Written by each site's owner or creator and approved by Yahoo editors, these descriptions will give you a quick handle on the nature and purpose of the Web site—something you don't always get when you use a search engine whose database is created by a spider or crawler program.

3. If the results list includes an exceptionally large number of Web sites, it will often be preceded by a section labeled "Most Popular" (**Figure 7.22**). Click a link to go to a site located by other users conducting searches similar to yours.

4. You may also encounter a section called "Inside Yahoo!" (**Figure 7.23**). Click a link here to go to a site created and maintained by Yahoo itself.

continues on next page

5. Click a link identified with a pair of sunglasses (**Figure 7.24**) to go to a Web site that Yahoo editors consider to be an especially noteworthy resource in its particular subject area. Only noncommercial sites qualify for the sunglasses designation.

Why sunglasses? Because in the early days of Yahoo, sites were chosen as noteworthy because they were considered to be "cool."

6. As you're working your way through the Yahoo directory, you can stop at any point and perform a search, using a form (**Figure 7.25**) that allows you to specify whether you want to search the entire Web or just the category that you're currently exploring.

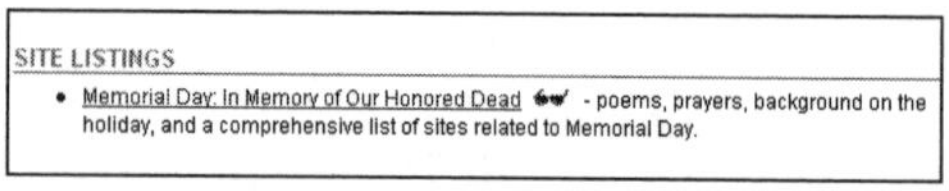

✔ Tips

■ If you have a subject in mind but aren't sure what topic to choose from the Yahoo Web directory, do a search first. For example, type collectibles in the Yahoo search form, and you'll be presented with categories within four major topics in the Web directory: Business & Economy, Entertainment, Recreation, and Regional.

■ As you move around the Yahoo directory, the category you're exploring will always be listed at the top of the page, with subtopics separated by the greater-than symbol (>) (**Figure 7.26**). You can go directly to any subtopic simply by clicking it.

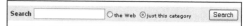

Figure 7.24 Yahoo uses the sunglasses icon to call your attention to exceptionally good (that is, "cool") Web sites.

Search		○ the Web ⦿ just this category	Search

Figure 7.25 You can choose to search for a phrase in just the current category instead of the entire Yahoo directory.

United States > Memorial Day
Directory > Regional > Countries > United States > Society and Culture > Holidays and Observances > **Memorial Day**

Figure 7.26 Yahoo helps you keep track of where you are in the directory by displaying your location. To go back to, say, Holidays and Observances, click its link.

Figure 7.27 My Yahoo is a customized version of the Yahoo home page, tailored to your particular interests.

Figure 7.28 Use the Personalize link on the Yahoo home page to access My Yahoo.

Customizing Yahoo

If you like Yahoo and decide to make it your primary search tool, you should either install the Yahoo! Toolbar for Internet Explorer or create your own special version of the Yahoo home page, tailored to your personal interests and information needs. That's what My Yahoo (**Figure 7.27**) is all about.

You can't change anything having to do with the way Yahoo searches and displays your results. But once you've signed up for My Yahoo—by selecting a user ID and password and providing some personal information—you can control the content, layout, and color scheme for the Yahoo home page.

More important, you can take advantage of these search-related features not available on the Yahoo home page:

◆ **Saved Searches:** Allows you to save frequently used searches and run them again with a single click.

◆ **News Clipper:** Similar to Saved Searches, but instead of running your query against the directory of Web sites, you'll be searching Yahoo's database of news articles.

To customize Yahoo:

1. Click the Personalize link (**Figure 7.28**) at the top of the Yahoo home page.

2. If you already have a Yahoo e-mail address, sign in with your username and password. Otherwise, click Sign Up Now and complete the form. You'll be asked to choose a user ID and password and to provide some personal information—name, birth date, e-mail address, zip code, gender, occupation, and industry affiliation.

continues on next page

Two words of warning on selecting your My Yahoo password: case counts! So whatever combination of uppercase and lowercase letters you use when you select your password, that's what Yahoo will expect when you access your My Yahoo page.

3. Once you've completed the questionnaire and submitted the information, continue on to your new My Yahoo page, which you can now personalize by clicking the Choose Content and Choose Layout buttons at the top of the page (**Figure 7.29**).

4. You can display up to 20 features on your My Yahoo page. Click the Choose Content button to open the Personalize Page Content page. To add a feature, click the box next to the feature so that a check mark appears (**Figure 7.30**). If you change your mind, click again, and the check mark will disappear. Once you've selected the features you want (and removed the ones you don't want), click Finished.

Rearrange the page layout by clicking the Choose Layout button.

5. Use the Edit button that appears with each feature to tailor things further.

For example, if you've chosen to include Saved Searches on your My Yahoo page, click its Edit button (**Figure 7.31**) to access the form that allows you to create and save a query (**Figure 7.32**). Click Create a New Search to open the Create Your Own Search Topic form. Type a name for your search and enter the keywords; then click Create. To edit a saved search, click Edit, make your changes, and then click Accept Changes (**Figure 7.33**). Click Finished and return to My Yahoo. (The News Clipper feature works the same way.)

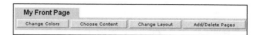

Figure 7.29 You can use these buttons to personalize both the content and layout of your My Yahoo page.

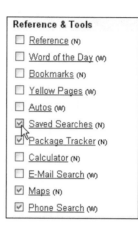

Figure 7.30 Select the features you want to include on your personalized page, such as Saved Searches.

Figure 7.31 Click Edit to further customize a feature (in this case, Saved Searches) on your My Yahoo page.

Figure 7.32 Edit, delete, or create new searches using the Save Your Searches page.

CUSTOMIZING YAHOO

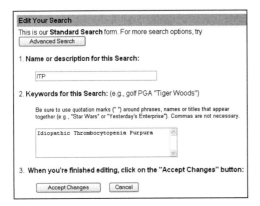

Figure 7.33 A similar form is used for creating new or editing existing searches. After entering a name for your search and the search keywords, click Accept Changes (or Create, if creating a new search) to return to the Save Your Searches page.

Figure 7.34 Having edited Saved Searches to include several queries, we can run any one simply by clicking it.

Once you've added a search to Saved Searches (or News Clipper), you can run it from your My Yahoo page simply by clicking it (**Figure 7.34**).

6. To make My Yahoo your browser's default home page, enter its complete address (http://my.yahoo.com) when you specify your home page or startup location. For specific instructions, see "Customizing Your Web Browser" in Chapter 4.

✔ Tips

- You can switch back and forth between the standard Yahoo home page and your personalized page using the Yahoo! link (to get back to standard Yahoo from your personalized page) and the My Yahoo! link (to get to your personal page from the Yahoo home page).

- If you have trouble setting up your personalized version of Yahoo, click Help at the top of the My Yahoo page for step-by-step instructions and answers to frequently asked questions.

CUSTOMIZING YAHOO

To use the Yahoo toolbar:

If you use Yahoo's portal or search engine, you'll want to use the Yahoo Companion toolbar (**Figure 7.35**). It includes a search field, a pop-up stopper, and links to many of Yahoo's featured sites. Go to companion.yahoo.com to download and install it.

The toolbar has three feature sets: Search Companion, Financial Companion, and My Companion. Each toolbar contains the search field and button and additional features, depending on the toolbar selected.

Enter your search words in the search field and click Search. Click the arrow next to the Search button to select another type of search (**Figure 7.36**).

To search the current site, enter your search words and click the Search This Site button. This performs the equivalent of a site: search.

Use the Highlight button to highlight the words in the search field on the current page. You can use Highlight instead of Edit > Find to look for words on a page.

Figure 7.36 Select different types of searches by clicking the Search button arrow.

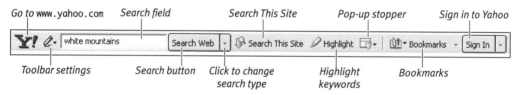

Go to www.yahoo.com   *Search field*   *Search This Site*   *Pop-up stopper*   *Sign in to Yahoo*

Toolbar settings   *Search button*   *Click to change search type*   *Highlight keywords*   *Bookmarks*

Figure 7.35 Install the Yahoo Companion toolbar for Internet Explorer if you use Yahoo often.

CUSTOMIZING YAHOO

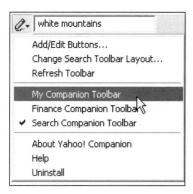

Figure 7.37 Change the toolbar features by clicking the Toolbar Settings button.

✔ Tips

- Click the Yahoo icon to return to the portal page at www.yahoo.com.

- Click the toolbar settings button (the pencil icon) and select a different toolbar from the menu (**Figure 7.37**).

- You don't need a Yahoo account to use the toolbar, but you do need one if you want to customize the toolbar.

To configure default search preferences:

1. To reach the Search Preferences page, click the Preferences link at the right of the Search button (**Figure 7.38**).

continues on next page

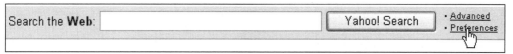

Figure 7.38 Click the Preferences link if you want to change your search preferences.

2. Yahoo has just a few search preferences that are configurable. You can configure any of the following search preferences (**Figure 7.39**):

▲ **New Window:** When you enable this option, clicking links in the search results opens the link in a new window, and you can refer to the search results as needed, without using the Back button or losing your place in the current page.

▲ **Number of Results:** Set the number of results displayed per page. The default is 20; you can select 10, 15, 30, 40, or 100 instead.

▲ **SafeSearch Filter:** The default setting is Moderate, which filters out explicit images only. Select Strict to filter explicit Web content as well as images, or select Off to turn off filtering.

▲ **Language:** Search for pages written in specified languages. The default setting is Any Language, but you can select one or more of the 33 languages listed to control the languages your results include.

3. Click Save Preferences when you are finished.

If you are logged on with a Yahoo ID, your preferences are saved with your ID and are used whenever and wherever you log on to Yahoo. Otherwise, your preferences are saved in a cookie to your local computer.

Figure 7.39 Yahoo lets you specify whether you want results links to open in a new window, the number of results displayed per page, the SafeSearch settings, and the language.

AOL Search

Good to Know

- ◆ AOL Search is the default search engine for America Online (AOL).

- ◆ The main benefit of AOL Search is that it allows you to search both the Web and AOL's proprietary content—assuming that you're an AOL subscriber.

- ◆ If you're *not* a subscriber, you can use AOL Search, but your results will be limited to information found on the Web.

- ◆ You can use Boolean operators and wildcards in your queries, but AOL Search offers little else in the way of power-search features.

Contact Information

America Online (AOL)
Dulles, VA
Phone: 703-265-1000
Fax: 703-918-1400
www.aol.com (AOL portal)
search.aol.com (AOL Search)

AOL Search is the creation of America Online (AOL), the world's largest online service. If you're one of AOL's 24 million subscribers—and you use the service not only for Internet access but also for its special proprietary content—you'll definitely want to learn some AOL Search basics. Why? It's the only search engine that allows you to simultaneously explore both the Web *and* AOL content. AOL Search is powered by Google, providing searchers with both the largest Internet search engine database and the AOL content.

Our advice is this:

- ◆ **If you're *not* an AOL subscriber:** Don't bother reading this chapter. Since it's powered by Google, there's little reason to consider AOL Search as an option for finding information on the Web. Use Google directly.

- ◆ **If you *are* an AOL subscriber:** Read on! In just a few short pages, we'll tell you what you need to know to use AOL Search to best advantage.

✔ Tip

- ■ For news and information about AOL and its parent company, AOL Time Warner, visit `media.aoltimewarner.com/media`.

The AOL Search Home Page

Figure 8.2 AOL subscribers can use the AOL toolbar's Search option to get to the AOL Search home page.

Nicely designed and refreshingly clutter-free, the AOL Search home page (**Figure 8.1**) provides you with several ways of finding information. You can search the Web by entering a query in a very basic search form, browse the Web by topic, or use a set of specialized tools for some of the most common search tasks.

As mentioned previously, anyone with Internet access can use AOL Search, which is located on the Web at search.aol.com. Subscribers to AOL's online service can also get to the AOL Search home page by signing on to AOL and then clicking the toolbar's Search button (**Figure 8.2**).

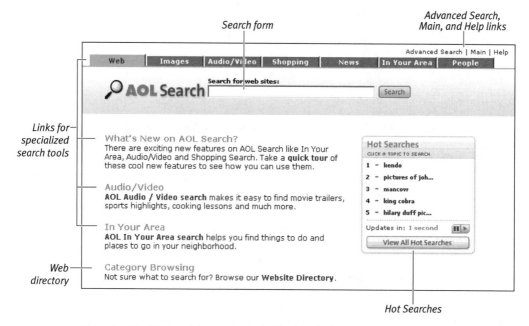

Figure 8.1. The AOL Search home page looks like this whether you access it via AOL or the Web.

Figure 8.3 There's nothing complicated about the AOL Search form—just type your query in the text box and click the Search button.

Search form

The search form for AOL Search (**Figure 8.3**) includes a box for entering your query and a Search button to submit it. AOL Search defaults to an AND search, looking for *all* the words and phrases you type, so you don't need to use plus signs (+) or the Boolean operator AND, but you can if you wish. AOL Search also supports OR and minus sign (–) operators.

✔ Tips

- You can use phrase connectors instead of double quotation marks. AOL Search treats words joined by hyphens, slashes, periods, equal signs, or apostrophes as phrases.

- Hot Searches is a list of popular searches, updated every 12 seconds.

Web directory

AOL Search's Web directory (**Figure 8.4**) comes from the Open Directory Project (`dmoz.org`), a human-compiled guide to the best Web sites, organized in outline fashion, with 16 main topics and hundreds of subtopics and sub-subtopics. Open the directory list by clicking the Website Directory link at the bottom of the search home page. You can click any topic (or subtopic) that appears in the directory list and then drill down through the various levels of the directory (**Figure 8.5**) to locate Web sites that might be of interest.

Figure 8.4 The Web directory is organized into 16 main categories, shown here in bold.

Main > Regional > North America > Canada > Prince Edward Island > Travel and Tourism

Sponsored Links: Provided by a third party and not endorsed by AOL What is this?

▶ **Vacation Rentals By Owner** - Prince Edward Isle Vacation Rentals Rent Direct From Owners and Save!

Sub Categories in Travel and Tourism:

▶ Attractions (2)   ▶ Parks (1)
▶ Charlottetown@ (3)   ▶ Summerside@ (4)
▶ Lodging (5)   ▶ Travelogues@ (1)

Sites in Category Travel and Tourism: What is this?

▶ **Avonlea Tours** New!
Tour operator that plans itineraries and travel packages for groups, individuals, families and reunions visiting Prince Edward Island. Information about tour packages and services.
http://www.avonleatours.com

▶ **Business and Vacation Guide**
A guide to the province's tourism industry and other Island businesses.
http://www.peisland.com

▶ **Canada Travel**
Information and reservation service covering everything travel: Hotels, Motels, Bed and Breakfast, Camping, Attractions, Adventure, Outdoors, Events, Festivals, Dining, and Tours.
http://www.canadatravel.ca/pei.asp

▶ **Cottage Canada - USA**
Listing of vacation rental of all types. From the rustic cabin on a lake to the luxurious homes.
http://www.cottage-canada-usa.com/prince_edward_island.htm

▶ **Destination PEI**
Information site including maps, accommodations, attractions and complete travel planning.
http://www.destination-pei.com

▶ **DiscoverPEI.ca**
Tourism guide Includes accommodations, maps, weather, and pictures.
http://www.discoverpei.ca

▶ **Island Visitor**
A destination guide featuring accommodations, dining, shopping, golf and attractions.
http://www.peivisitor.com

Figure 8.5 The Regional category includes Canada, which is further broken down into more than two dozen subcategories. The numbers tell you how many Web sites you'll find by clicking each link.

Figure 8.6 Use the Quick Start menu to access specialized search tools. Click Find It Fast to open the menu for additional search types.

Figure 8.7 Clicking this logo takes you back to the AOL Search home page.

✔ Tips

■ Unlike Yahoo (www.yahoo.com), AOL Search doesn't give you the option of limiting your search to topic categories in the Web directory. But it *does* include matching Web-directory topic categories in your search results.

■ The Open Directory Project is owned by AOL, which acquired it along with Netscape Communications in 1998. Despite the change in ownership, the process for building the directory remains the same: volunteer editors from around the world who are knowledgeable about a particular topic take responsibility for reviewing Web sites and selecting the best ones for inclusion in the directory.

Specialized search tools

The AOL Quick Start menu includes links for a set of specialized tools that come in handy for everyday search tasks: looking up e-mail addresses and phone numbers in Yellow Pages and White Pages directories, checking stock prices, getting maps and driving directions, locating product information, and so forth (**Figure 8.6**). You can click any of the buttons with arrows to expand the menus; click Find It Fast to expand the search menu.

✔ Tips

■ To make AOL Search your Web browser's default home page, see "Customizing Your Web Browser" in Chapter 4.

■ You can return to the AOL Search home page at any time by clicking the AOL Search logo (**Figure 8.7**), which appears on every page, or the text link Main, found at the top right of every search page.

Searching with AOL Search

There are two important points to keep in mind when searching with AOL Search:

◆ AOL's overall goal is to help you find what it considers to be the *best* information related to your search. Consequently, it lists its own proprietary content, where available, ahead of results provided by Google.

◆ Anyone with Internet access can use AOL Search, but unless you're an AOL subscriber and you have signed in with your screen name and password, you won't be shown AOL content.

To enter a query:

1. If you're an AOL subscriber, sign on to AOL and use the toolbar's Search option to go to the AOL Search home page. Subscribers and nonsubscribers alike can access the home page by going directly to search.aol.com.

2. Type your query—expressed as a plain-English question or one or more unique keywords—in the search form (**Figure 8.8**).

3. To look for an exact phrase, *do one of the following:*

▲ Enclose the words in double quotation marks: "digital photography".

▲ Use phrase connectors: brother-in-law.

Figure 8.8 AOL Search defaults to an AND search, so it would interpret a query like this to mean that you want to find items with all the words.

4. You can use the Boolean operators AND and OR (uppercase *not* required) to look for all words or only some of them. AND isn't really necessary, however, because AOL Search defaults to an AND search.

You can also use plus signs (+) in front of required words and phrases, though, like AND, it is not required.

5. To *exclude* a word or phrase from your results, type a minus sign (–) directly before the word to exclude: photography -fashion. Remember: *Don't* enter a space between the minus sign and word.

✔ Tips

- Instead of going to the AOL Search home page, AOL subscribers can simply enter a query in the AOL navigation bar's text box and click Search to submit it (**Figure 8.9**).

- Use the search form on the Welcome page or click the Search button in the Quick Start window to open a simple search form.

- AOL Search is *not* case sensitive, so you'll get the same results whether you type your queries in uppercase, lowercase, or a mix of the two.

Figure 8.9 AOL subscribers don't have to go to the AOL Search page. They can type a query in the AOL navigation bar's text box and click Search to submit the query.

To view your search results:

◆ Click the Search button (or press Enter) to submit your query.

Your search results (**Figure 8.10**) will be organized into as many as four sections:

Sponsored Links: These are paid listings for sites offering products and services related in some way (often quite loosely) to your search words.

Recommended Sites: The items here include AOL's proprietary content, "official" Web sites for companies and celebrities, and other Web sites selected by AOL's editorial staff.

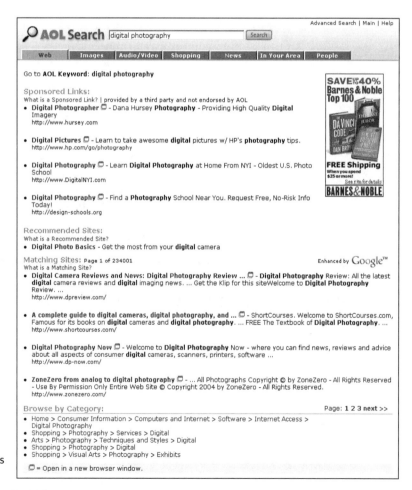

Figure 8.10 Here's an example of how AOL Search presents results.

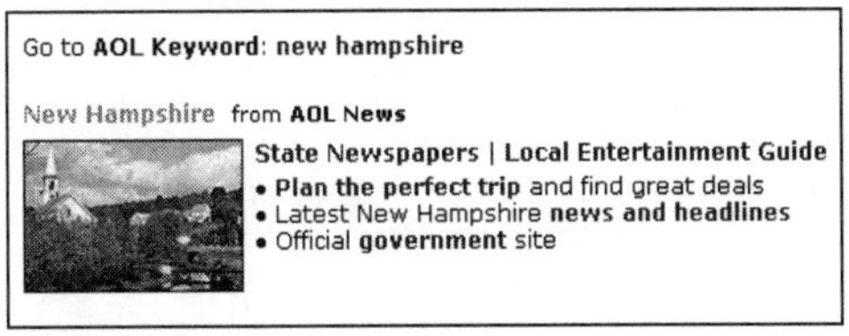

Go to **AOL Keyword**: new hampshire

New Hampshire from **AOL News**

State Newspapers | Local Entertainment Guide
• **Plan the perfect trip** and find great deals
• Latest New Hampshire **news and headlines**
• Official **government** site

Figure 8.11 Occasionally, the first result listed is from AOL News and contains links to news sources and other official information. When your search word is also an AOL keyword, you'll see a link at the top of the page.

Matching Sites: Typically the largest section, this includes AOL and Google content and Web sites from the Open Directory Project.

Browse by Category: These are topic categories from the Open Directory Project that may be relevant to your search.

✔ Tips

- You can increase the likelihood of being presented with all four categories of AOL Search results by limiting the number of words you type in the search box.

- AOL Search doesn't give you any control over how your results are displayed.

- When AOL News appears at the top of a listing, it includes links to AOL-sponsored news and information sites and official sites (**Figure 8.11**).

To refine an AOL Search query:

1. One way to refine a query is simply to add another unique keyword or phrase and run the search again. AOL Search looks for *all* the words that you type in the search box, so this has the effect of searching *within* your original results (also referred to as *set searching*).

2. Use the Browse by Category section to get ideas for additional keywords.

✔ Tips

- For a summary of search rules and examples for AOL Search, see the AOL Search Quick Reference (**Table 8.1**).

- For AOL Search's own help information, click the Help link at the top of the AOL Search page (**Figure 8.12**).

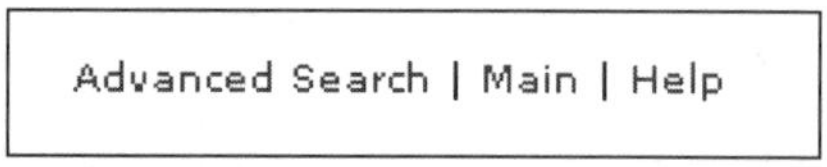

Advanced Search | Main | Help

Figure 8.12 To learn more about AOL Search, including new features that may have been added, click the Help link.

Table 11.1

AOL Search Quick Reference

FOR THIS TYPE OF SEARCH:	DO THIS:	EXAMPLES:
Plain-English Question	Type a question that expresses the idea or concept, using as many words as necessary.	Does Norm Abram have a Web site
Phrase Search	Type the phrase enclosed in double quotation marks or use phrase connectors.	"New Yankee Workshop" or brother-in-law
AND Search (multiple words and phrases, each of which *must* be present)	Type words or phrases separated by a space. You can also use the Boolean operator AND (uppercase or lowercase) to connect two or more search terms or put plus signs (+) directly in front of required search terms. All three examples will produce the same results.	"paint shaver" clapboard "paint shaver" AND clapboard +"paint shaver" +clapboard
OR Search (multiple words and phrases, *any* one of which may be present)	Use the Boolean operator OR (uppercase or lowercase) to combine words and phrases.	woodworking OR cabinetry
NOT Search (exclude a word or phrase)	Use a minus sign (–) to exclude a word or phrase.	"custom windows" –software
Case-Sensitive Search	Not available.	
Date Search	Advanced Search option.	
Field Search	Advanced Search option.	

SEARCHING WITH AOL SEARCH

Using Advanced Search

AOL Search offers many of the same basic advanced searching features as Google.

To use AOL Advanced Search:

1. Click Advanced Search at the top of the page to open the Advanced Search page (**Figure 8.13**).

continues on next page

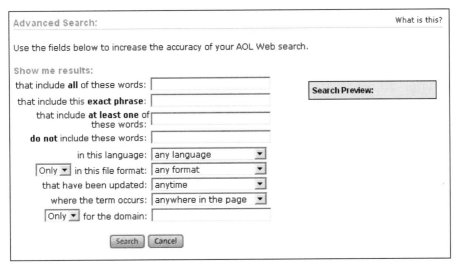

Figure 8.13 Use Advanced Search when you need to refine your search.

2. Select the options to *do any of the following:*

▲ Search for all words, an exact phrase, any of the words, or none of the words. As you tab out of the fields, the Search Preview box shows you what the search looks like (**Figure 8.14**).

▲ Restrict your search to pages written in a specific language by selecting the language from the menu (**Figure 8.15**),

Figure 8.15 Use Advanced Search to return results only from pages written in a specific language.

Show me results:

that include **all** of these words: white mountain

that include this **exact phrase**:

that include **at least one** of these words: lake ski

do not include these words:

Search Preview:
You are searching for white mountain, and at least one of the words lake ski

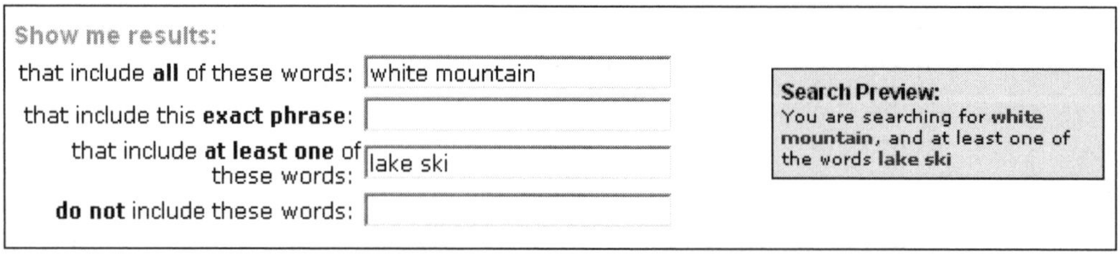

Figure 8.14 As you enter search terms and tab out of the fields, Search Preview shows you what your query looks like.

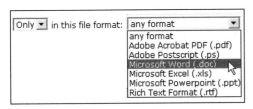

Figure 8.16 Control the types of documents that the search returns.

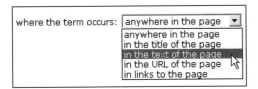

Figure 8.17 Use Advanced Search to search for keywords in specific parts of a page.

▲ Search for a specific file format or don't include a specific file format in the results (**Figure 8.16**).

▲ Include in the results pages that have been updated any time or that were updated within the last three months, six months, or year.

▲ Search for the search terms anywhere on the page or only in the title, in the text, in the URL of the page, or in links on the page (**Figure 8.17**).

▲ Restrict the search to a specific domain or don't include results from a specific domain. You can enter top-level domains, such as .edu or .net, or a specific domain, such as unh.edu.

3. After entering your search criteria (**Figure 8.18**), click the Search button or press Enter to begin the search.

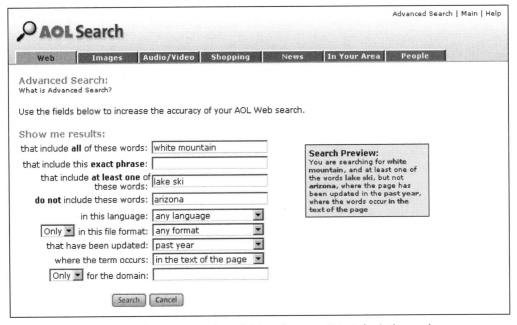

Figure 8.18 When your advanced query is complete, click Search or press Enter to begin the search.

MSN Search

Good to Know

- MSN Search is the default search engine for Internet Explorer (IE) and Microsoft Network (MSN).

- At the time of this writing, MSN Search is powered by Inktomi's 3-billion-page database and uses LookSmart for its Web directory.

- MSN Search encourages you to keep your queries simple. Boolean operators and most other power-search features are available only with Advanced Search.

- Despite its limited search options, MSN Search does a surprisingly good job of returning high-quality results.

Contact Information

Microsoft Network
Redmond, WA
Customer Service: 800-386-5550
Technical Support: 877-635-7019
search.msn.com (MSN Search)

MSN Search is among the most heavily used search sites on the Internet. But its popularity is due in large measure to the fact that it's on Internet Explorer's default start page.

Many users have no idea that they can change IE's default home page from MSN (www.msn.com) to some other Web site of their choosing. Others aren't aware of other search engines. Still others simply haven't bothered to change their search settings. Consequently, people leave their setup the way it is, and whenever they click Internet Explorer's Search button, they're presented with an MSN Search form.

Fortunately, it's possible to get fairly good results with MSN Search, using the simplest of queries. The creators of the site have chosen to emphasize quality versus quantity of search results—their objective is to present a small number of highly relevant Web pages on the very first results page. And they discourage the use of power-search capabilities— Boolean expressions, field searching, limiting a query by date and language—by relegating these features to the Advanced Search form.

continues on next page

MSN Search even tries to accommodate poor spellers and those prone to typing errors with what it calls a "what you mean is what you get" approach to searching. They've designed their software to recognize common misspellings, so that a search for, say, Brittany Spears or Britney Speers will nevertheless return Web pages featuring pop singer Britney Spears (**Figure 9.1**).

The biggest drawback to MSN Search, in our opinion, is that it doesn't allow you to search with much precision. And features like the "what you mean is what you get" approach to common misspellings may work most—but not all—of the time.

✔ Tips

■ Out of curiosity, we did an MSN Search for the "what you mean is what you get" acronym WYMIWYG (which could be pronounced "why-me-wig," but we're just guessing!). Turns out the acronym has been used since the mid-1990s in educational measurement circles to refer to "What You Measure Is What You Get." An obscure fact and a relatively small database—but we found what we wanted quickly and easily by simply typing wymiwyg in the MSN Search form.

■ You won't find an About link on the MSN Search page, but if you're interested in reading up on the latest Microsoft and MSN corporate news and information, visit www.microsoft.com/mscorp.

Figure 9.1 Spelling and typing errors are often not a problem for MSN Search. Even though we spelled the name incorrectly, the search engine located several "official" Britney Spears fan pages.

The MSN Search Home Page

If you're an MSN or IE user, you've probably already figured out that clicking any button labeled "Search"—on the MSN home page (www.msn.com) or on the IE toolbar—takes you to the MSN Search home page (**Figure 9.2**) or some version of the MSN Search form.

You can also go to MSN Search directly, of course, by typing the Web address search.msn.com in your browser's Address or Location box.

The MSN Search home page is devoted exclusively to searching. The key features to zero in on are the search form, Web directory, and Advanced Search option.

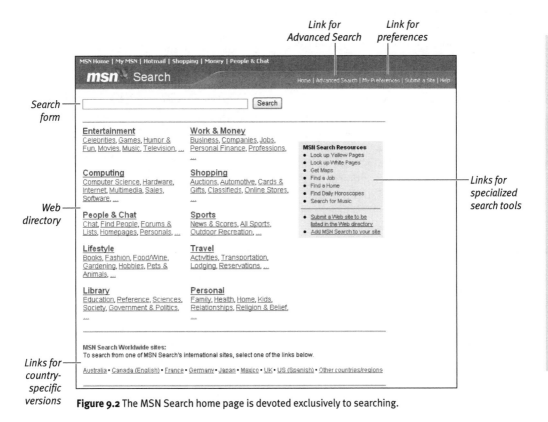

Figure 9.2 The MSN Search home page is devoted exclusively to searching.

Search form

The MSN Search form (**Figure 9.3**) is about as simple as they get: a box for entering your query and a Search button to submit it. MSN Search automatically looks for *all* the words in your query, so it's not necessary to put plus signs (+) in front of required terms.

✔ Tip

■ Boolean operators aren't recognized on this search form. If you combine search terms with AND or OR (in full caps or lowercase) on the MSN Search home page, the Boolean operators will simply be ignored.

Web directory

The Web directory (**Figure 9.4**) on the MSN Search home page is created and maintained by LookSmart (www.looksmart.com), a company that employs a staff of editors to identify the best Web sites and organize them into meaningful categories.

When you perform an MSN Search, your results include matches from the LookSmart Web directory as well as the Inktomi database of Web pages. But you can also *browse* the directory by clicking the link for one of the 10 major categories (Entertainment, Work and Money, Computing, and so on) or the dozens of subcategories and then drill down through topics of greater specificity.

✔ Tip

■ Unlike Yahoo (search.yahoo.com), MSN Search doesn't give you the option of limiting your search to the Web directory. But you can increase the likelihood of finding Web directory matches by using a fairly general word or phrase as your search term.

Figure 9.3 MSN Search would interpret this query to mean that you want to find Web pages with *all the* words, even though you haven't used plus signs or AND.

Figure 9.4 The Web directory on the MSN Search home page comes from LookSmart, a human-compiled guide to the best Web sites, organized by topic.

Figure 9.5 The Advanced Search link takes you to a page that gives you access to power-search features not available on the MSN Search home page.

MSN Search Resources

- Look up Yellow Pages
- Look up White Pages
- Get Maps
- Find a Job
- Find a Home
- Find Daily Horoscopes
- Search for Music

- Submit a Web site to be listed in the Web directory
- Add MSN Search to your site

Figure 9.6 Use the MSN Search Resources tools for specialized searches.

Figure 9.7 If you live outside the United States—or if you simply want to explore the Web from the perspective of another country and language—try one of MSN Search's country-specific versions.

Figure 9.8 Use this link, which you'll find at the top of most pages within the MSN site, to get back to the MSN Search home page.

- Download and install the MSN Search toolbar to add a search field to Internet Explorer's toolbars. In addition to providing the search form, the toolbar highlights your search keywords and blocks annoying pop-up windows. (For more information, see "Using the MSN Search Toolbar" later in this chapter.)

- You can get back to the MSN Search home page by clicking the Web Search link (**Figure 9.8**) that appears at the top of most pages within MSN and Hotmail sites.

Advanced Search option

When you want to search with more precision or exercise some control over how your results are presented, click Advanced Search (**Figure 9.5**) and use the form presented there.

With Advanced Search, you can enter Boolean expressions, change the sort order, do field searches (titles, links, and domains), and limit your queries in a variety of ways: by language, date modified, and multimedia file type, among others.

✔ Tips

- Use the MSN Search Resources links on the MSN Search home page (**Figure 9.6**) for help with common search tasks: looking up e-mail addresses and phone numbers, getting maps and driving directions, and so on.

- Submit a Web Site to Be Listed in the Web Directory does not allow you to submit a site to the MSN Search database as you can in other search engines. It's a link for paid placement services.

- MSN Search is offered in several country-specific versions that you can access from the home page (**Figure 9.7**). In addition to being presented in the country's native language, the content is also tailored to the country. (For more information, see "To refine an MSN Search query" later in this chapter.)

- To make MSN Search your Web browser's default home page, see "Customizing Your Web Browser" in Chapter 4.

Searching with MSN Search

As we've said, the search form on the MSN Search home page is quite simple to use and offers very few options. There are just a few basic rules to keep in mind:

- ◆ You can type up to 150 characters in the search form's text box.

- ◆ There's no need to use plus signs (+) to combine words and phrases, because MSN Search automatically looks for *all* the words in your query.

- ◆ Boolean operators aren't allowed, and including them is likely to result in a "no results found" message.

- ◆ Searches are *not* case sensitive, so you'll get the same results whether you type your search terms in uppercase, lowercase, or a combination of the two.

To enter a query:

1. Go to MSN Search (`search.msn.com`) and type a plain-English question or several unique keywords in the search form (**Figure 9.9**).

2. To look for an exact phrase, enclose the words in double quotation marks: `"reading maketh a full man"`.

3. If you want to *exclude* a word or phrase from your search results, try putting a minus sign (–) in front of it: `bacon -francis` (no space between the minus sign and the search word).

   This may or may not actually eliminate the word from your search results, but it's likely at least to push pages containing the excluded word farther down in the list.

Figure 9.9 With MSN Search, it's often best to start with a simple query like this.

✔ Tip

- ■ A more effective way to exclude a word or phrase from your search results is to go to the Advanced Search page, type your query in the search box using the Boolean operator AND NOT (in full caps), and choose Boolean Phrase from the Find menu. (For more information, see "To refine an MSN Search query" later in this chapter.)

To view your search results:

1. Click the Search button (or press Enter) to submit your query.

Your results will be presented 15 to a page (unless you set a difference preference; see "Customizing MSN Search" later in this chapter), along with a count of the total number of matches found (**Figure 9.10**). They'll be organized into as many as five categories:

continues on next page

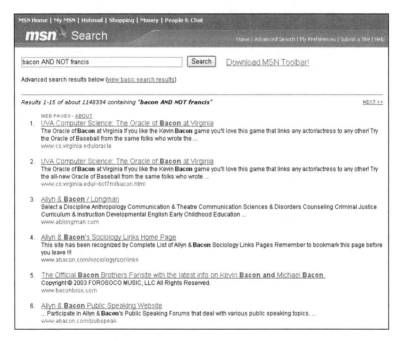

Figure 9.10 For searches that involve *excluding* a word, we've found that using AND NOT on the Advanced Search form works better than using a minus sign (–) on the regular search form.

Featured Sites are Web sites from MSN.com and MSN sponsors, some of whom pay for appearing in this section. A special icon is used to identify sites popular among MSN Search users (**Figure 9.11**).

Web Pages come from the 3-billion-page Inktomi database. MSN Search does *not* cluster search results, so if multiple pages within a Web site match your query, they will all be included in your results.

2. To visit any Web site on the search results page, click its title link.

✔ Tip

■ Don't enter a long phrase or a plain-English question in the search box. MSN Search's objective is to direct you to the "most popular" or "best" Web sites on a given topic, and the search engine has been designed to do that most effectively when you enter just a couple of search words.

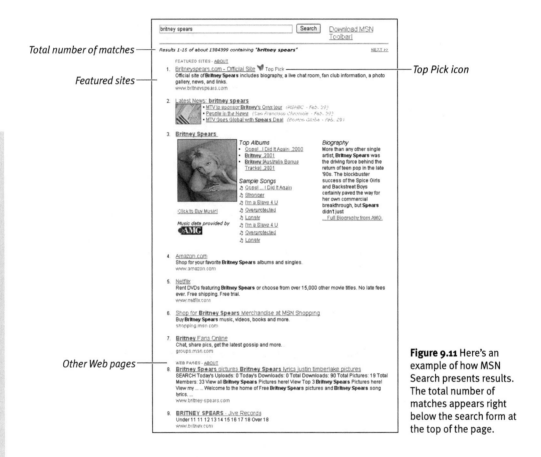

Total number of matches

Featured sites

Top Pick icon

Other Web pages

Figure 9.11 Here's an example of how MSN Search presents results. The total number of matches appears right below the search form at the top of the page.

To refine an MSN Search query:

1. To refine an MSN Search, simply add another unique keyword or phrase to your original query.

   Since MSN Search looks for *all* the words, this has the effect of searching *within* your original results (also referred to as *set searching*).

2. You can also click Advanced Search on the results page and select from the options to refine your query. Advanced Search offers a number of power-search features not available on the MSN Search home page (**Figure 9.12**):

continues on next page

Use Boolean operators or perform field search ——

Enable stemming ——

Show one page per domain ——

Sort results ——

Restrict search to specific languages and regions ——

Restrict search to specific domain ——

Control how deep to search ——

Restrict search to specific file types ——

Return pages containing links to these file types ——

Figure 9.12 To make changes in the way MSN Search looks for and displays results, use these options on the Advanced Search form. Unfortunately, you have to make the changes each time you search.

SEARCHING WITH MSN SEARCH

▲ **Use Boolean operators**: Select Boolean Phrase in the Find menu (**Figure 9.13**), and you can use AND, OR, AND NOT, and parentheses in your queries to create Boolean expressions and nested searches. Just be sure to type the Boolean operators in *uppercase* in your searches.

▲ **Perform field search**: Select the Find menu's Words in Title and Links to URL options to look for words in Web page titles and links. For links, be sure to type the *complete* URL (including `http://`) in the Advanced Search form's search box: `http://www.bartleby.com`.

▲ **Enable stemming**: You can turn on stemming (a type of wildcard searching), so that MSN Search will automatically look for both root words and variations.

▲ **Show one result per domain**: The Advanced Search display options let you cluster results so that you'll be shown only one page per Web site.

▲ **Sort results**: Sort the results by Date Descending (newest pages first), Title Ascending (alphabetically by title), or Depth Ascending (how far down in the Web site the page is located). By default, MSN Search lists results by popularity.

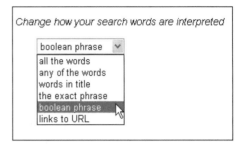

Figure 9.13 You can use Boolean operators on the Advanced Search form. Just remember to type them in *uppercase* and choose Boolean Phrase from the Find menu.

Figure 9.14 Typing edu in the Domain search box tells MSN Search to limit the query to education Web sites (sites whose domain names end in .edu).

▲ **Restrict search by region**: Limit your search to Web pages originating in a particular region of the world.

▲ **Restrict search by language**: You can limit your search to Web pages written in a specific language; choose a language from the menu.

▲ **Restrict search by domain**: To limit a search to a specific domain or domain type, enter that information (com for commercial, edu for education, org for nonprofit organization, and so on) in the Domain text box (**Figure 9.14**).

▲ **Restrict search by file type**: Uncheck the file types you do not want included in the search results.

▲ **Search multimedia files**: The final Advanced Search option is for links to multimedia types. You can search for Web pages that include links to specific types of files (images, audio, video, VBScript, and so on).

continues on next page

SEARCHING WITH MSN SEARCH

159

✔ Tips

- For a summary of search rules and examples, see the MSN Search Quick Reference for the regular search form (**Table 9.1**) and the Advanced Search form (**Table 9.2**).

- MSN Search's own help information, which you can access by clicking Help on the home page and the Advanced Search form, is rather skimpy. It appears in a frame on the right side of your screen (**Figure 9.15**), and you have to right-click (Windows) or Control-click (Mac) the frame to print a topic. Fortunately, the window is resizable; just drag the inside edge to make it wider, or double-click the title bar to maximize the window.

Figure 9.15 The MSN Search help information is accurate and searchable, but you may want to resize the window.

Table 9.1

MSN Search Basic Search Quick Reference		
FOR THIS TYPE OF SEARCH:	DO THIS:	EXAMPLES:
Plain-English Question	Simply type a question that expresses the idea or concept, using as many words as necessary.	`What's the best place for cross-country skiing in Minnesota?`
Phrase Search	Type the phrase enclosed in double quotation marks.	`"Gunflint Lodge"`
AND Search (multiple words and phrases, each of which *must* be present)	Type words or phrases separated by a space. MSN Search automatically searches for *all* the words, so plus signs (+) aren't necessary.	`skiing snowboarding`
OR Search (multiple words and phrases, any one of which may be present)	Not available. Use Advanced Search.	
NOT Search	Use a minus sign (–) directly in front of the word or phrase you want to exclude from your results. (Note that there's no space between the minus sign and the search word.)	`skiing -downhill`
Case-Sensitive Search	Not available.	
Date Search	Not available. Use Advanced Search.	
Field Search	Not available. Use Advanced Search.	
Nested Search	Not available. Use Advanced Search.	
Proximity Search	Not available.	
Wildcard Search	Not available. Use Advanced Search.	

Table 9.2

MSN Search Advanced Search Quick Reference		
FOR THIS TYPE OF SEARCH:	DO THIS:	EXAMPLES:
Plain-English Question	Type a question that expresses the idea or concept and choose All the Words on the Find menu.	`When was the Mir space station launched"?`
Phrase Search	Type the phrase without any special punctuation and choose The Exact Phrase on the Find menu.	`Hubble space telescope`
AND Search (multiple words and phrases, each of which *must* be present)	Type words or phrases separated by a space and choose All the Words on the Find menu.	`"space camp" scholarships`
	Alternatively, you can combine words and phrases with the Boolean operator AND (full caps required) and choose Boolean Phrase on the Find menu.	`"space camp" AND scholarships`
OR Search (multiple words and phrases, any one of which may be present)	Type words or phrases separated by a space and choose Any of the Words on the Find menu.	`NASA "space program"`
	Alternatively, you can combine words and phrases with the Boolean operator OR (full caps required) and choose Boolean Phrase on the Find menu.	`NASA OR "space program"`
NOT Search (to exclude a word or phrase)	Use the Boolean operator AND NOT (full caps required) with the word or phrase you want to exclude and choose Boolean Phrase on the Find menu.	`shuttle AND NOT challenger`
Case-Sensitive Search	Not available.	
Field Search	Three types of field searches are possible:	
	Titles. Type search words or phrases in the search box and choose Words in Title on the Find menu.	`astronaut hall of fame`
	Links. Type the complete URL (including `http://`) in the search box and choose Links to URL on the Find menu.	`http://www.astronaut.org`
	Domain. Use the Domain text box on the form to limit your search to a domain type (com, edu, gov, org, and so on) or to a specific domain.	`Domain: nasa.gov` `Domain: com`
Nested Search	Combine search terms with Boolean operators and parentheses and choose Boolean Phrase from the Find menu.	`(NASA OR "space program")` `AND budget AND 2001`
Proximity Search	Not available.	
Wildcard Search	Use the Enable Stemming option to automatically search for both *root* words and *variations*. With stemming enabled, a search for *budget* would also find references to *budgets*, *budgetary*, and *budgeting*.	`budget`

Using IE's Search Explorer Bar

Internet Explorer includes an Explorer bar on the left side to display your Favorites, History, Media Player, or Search results. Show, hide, or change the contents of the Explorer bar by selecting the appropriate button.

The Explorer bar includes a unique feature when you use MSN Search: Search Preview.

When you use Search Preview, Internet Explorer displays small preview images of Web sites for the first six search results on each results page (**Figure 9.16**). These preview images can help you decide whether a site might have the information you are searching for. When you click Previous or Next to display another set of results, previews of the first six sites in the set are displayed.

To enable or disable Search Preview, add or remove the check for Show Search Preview (Right) (**Figure 9.17**) at the bottom of the Search Explorer bar

Search Preview works only when MSN Search is set as your default search provider for the Search Explorer bar. (See Chapter 4 to learn more about the Search Explorer bar.)

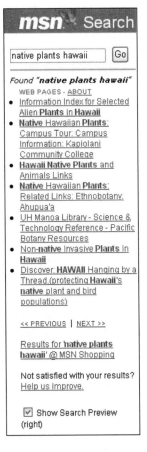

Figure 9.17 You can disable Search Preview images at the bottom of the Search Explorer bar.

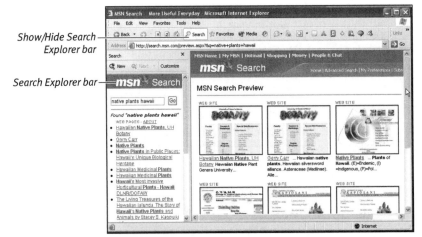

Show/Hide Search Explorer bar

Search Explorer bar

Figure 9.16 Searching from the Search Explorer bar lets you look at previews of Web pages.

USING IE'S SEARCH EXPLORER BAR

Figure 9.18 You need to use the Search Assistant, not the Search Companion, and the MSN search engine to see the page previews.

✔ Tips

- The Search Explorer bar must be configured to use the Search Assistant for you to view Search Preview images. If your version of Windows uses the Search Companion (usually with an animated character), you'll need to switch to the Search Assistant. From the Search Explorer bar, choose Change Preferences > Change Internet Search Behavior; then select With Classic Internet Search (**Figure 9.18**). Choose MSN as the default search engine and click OK. Close all IE windows and then reopen them. The Search Assistant should now be active.

- Although the preview feature helps people looking for sites, Webmasters may not want certain pages, such as ones that change often, indexed with a preview. To prevent individual page previews, add this meta tag to the page header:
  `<meta name="robots"`
  `content="noimageindex, nomediaindex">`

- Webmasters can prevent their entire site from being indexed with page previews by add the following line to robots.txt:
  `User-agent: searchpreview Disallow: /`

Using the MSN Search Toolbar

Like most other search engines, MSN Search has a toolbar for Internet Explorer that you can download using a link on the search page (**Figure 9.19**). And like the other search toolbars, it does more than just add a search field to your browser. For instance, you can highlight your search words and search the MSN dictionary and Encarta encyclopedia and the MSNBC news site (**Figure 9.20**).

One interesting feature of the toolbar is the Highlight Viewer (**Figure 9.21**). When you click the Highlight button, a small window opens, showing you where on the page the search terms are found. Each search word is highlighted in a different color so you can get an idea of how many times each word is used on the page and where on the page the words are used.

Figure 9.19 Use the MSN Search toolbar and you won't need to open the search page to begin a search.

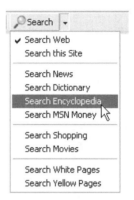

Figure 9.20 Choose from different types of searches.

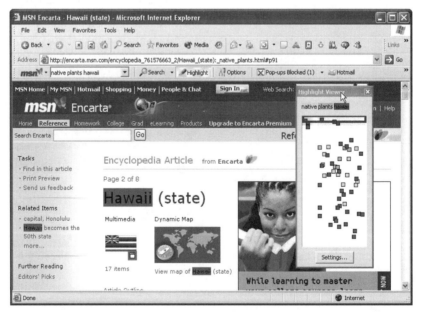

Figure 9.21 Highlight your search terms and use the Highlight Viewer to see a map of the search words on the page.

USING THE MSN SEARCH TOOLBAR

Figure 9.22 Select My Preferences to go to the MSN Search preferences Web page.

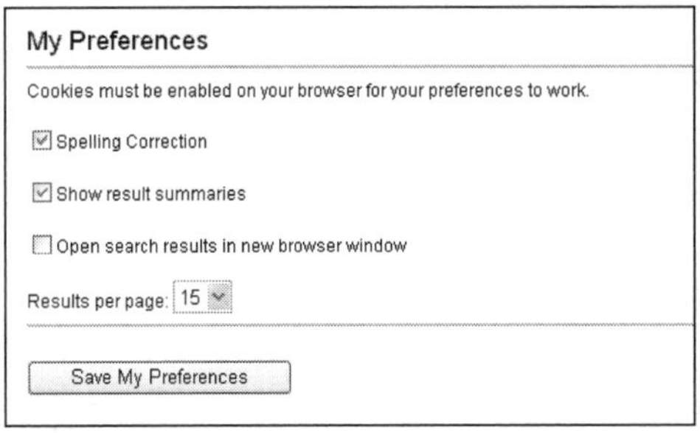

My Preferences

Cookies must be enabled on your browser for your preferences to work.

☑ Spelling Correction

☑ Show result summaries

☐ Open search results in new browser window

Results per page: 15 ▾

[Save My Preferences]

Figure 9.23 MSN Search has limited preferences for searchers to change.

Customizing MSN Search

MSN Search has just four preferences you can set, related to the spelling correction feature and the way that results are displayed. Since Preferences are saved in cookies on your computer, you'll need to allow cookies.

To change your preferences:

1. Select My Preferences (**Figure 9.22**) to open the My Preferences page.

2. Set any of the preferences you want (**Figure 9.23**):

   ▲ **Spelling Correction:** Uncheck this option if you don't want MSN Search to correct misspellings in your search entries.

   ▲ **Show Result Summaries:** If you don't select this option, MSN Search lists only URLs, without a brief description of the site.

   ▲ **Open Search Results in New Browser Window:** When this option is selected, you can view results from several URLs in new browser windows without having to specifically open a new window.

3. Choose the number of results to display per page. The default is 15.

4. Click Save My Preferences, and your preferences are saved to a cookie on your computer.

CUSTOMIZING MSN SEARCH

165

ASK JEEVES

Founded in 1996, at a time when the Internet was in its infancy, Ask Jeeves's friendly butler named Jeeves helps users find the best answers on the Web, answering millions of queries each day.

Don't let its position as the fifth most popular search engine make you think it's not as good as the others. Remember that three of the search engines ahead of it draw users through their portal or ISP businesses. Ask Jeeves's only business is the search business.

Ask Jeeves Kids (`AJKids.com`) offers a kid-friendly way for children to find answers to their questions or help with their homework while learning about the online world. Children can ask Jeeves natural-language questions, just as they would ask a parent, friend, or teacher.

Good to Know

- ◆ Popular and safe search engine for children to use.

✔ Tip

- ■ Ask Jeeves uses natural-language technology, allowing you to ask Jeeves questions just as you would a real person.

Contact Information

Ask Jeeves, Inc.
Emeryville, CA
Phone: 510-985-7400
Fax: 510-985-7412
www.ask.com

Searching with Ask Jeeves

As with the other search-engine-only sites, the Ask Jeeves home page is simple, clean, and exceptionally easy to use (**Figure 10.1**). Type your question in the search form and click Ask. Ask Jeeves uses AND as the default Boolean operator and returns the results quickly.

Ask Jeeves is well known for its natural-language technology, and you can type a question or enter your search words as a phrase.

✔ Tip

■ Click the Ask Jeeves logo or Home link on any page to return to the home page.

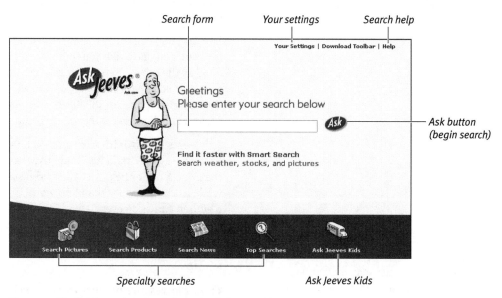

Figure 10.1 The Ask Jeeves home page is used only for searching.

To enter a basic search query:

1. Go to the Ask Jeeves home page at www.ask.com and enter your search phrase or question (**Figure 10.2**).

2. You can use the minus sign (–) on the basic form to exclude words. Use double-quotation marks around phrases or punctuation marks between the words to search for an exact phrase.

✔ Tips

- Always enter keywords in a logical order, using the same order as if you were speaking the keywords to someone. For example, enter `father's day gift ideas for dad`, not `dad gift ideas father's day`.

- Be specific. Use categories to help Jeeves pinpoint the information. For example, `I want information on Cheers` will return results that include cheerleading, while `I want information on Cheers, the TV show` brings up only pages about the TV show *Cheers*.

- When you use the AND operator, Ask Jeeves includes it in the results—that is, searching for `art AND museum` finds entries containing all three words.

Figure 10.2 Ask Jeeves, the friendly Internet butler, a question.

To view your search results:

1. Click the Ask button or press Enter to search.
2. The search results are grouped into three well-defined groups: Sponsored Web Results, Web Results, and Related Searches. If the question or phrase is a popular one, you may see a Do You Want to Know section at the top of the page (**Figure 10.3**). Select a person or word from the menu to begin a search.
3. Ask Jeeves displays limited information about the link—just the page title, which links to the page, a two-line description, and the actual URL (**Figure 10.4**). Click the link to view the page.

Home
Your Settings | Editorial Guidelines | Help
Ask Jeeves
richard harris, the actor
Advanced Options
Search: Web Pictures News Products
Do you want to know:
Where can I find fan pages for Richard Harris ?
Sponsored Web Result
About
Richard Harris Movies
Find the Best Price on Videos, DVDs Compare Products & Stores to Save
From: http://www.pricegrabber.com
Web Results
About
CNN.com - Actor Richard Harris dead at 72 - Oct. 25, 2002
Richard Harris, the classically trained actor whose roles ranged from King Arthur in Camelot to Headmaster Albus Dumbledore in the Harry Potter...
From: www.cnn.com/2002/SHOWBIZ/Movies/10/25/harris.obit/index.html
BBC NEWS | Entertainment | Film | Obituary: Richard Harris
The Irish actor, Richard Harris, was a well known for his hell-raising lifestyle as his considerable abilities as an actor.
From: news.bbc.co.uk/1/hi/entertainment/film/2361801.stm
BBC NEWS | Entertainment | Film | Actor Richard Harris dies
Irish actor Richard Harris has died in hospital where he was being treated for cancer, his family has confirmed.
From: news.bbc.co.uk/1/hi/entertainment/film/2362935.stm
Richard Harris
Actor - filmography (2000s) (1990s) (1980s) (1970s) (1960s ... Find where Richard Harris is credited alongside another name. Richard Harris &
From: us.imdb.com/Name?Harris,+Richard
Related Searches
1970 S Movie Of Richard Harris
Movie Richard Harris
Man Called Horse Film
Clint Eastwood Obituary
Harry Potter Actor Dies
Tall Was Actor Richard Harris
Actor Richard Harris Pictures
Richard Harris The Actor
Macarthur Park Richard Harris
Richard Harris Dead

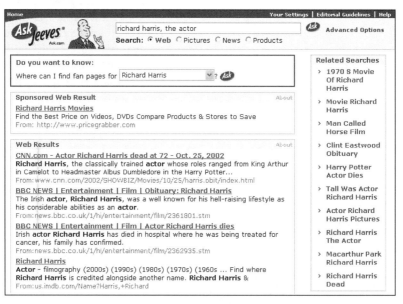

Figure 10.3 Search results are easy to read at Ask Jeeves, with sponsored results clearly identified and a Related Searches section listing additional sites that may interest you.

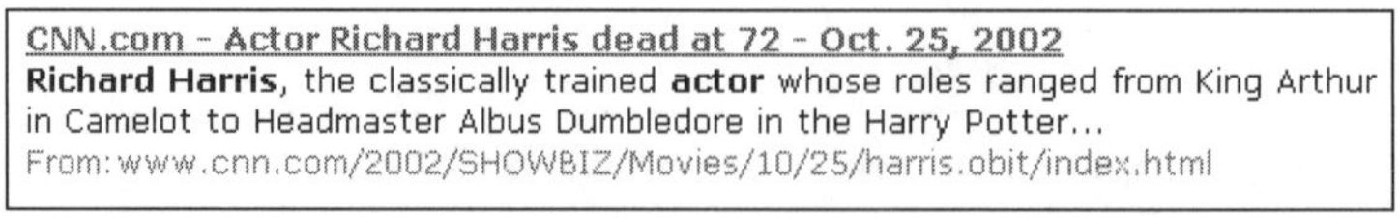

CNN.com - Actor Richard Harris dead at 72 - Oct. 25, 2002
Richard Harris, the classically trained actor whose roles ranged from King Arthur in Camelot to Headmaster Albus Dumbledore in the Harry Potter...
From: www.cnn.com/2002/SHOWBIZ/Movies/10/25/harris.obit/index.html

Figure 10.4 Ask Jeeves doesn't add options to the search results—just the page title, a short description of the page, and the complete URL.

Figure 10.5 Search for pictures, news, or products using your keywords by selecting a radio button.

4. To see pictures, news, or products related to your search phrase, select the appropriate radio button below the search form (**Figure 10.5**).

5. Ask Jeeves displays pages in a framed window, with the Ask Jeeves search form at the top of the page. Click the Back to Your Results link to go back to your search results, click the page URL to view the site without a frame, or click Remove Frame to close the frame (**Figure 10.6**).

✔ Tips

■ The News search archive goes back just one month and has filters to let you narrow your search to today/yesterday, last week, the last two weeks, or the last month (**Figure 10.7**).

■ If you don't want framed pages, you can change your settings as described in "Customizing Ask Jeeves" later in this chapter.

Back to results page   Page URL   Remove frame

Figure 10.6 Pages are displayed in a frame by default. The frame includes a link to return to the results page (on the left), to view the current page (in the center), and to remove the frame (on the right).

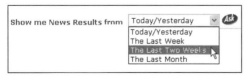

Figure 10.7 News results are limited to time frames within the last month.

Using Advanced Search

Unlike many other search engines, Ask Jeeves has very limited advanced search options. It's very easy to create an advanced search using the point-and-click interface.

To do an advanced search:

1. Click the Advanced Options link on the Ask Jeeves home page (**Figure 10.8**).

2. Choose one or more advanced options to refine your search (**Figure 10.9**):

Figure 10.8 Use Advanced Options to use Ask Jeeves's advanced search features.

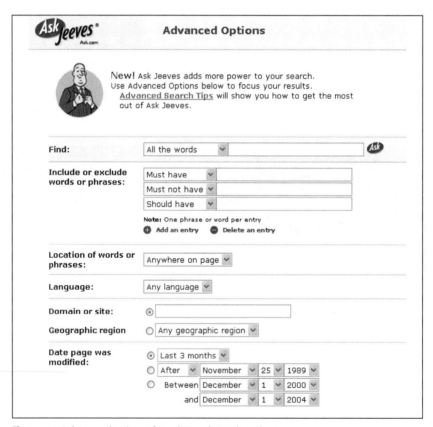

Figure 10.9 Ask Jeeves has just a few advanced search options.

▲ **Find:** Look for all of the words or the exact phrase.

▲ **Include or Exclude Words or Phrases:** Specify words that the results must have, must not have, or should have. Use these options when you want to do an AND, NOT, or OR search.

▲ **Location of Words or Phrases:** Look for search words anywhere on the page, in the page title, or in the URL.

▲ **Language:** Select a language from the list to search for pages written in one of the 10 languages that Ask Jeeves supports.

▲ **Domain or Site:** Enter any domain (com, net, edu, and so on) or site name (microsoft.com) to restrict searches to that domain or site. Or choose to search only pages from a specific geographic region of the world.

▲ **Date Page Was Modified:** Choose one of the three options: search using a relative time frame (any time, last week, last month, and so on, through the last two years), before or after a specific date, or between two dates.

3. Scroll to the top of the page and click Ask when you are ready to begin your advanced search.

Using Smart Search

Ask Jeeves has a new feature called Smart Search. Sample Smart Searches are shown on the home page, below the search form (**Figure 10.10**). The Smart Search links rotate after a few uses, so your page may have different links.

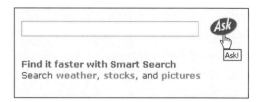

Figure 10.10 Click one of the Smart Search links on the Ask Jeeves home page.

Click one of the links to see how to use the Smart Search. For example, clicking the Weather link brings up a page with Seattle's current conditions (**Figure 10.11**). As you can see in the search bar, the keywords used were `weather seattle` or `boston weather`. Ask Jeeves supports city names or zip codes in a Weather Smart Search. You can also ask Jeeves about current conditions: `Is it snowing in Chicago?`

Figure 10.11 Get local weather conditions using the Weather Smart Search.

Other special searches include:

◆ **Famous People:** Type the name of a famous person, and Jeeves includes a picture and bibliographical information as well as relevant links (**Figure 10.12**).

◆ **Stocks:** Search for stock quotes for all publicly traded U.S. companies on all U.S. markets by including either the stock ticker symbol or the company name plus the phrase stock quote (**Figure 10.13**). You're limited to one quote at a time.

continues on next page

Figure 10.12 Type a famous person's name in the search form, and the first result is a picture, biography, and links to more information about the person.

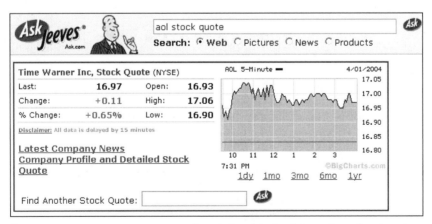

Figure 10.13 Enter a company name or stock symbol, and the Stock Quote Smart Search returns the latest information on the company.

USING SMART SEARCH

◆ **Weights and Measures Conversions:**
Use the simple conversion calculator to
convert weights and measures (**Figure
10.14**). Ask Jeeves currently supports
time, data, weight, length, area, volume,
and temperature conversions.

✔ Tip

■ For a summary of Ask Jeeves's search
tools, see **Table 10.1**.

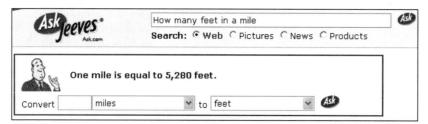

Figure 10.14 Ask Jeeves a weight or measurement question or use the conversion form to
convert weights and measures to other units.

Table 10.1

Ask Jeeves Quick Reference

FOR THIS TYPE OF SEARCH:	DO THIS:	EXAMPLES:
Word or Phrase Search	Type the phrase enclosed in quotation marks or use punctuation marks to separate words.	"detroit tigers" or detroit.tigers
AND Search (multiple words and phrases, each of which must be present)	The default search type; AND is not required.	Asia business
OR Search (multiple words and phrases, any one of which may be present)	Use OR to connect two or more words or phrases, either one of which may appear in the guide's title or keywords.	justice OR judicial
Wildcard Search	Not supported.	
Nested Search	Use parentheses to group search expressions into more complex queries. The example would find references to *art museum* and *art gallery.*	art (museum OR gallery)
Weather	Get local weather forecasts. Enter weather and the city name or zip code in the search form, in either order.	weather Austin or 37601 weather
Stock Quotes and Information	Enter the stock symbol or company name and stock quote.	Msft stock quote
Famous People	Enter the person's name to get pictures, bibliographical information, and related links a famous people.	Abe Lincoln
Weights and Measures	Enter a phrase or question about weights or measures to open the weights and measures converter. Time, data, weight, length, area, volume, and temperature conversions are supported.	how many feet in a mile

Figure 10.15 Click the Your Settings link to open the custom settings dialog box.

Customizing Ask Jeeves

Ask Jeeves offers only minimal user-controlled preferences, display options, and content filtering.

To customize Ask Jeeves:

1. Open the Your Settings page by clicking Your Settings at the top of any page (**Figure 10.15**).

2. You can configure the results display and filtering (**Figure 10.16**):

   ▲ Display options are limited; you can choose the number of results displayed per page, specify whether to open links in new windows, and disable framed browsing.

   ▲ Choose one of three options for the content filtering level: limit exposure to adult content, display a warning before showing adult content, or don't display a warning.

3. Click Save My Settings after you are finished making changes to return to the search page.

Figure 10.16 Change the number of pages displayed by default, open results in new windows, or disable the frame.

Ask Jeeves Kids

Parents of school-age children will appreciate Ask Jeeves Kids (**Figure 10.17**). It's a kid-friendly search engine with study tools and educational games for children.

To open Ask Jeeves Kids, click the Ask Jeeves Kids link at the bottom of the Ask Jeeves home page (**Figure 10.18**).

The Ask Jeeves Kids home page has a search form and, in the center of the page, a text box displaying questions that other kids are asking right now. The left side has links to games, news resources, and Encarta, and links to a wide range of research tools are on the right (**Figure 10.19**).

Figure 10.17 Click Ask Jeeves Kids on the home page if you want to visit the Ask Jeeves Kids site.

Figure 10.18 Jeeves provides a safe site for children to search.

Figure 10.19 Type a question or peek at the answers to questions other kids are asking.

The search form works like any other search form—type a question or phrase in the form and click Ask. Or to find the answers to questions other kids are asking, click the Ask button beside the Peek form.

Instead of listing a page full of results, Ask Jeeves Kids uses an answers page, where children can select an answer (**Figure 10.20**) or refine their searches.

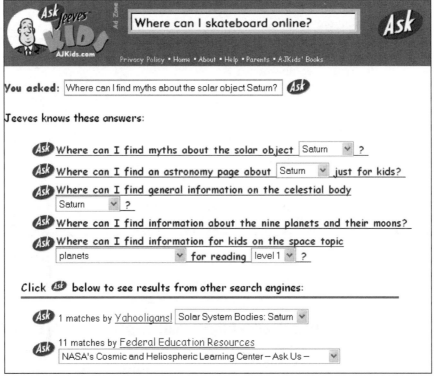

Figure 10.20 Ask Jeeves Kids returns the results in a format that is easy for even the youngest child to understand.

Using the Ask Jeeves Toolbar

Not to be outdone by the other search engines that have toolbars for Internet Explorer, Ask Jeeves has a toolbar, too.

If you (or your children) plan to use Ask Jeeves as your search engine, you'll want to install the toolbar. Look for links to download the toolbar at the bottom of every results page (**Figure 10.21**).

After the installation is complete, the toolbar will be added to your browser (**Figure 10.22**). Like many other search toolbars, it has a search field, a button to highlight your search words on the page, a pop-up stopper, and links to Ask Jeeves's other specialty search areas.

It also has a unique feature: zoom. The zoom control zooms Web pages in and out—handy if you need to see more of a page on the screen or want the text larger (**Figure 10.23**).

Figure 10.21 If you plan to use Ask Jeeves often, you'll want to download and install the Ask Jeeves toolbar.

Figure 10.22 The toolbar includes a search field, highlight, zoom, and pop-up blocker. It also has shortcuts to other Ask Jeeves sections.

Figure 10.23 Click the zoom button to zoom in and out of the current Web page. Here we zoomed in to make the page easier to read.

Click the Ask Jeeves button at the far left to view various options available to you, including options to open the Ask Jeeves or Ask Jeeves Kids home page, hide or show buttons, and clear your search history (**Figure 10.24**).

Enter your search phrase or question in the search field and click Ask to search the Ask Jeeves site. Click the arrow to select other search options (**Figure 10.25**). Search This Site initiates a domain search of the site you are viewing.

✔ Tip

- Enter a word in the search field and select Search Dictionary to find the definition of a word.

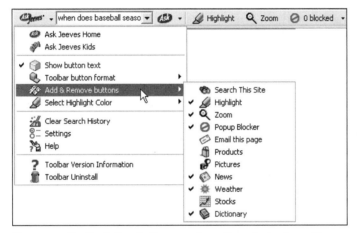

Figure 10.24 Use the Options button menu to configure the toolbar settings.

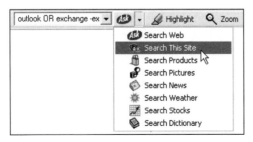

Figure 10.25 Use the Ask button menu to begin different types of searches.

ALTAVISTA

Good to Know

◆ AltaVista is a favorite of professional searchers because of its powerful search features.

◆ AltaVista is one of the few search engines that offers full Boolean and case-sensitive searching, along with a variety of field-search and language options, to help you target your searches.

◆ Developed in 1995 at Digital Equipment Corporation in Palo Alto, California, AltaVista has been awarded more search-related patents than any other company in the world.

Contact Information

AltaVista Company
Palo Alto, CA
Phone: 650-320-7700
Fax: 650-320-7720
www.altavista.com

AltaVista is one of the most powerful and comprehensive search engines available today. Launched in 1995 as a pioneering effort to index the full text of the World Wide Web, it has evolved over the years from a pure search engine to a portal service and is now back to being just a search engine.

You'll be pleased to discover how quickly and precisely you can find information with AltaVista. All it takes is a little practice and the mastery of a few simple techniques, which we'll cover in this chapter.

Experienced searchers will appreciate the fact that AltaVista offers full Boolean search capabilities, case-sensitive searching, and a range of field-search options that is second to none. With AltaVista, you can tailor the search form to limit your queries to pages written in a particular language. And you can specify the amount of detail presented in your search results as well as the number of items presented on each page.

To take full advantage of AltaVista's power and sophistication, you'll need to spend some time familiarizing yourself with its various search forms. Once you've learned your way around, you may well decide to join the legions of professional searchers who've made AltaVista their search engine of choice.

continues on next page

✔ Tips

- The AltaVista database is created by a spider program known as Scooter, which constantly roams the World Wide Web, collecting some 10 million Web pages each day and delivering them to AltaVista, where special software indexes every word. Scooter's work is supplemented by information provided to AltaVista by Web site creators.

- To save keystrokes, you can reach the AltaVista home page using the Web address www.av.com.

- To make AltaVista your default home page, follow the instructions in "Customizing Your Web Browser" in Chapter 4.

- You can get back to the AltaVista home page at any time by clicking the AltaVista logo at the top of most pages.

Searching with AltaVista

The AltaVista (www.altavista.com) home page is simple and clean (**Figure 11.1**), but as you'll soon discover, AltaVista offers a range of options for finding information on the Web. So whether you're a complete novice, a seasoned researcher, or somewhere in between, chances are good that you'll find that AltaVista has you covered.

Despite its name, the Basic Search form is actually quite powerful. If you take full advantage of the tools that AltaVista makes available to you for use with Basic Search, you'll be amazed at how easily you can zero in on the information you're looking for on the Web.

continues on next page

Figure 11.1 You will probably do most of your AltaVista searches using the Basic Search form.

In this section, we'll show you in step-by-step fashion how to enter search terms and special punctuation on the Basic Search form. For a summary of the material covered here, see the AltaVista Basic Search Quick Reference (**Table 11.1**).

Table 11.1

AltaVista Basic Search Quick Reference		
FOR THIS TYPE OF SEARCH:	DO THIS:	EXAMPLES:
Plain-English Question	Simply type the question in the search form text box. Use as many words as necessary.	`What is the date of the Battle of Trafalgar?`
Phrase Search	Type the phrase as a sequence of words surrounded by double quotation marks.	`"Battle of Trafalgar"`
AND Search (multiple words and phrases, each of which must be present)	Use a plus sign (+) in front of each word or phrase that must appear in the results.	`+London + "art museum"`
OR Search (multiple words and phrases, any one of which may be present)	Type words or phrases separated by spaces, without any special notation.	`Stratford Shakespeare`
NOT Search (exclude a word or phrase)	Use a minus sign (–) in front of a word or phrase you want to exclude from the results.	`+python –monty`
Case-Sensitive Search	Use lowercase to find any combination of uppercase and lowercase letters. Use capital letters (initial caps or a combination of uppercase and lowercase) to force an exact match of your search term. The first example would match *Bath* (but not *bath* or *BATH*). The second example would match *BATH* only.	`Bath     BATH`
Date Search	Not available on the Basic Search form. Use Advanced Search.	
Field Search	Type the field-search keyword in lowercase, followed by a colon and your search word or phrase. (See Table 11.2 later in this chapter for a complete list of field-search keywords.)	`title:"Victoria and Albert Museum" host:cambridge.edu domain:com`
Nested Search	Not available on the Basic Search form. Use Advanced Search.	
Proximity Search	Not available on the Basic Search form. Use Advanced Search.	
Wildcard Search	Use an asterisk (*) at the end of or within a word, along with at least three letters at the beginning of the search term.	`Brit*     col*r`

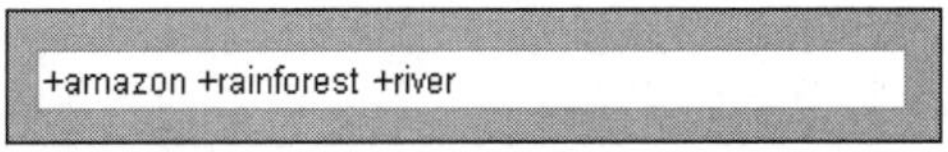

+amazon +rainforest +river

Figure 11.2 To do an AND search on the Basic Search form, put a plus sign (+) in front of each term.

London museums -Victoria -Albert

Figure 11.3 A minus sign (–) in front of a search term tells AltaVista to exclude Web pages containing that word or phrase.

To enter a Basic Search query:

1. Go to www.altavista.com and type several unique keywords, a phrase in quotation marks, or a combination of words and phrases in the Basic Search form.

   ▲ To look for Web pages with references to *any* (but not necessarily *all*) of the terms in your query, type words or phrases with a space between them.

   ▲ Use a plus sign (+) in front of each word or phrase to tell AltaVista that they must *all* appear in your search results (**Figure 11.2**).

   ▲ Use a minus sign (–) in front of any word or phrase you want to *exclude* from the search results. To find London museums *other than* the Victoria and Albert, use a search like the one shown in **Figure 11.3**.

   ▲ Use an asterisk (*) at the end of (or within) a word to perform a wildcard search. Be sure to use at least three letters at the beginning of the search term or AltaVista will ignore the request. Using Brit* as a search term will find references to *Britain, British,* and *Britannia,* as well as *Britney* and other similar words. To narrow your search, combine a wildcard search term with at least one other keyword or phrase.

2. When you've finished entering your query, click the Search button to submit it.

continues on next page

SEARCHING WITH ALTAVISTA

✔ Tips

- You'll typically get much better results with AltaVista if you search for a phrase, or a combination of words and phrases, rather than a single word.

- AltaVista uses an automated process to detect commonly used phrases in your queries, even if you haven't enclosed the words in quotation marks. Consequently, you'll sometimes get the same results with or without quotation marks (**Figure 11.4**). Still, you should get into the habit of always enclosing phrases in quotation marks on the Basic Search form. After all, there's no way of knowing for sure exactly what AltaVista considers a "common phrase."

- AltaVista treats words with punctuation marks between them as phrases. This means that you can type a period between words instead of using double quotation marks: `"princess of wales"` and `princess.of.wales` will both return the same results.

- AltaVista performs case-sensitive searches only when you enter a phrase search.

Figure 11.4 Common phrases like this are included in AltaVista's phrase dictionary, so you'll get the same results with or without quotation marks.

To limit your search to a particular language:

1. Click the English, Spanish link on the Basic Search form (**Figure 11.5**) to change the language selection. (English and Spanish is the default setting for systems using English.)

   Choose English, for example, to tell AltaVista to include only Web pages written in English in your search results (**Figure 11.6**). You can choose more than one language.

   To search pages written in any language, select the All Languages radio button.

2. Click OK to return to the Basic Search form or X (at the upper right) to close the form.

   The default language (or languages) for your searches will now be the one you selected.

continues on next page

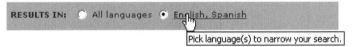

Figure 11.5 If a particular search returns a lot of foreign-language pages, you can eliminate them by using the Search Languages menu.

Figure 11.6 Once you've customized the language option, AltaVista will automatically search for pages in your chosen language(s).

✔ Tips

■ You can also change the default language setting by clicking Settings and then Language of Search Results. Make your language selections and then click OK.

■ Another way of dealing with unfamiliar languages is to use AltaVista's translation tool, Babel Fish. If your results include a Web site in French, German, Italian, Portuguese, Russian, or Spanish, click the Translate link (**Figure 11.7**) for an instant translation to English. It won't be perfect, but it could give you enough information to go on.

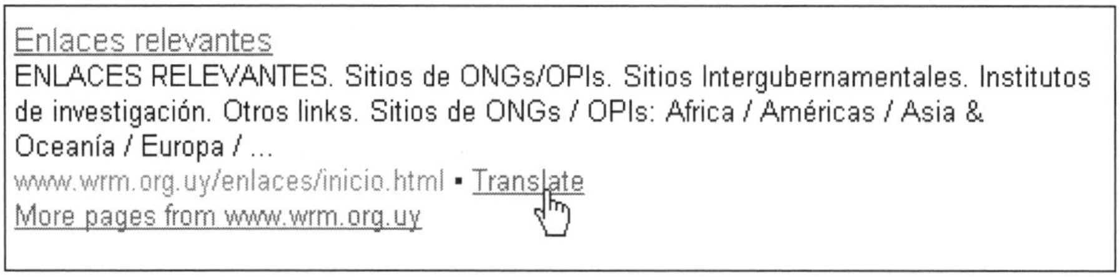

Enlaces relevantes
ENLACES RELEVANTES. Sitios de ONGs/OPIs. Sitios Intergubernamentales. Institutos de investigación. Otros links. Sitios de ONGs / OPIs: Africa / Américas / Asia & Oceanía / Europa / ...
www.wrm.org.uy/enlaces/inicio.html • Translate
More pages from www.wrm.org.uy

Figure 11.7 For an instant translation to English, click the Translate link in your search results.

To view your search results:

1. Click the Search button to the right of the search form text box.

By default, AltaVista presents your results, 10 to a page, with sponsored matches listed first and then the best matches from its database (**Figure 11.8**). AltaVista also tells you exactly how many matches it found in its database, and it boldfaces your search terms to make them easy to spot in the site descriptions.

continues on next page

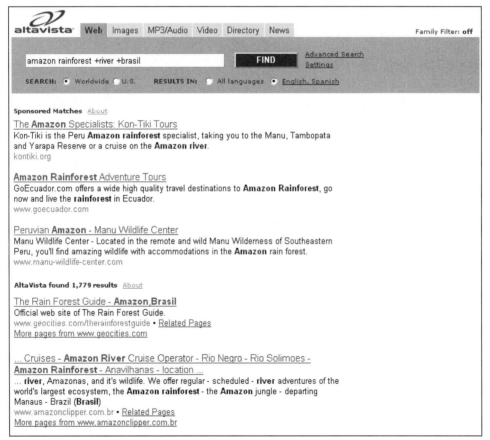

Figure 11.8 AltaVista presents your results with the best matches listed first, highlighting your search terms in bold to make them easy to spot. The first page of your search results includes the total number of pages found.

2. A typical entry (**Figure 11.9**) on the results page includes the title of the document, a brief description provided by the person who created it (or, if a description has not been provided, the first few lines of text on the page), and the URL. Click the title to go to the page.

3. If AltaVista finds similar pages, it includes a link for Related Pages. Click the link to display pages that are similar to the page shown in the results.

4. If your query matches multiple pages at a single Web site, AltaVista clusters the results and presents only two pages from that Web site—a neat feature that allows you to get more variety in your results. To look at other pages from the site that match your query, click the More Pages From link.

5. With a single click, you can also direct your query to one of AltaVista's other search options (Images, MP3/Audio, Video, Directory, and News) located above the search form on the search results page (**Figure 11.10**). These options return images, MP3/audio files, or video files that contain your keywords in the title or description. The News link returns news stories containing your keyword, while the directory search lists the categories your keyword is found in.

AltaVista found 1,779 results   About

The Rain Forest Guide - **Amazon,Brasil**
Official web site of The Rain Forest Guide.
www.geocities.com/therainforestguide • Related Pages
More pages from www.geocities.com

Figure 11.9 Each match includes a link to the page, a description, and links to similar pages and to more pages at the same site.

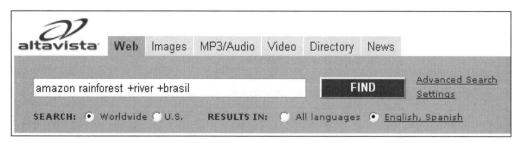

Figure 11.10 Click any of the tabs to direct your search to other media types.

Refine Your Search [?]
Click a term to focus your search. Click >> to replace your search.

Amazon Basin >>

Amazon Rain Forest >>

Amazon River >>

Tropical Rainforests >>

Rain Forest >>

South America >>

Brazil >>

Ecuador >>

Iquitos >>

Manaus >>

Peru >>

Protect >>

Figure 11.11 AltaVista often suggests additional words you can use to refine your search.

✔ Tips

- If your original search is quite general, your results may include a Refine Your Search section to help you narrow the focus and home in on the information you're looking for (**Figure 11.11**). Click the underlined words to add them to the search, or click the double-arrow link (>>) to create a new search using the words.

- AltaVista allows you to control the amount of detail included in your search results, as well as the number of items presented on each page. You can also turn bold highlighting of your search terms on or off. For more information, see "Customizing AltaVista" later in this chapter.

- For additional guidance in using the Basic Search form, click the Help link at the bottom of each page. AltaVista's help information is nicely organized and well written, with search examples and suggestions for getting better results from your AltaVista queries.

Improving Results with Field Searching

It's not uncommon to enter a query on the AltaVista Basic Search form that returns hundreds, if not thousands, of Web pages— many of which have little or nothing to do with the information you're looking for.

When that happens, try adding one of AltaVista's *field-search* terms to your query. Field-search terms allow you to limit your search to specific parts (or *fields*) of Web pages.

You'll find a complete list of field-search terms that you can use on both the Basic Search and Advanced Web Search forms in the AltaVista Field Search Quick Reference (**Table 11.2**). The ones you are likely to find most useful are title:, domain:, host:, and link:.

✔ Tip

■ For point-and-click field searching, use AltaVista's Advanced Web Search form. It gives you the ability to incorporate some of the field-search terms into your queries by filling in blanks.

Table 11.2

AltaVista Field Search Quick Reference		
SEARCH TERM:	DESCRIPTION:	EXAMPLES:
anchor:	Searches for Web pages that contain the specified hyperlink.	anchor:"free product samples"
applet:	Searches for Java applets. If you don't know the name of the applet, try combining an applet wildcard search with some other search term.	applet:beeper +applet:* +Java
domain:	Searches Web addresses for a specific domain (com, edu, gov, net, org, and so on) or two-letter Internet country code. (See Appendix B for a complete list.)	domain:edu domain:uk
host:	Searches just the host name portion of Web addresses.	host:beatlefest.com host:oxford.edu host:BBC
image:	Searches Web pages for the file names of images that match your search term.	image:ringo.gif image:*.gif
like:	Searches for Web pages similar to (or related in some way to) the specified URL.	like:www.beatle.net
link:	Searches for hypertext links (URLs) embedded in a Web page.	link:www.songlyrics.com
text:	Searches for text in the body of the Web page.	text:"Strawberry Fields"
title:	Limits the search to the part of the Web page that the author labeled as the title.	title:"John Lennon"
url:	Searches for text in complete Web addresses (URLs).	url:beatles.html

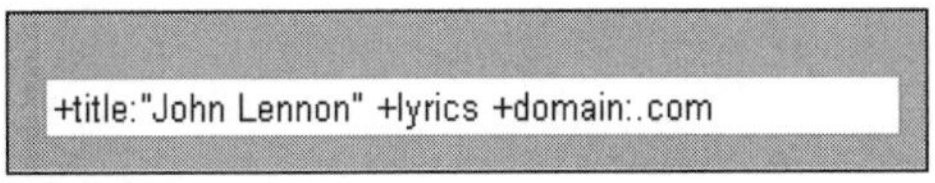

```
+title:"John Lennon" +lyrics +domain:.com
```

Figure 11.13 A search like this would help you locate Beatles-related sites in the U.S. that are commercial in nature.

To search Web page titles:

◆ Add a Title field search to your query. Let's say your initial search for +"John Lennon" +lyrics results in too many hits. Try restricting your query to Web pages that include the singer/song-writer's name in the title: +title:"John Lennon" +lyrics (**Figure 11.12**). In most cases, you'll find that your search returns a much more manageable list of results.

To limit your search by Internet domain:

◆ Include a Domain field search in your query. For example, to focus on Web pages of commercial establishments, include +domain:com in your search request (**Figure 11.13**). You can also limit your search to Web pages for a *specific* domain name by including the entire name with the Domain search term. For example, using +domain:beatlefest.com in your query would limit your search to the Beatlefest Web site.

Here are the field-search terms for the most common Internet domains:

continues on next page

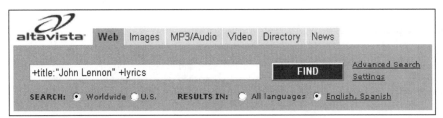

Figure 11.12 A search for *John Lennon* in the titles of Web pages reduced the number of hits from several thousand to 1,122.

▲ domain:com (commercial establishments)

▲ domain:edu (educational institutions)

▲ domain:gov (government agencies)

▲ domain:mil (U.S. military)

▲ domain:net (networks, such as
EarthLink and Comcast)

▲ domain:org (nonprofit organizations)

To limit your search by country:

◆ Do a Domain search for the country's
two-letter country code. For instance,
adding +domain:uk to a Beatles search
would limit the query to sites based in
the United Kingdom (**Figure 11.14**).

✔ Tip

■ See Appendix B for a complete list of
Internet domains and country codes.

Figure 11.14 If you include +domain:uk in your query, your search will be limited to Web sites in the United Kingdom, as shown here.

Harvard University -host:harvard.edu

Figure 11.15 To exclude Web pages from a particular host system, use a Host field search preceded by a minus sign (–).

To limit your search by host name:

1. Use a Host field search to find all the Web pages hosted on a particular computer. A search for +host:harvard.edu, for example, would find Web pages hosted by a computer at Harvard University.

2. To exclude all such pages, put a minus sign (–) in front of the field-search term. A search like the one in **Figure 11.15**, for example, would help you locate sites that mention Harvard University while avoiding Harvard's own Web site.

To search for embedded links:

◆ Use a Link field in your query. For example, the search term +link:www.songlyrics.com would help you identify Web pages that include embedded links to the Song Lyrics Web site.

✔ Tip

■ Webmasters and Web site creators often use Link searches to find out who is sending traffic to their Web sites. Link searches also provide a rough indication of a site's popularity—the more links, the more popular the site.

IMPROVING RESULTS WITH FIELD SEARCHING

Using Advanced Search

Many AltaVista fans never venture beyond the search engine's main page. They master the Basic Search form and use it exclusively for most of their Internet searches.

But power users and professional searchers will tell you that AltaVista's Advanced Web Search form (**Figure 11.16**) is worth taking the time to learn. In fact, some of what you've learned already about Basic Search applies to Advanced Search as well. The techniques for using wildcards, performing a case-sensitive search, and field searching are the same on both the Basic Search and Advanced Web Search forms.

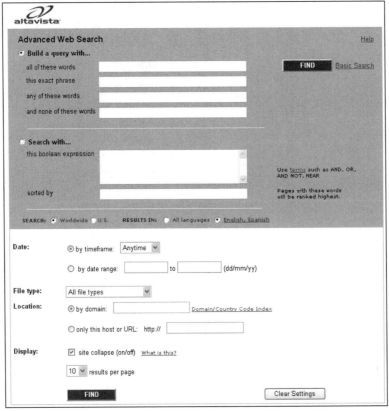

Figure 11.16 AltaVista's Advanced Web Search form offers a number of search options not offered on the Basic Search form, including the use of Boolean operators and date searching.

AltaVista's Advanced Web Search form gives you a choice in how to enter the keywords: using the Build a Query With fields or the Search With field, where you enter a Boolean query.

Using the Build a Query With fields is straightforward: enter your keywords in the appropriate fields to search for all of the specified words, the exact phrase, any of the specified words, and none of the specified words (that is, to find sites that don't include the specified words).

Or you can build your own queries using the Search With field. Instead of using plus and minus signs to require and exclude keywords and phrases, you must use the traditional Boolean operator AND (to require a term) and the somewhat less traditional AND NOT (to exclude a term) when building queries in the Search With field. To search for several words or phrases, any of which *may* be present in your search results, you must link the terms with the Boolean operator OR.

The Search With option gives you more power-search capabilities. You can group search words and phrases in parentheses to form more complex queries: (mystery AND (author OR novelist)) AND bestseller. You can enter a proximity search, using NEAR to find terms that appear within 10 words of each other: Catherine the Great NEAR biography.

When you search using the Basic Search form, AltaVista sorts and ranks your results according to relevance. But with the Search With option, *you* control the sort order by specifying the words or phrases that should be given the greatest weight.

USING ADVANCED SEARCH

To search with Advanced Search:

1. On the AltaVista home page (www.altavista.com), click Advanced Search (**Figure 11.17**).

2. Type your search request in the area labeled Search With This Boolean Expression (**Figure 11.18**). Use AND, OR, and NEAR to combine words and phrases. To exclude a word, be sure to use AND NOT: Oxford AND NOT shoes. You can also use parentheses in your query to group words and phrases.

3. If there's any particular word or phrase that should be given greater weight in the presentation of search results, enter it in the Sorted By field. Boolean expressions are not allowed in this part of the search form.

4. To limit your search to documents created within a range of dates, select a time frame from the drop-down menu—you can choose the last week, the last month, the last four or eight months, or the last year—or enter the specific dates in the date range fields. Be sure to use a two-digit number for day, month, and year (**Figure 11.19**). Note that the day (rather than the month) comes first.

5. Select Site Collapse (On/Off) if you prefer not to see multiple pages from the same site (**Figure 11.20**).

6. Click Search to enter your query.

   Your results will be presented in random order, unless you entered a word or phrase in the Sorted By field, as explained in step 3. In all other respects, search results for Advanced Search are identical to what you get when you use the Basic Search form, described earlier in this chapter.

Figure 11.17 Clicking this link on the AltaVista home page takes you to the Advanced Web Search form.

Figure 11.18 Compose a Boolean query in the field. If you enter words in the Sorted By field, they are given greater weight when AltaVista organizes your search results, and pages containing those words will be listed first.

Figure 11.19 Specifying a range of dates like this would limit your search to Web pages created or modified between January 15, 2004, and March 31, 2004.

Figure 11.20 The check mark here tells AltaVista to cluster your results and show you only two pages per Web site.

✔ Tips

■ AltaVista supports specific file type searches only for HTML and PDF files.

■ You can use uppercase or lowercase letters for Boolean operators on the Advanced Web Search form.

■ The AltaVista Advanced Search Quick Reference (**Table 11.3**) summarizes the Advanced Search features and how to use them.

■ For more tips and search examples, click Help.

Table 11.3

AltaVista Advanced Search Quick Reference

FOR THIS TYPE OF SEARCH:	DO THIS:	EXAMPLES:
Plain-English Question	Not recommended on Advanced Web Search form. Use Basic Search instead.	
Phrase Search	Just type the phrase in the search box (*without* quotation marks). AltaVista interprets as a phrase any words that appear together without a search operator between them.	`Tower of London`
AND Search must be present) (multiple words and phrases, each of which	Use AND between words or phrases to specify that both must be present in the results.	`Oxford AND Cambridge`
OR Search (multiple words and phrases, any one of which may be present)	Use OR between words or phrases to specify that you want to find references to either or both terms.	`Oxford OR Cambridge`
NOT Search (exclude a word or phrase)	Use AND NOT in front of the word or phrase you want to exclude from the query.	`Oxford AND NOT Cambridge`
Case-Sensitive Search	Use lowercase to find any *combination* of uppercase and lowercase letters. Use capital letters (initial caps or a combination of uppercase and lowercase) to force an *exact match* of your search term, as shown in the example.	`Round Table`
Date Search	Type the range of dates you want to search in the From and To boxes, using the format *DD/MM/YY*. The example would search for dates between January 1, 2001, and December 3, 2001 (not March 12, 2001).	`From: 01/01/01 To: 03/12/01`
Field Search	Type field-search keyword in lowercase, immediately followed by a colon and your search word or phrase. (See Table 11.2 for a complete list of field-search keywords.)	`title:Castle Howard` `domain:com` `host:cambridge.edu`
Nested Search	Use parentheses to group search expressions into more complex queries. The example would find *Queen Mother* as well as *Queen Mum*.	`Queen (Mother OR Mum)`
Proximity Search	Use NEAR to find words or phrases that appear within 10 words of each other. The example would find *bed and breakfast* as well as *bed & breakfast* and *breakfast in bed*.	`bed NEAR breakfast.`
Wildcard Search	Enter an asterisk (*) at the end of or within a word and at least three letters at the beginning of the search term.	`bicycl*    col*r`

USING ADVANCED SEARCH

Customizing AltaVista

If you use AltaVista a lot, you'll want to take advantage of its customization features.

Here's a brief summary of the AltaVista features you can customize:

◆ **Language options:** You can change AltaVista's default language setting from Any Language to English, or whatever languages you want. Once you've specified your language preferences, AltaVista will automatically screen out Web pages written in other languages.

◆ **Family Filter options:** You can set preferences to screen out objectionable material from your Web searches.

◆ **Display of Web Results options:** These options give you complete control over the amount of detail displayed in your search results. They also allow you to specify the number of search results presented on each page, and whether your search terms should be presented in boldface so that they are easy to locate.

To set language options:

1. Click Settings on the AltaVista Basic Search form to open the Settings page (**Figure 11.21**).

continues on next page

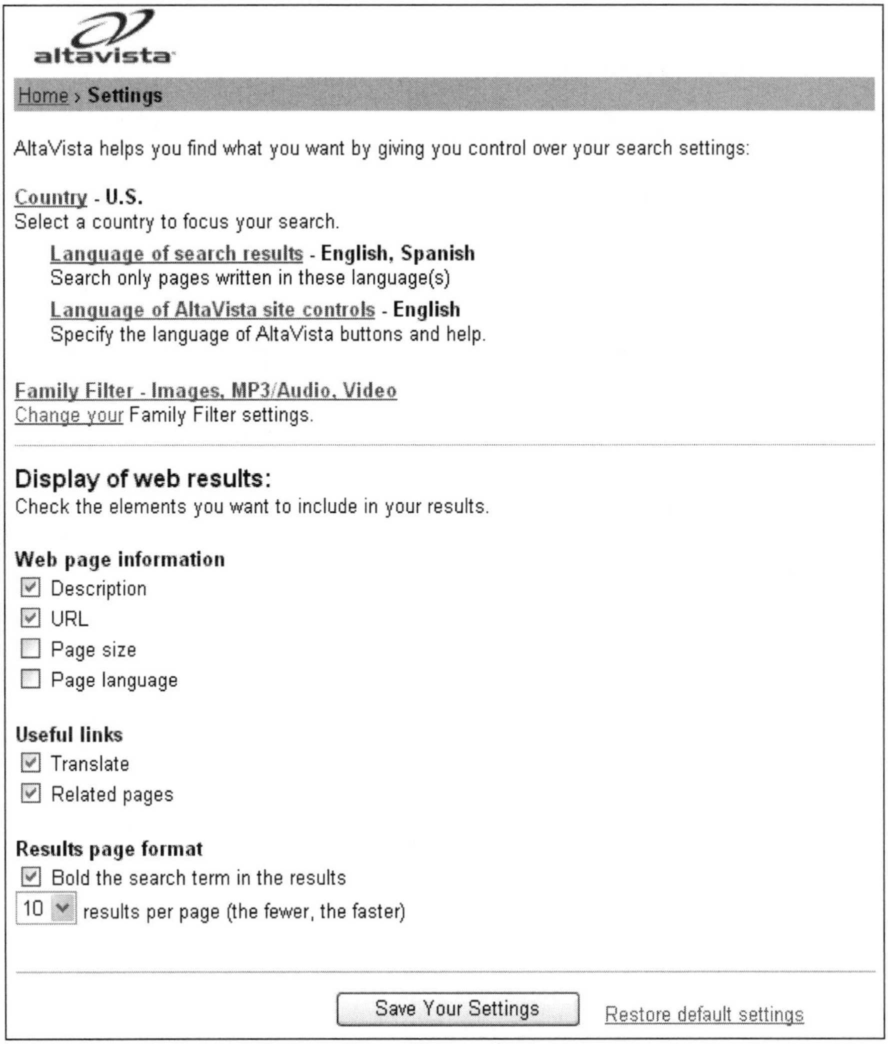

altavista

Home > **Settings**

AltaVista helps you find what you want by giving you control over your search settings:

Country - **U.S.**
Select a country to focus your search.

Language of search results - **English, Spanish**
Search only pages written in these language(s)

Language of AltaVista site controls - **English**
Specify the language of AltaVista buttons and help.

Family Filter - Images, MP3/Audio, Video
Change your Family Filter settings.

Display of web results:
Check the elements you want to include in your results.

Web page information
☑ Description
☑ URL
☐ Page size
☐ Page language

Useful links
☑ Translate
☑ Related pages

Results page format
☑ Bold the search term in the results
[10 ▾] results per page (the fewer, the faster)

[Save Your Settings]   Restore default settings

Figure 11.21 You can customize your language, filter, and display settings.

2. To change the focus of your searches to another country, click the Country link. Select from the list of countries (**Figure 11.22**) Click OK; AltaVista then loads the next language option, allowing you to choose the language of search results.

3. Make your language selections by clicking the box next to any language (**Figure 11.23**). Select as many languages as you desire. If you plan to select many languages, you should select the All Languages radio button on the search page instead; it's easier than adding checks to a large number of boxes and won't appreciably increase the number of results.

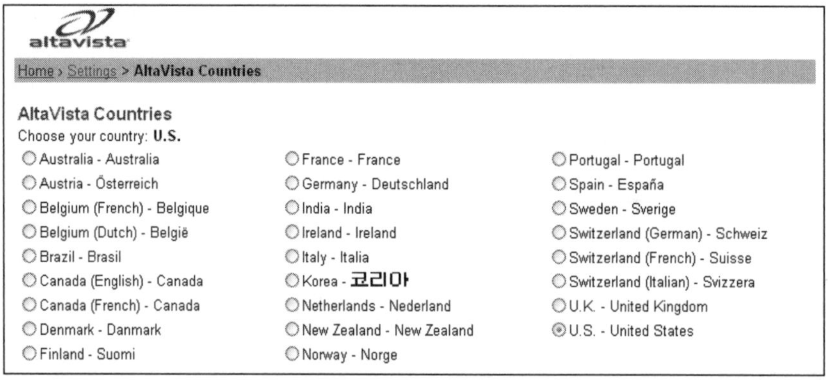

Figure 11.22 You can target your searches to a specific country. AltaVista will still search pages created in other countries, based on the Search Languages settings.

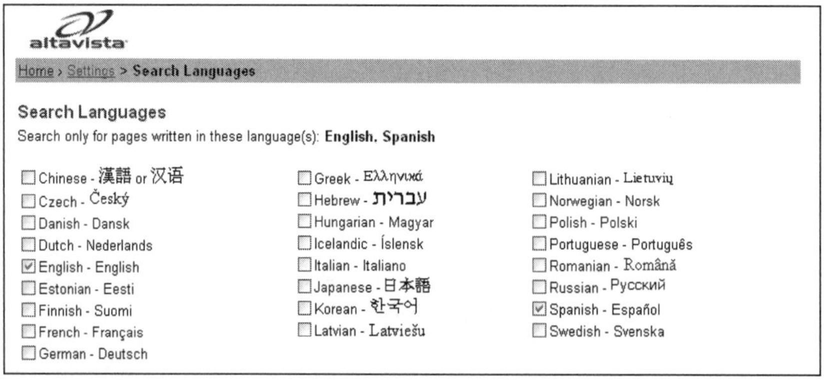

Figure 11.23 After you set the search language, your searches will automatically default to your chosen languages.

Figure 11.24 Click here to access the Search Languages page instead of following the links on the Settings page.

AltaVista USA ▼

Most Web pages are presented in English, but if you want to ensure that your results include *only* English-language pages, click the box for English and uncheck any other boxes. Then click OK.

4. AltaVista next loads the Interface Language form. In most cases, you'll want to use the default, but you can use this option to set the controls to a different language.

5. Click OK, and your settings are applied and you're returned to the Settings page.

✔ Tips

- You can change the country selection by clicking the AltaVista country link in the upper-right corner of the home page. In **Figure 11.24**, it's AltaVista USA, since my Country setting is USA.

- You can change the language by clicking the language link on the home page, as shown earlier in Figures 11.5 and 11.6.

To set Family Filter preferences:

1. Click Family Filter - Images, MP3/Audio, Video on the Settings page or Family Filter: Off (or Family Filter: On) on any search results page (**Figure 11.25**) to open the Family Filter Setup page.

2. Choose your filter preferences (**Figure 11.26**) by clicking the radio button to indicate whether you want to screen multimedia content only (the default) or all Web content. To eliminate filtering completely, click the radio button for None.

3. To activate password protection—optional, but probably a good idea if your objective is to prevent young family members from accessing inappropriate material—choose a password and enter it twice in the boxes provided.

Family Filter: **off**

Figure 11.25 Click here to set up the Family Filter options, or follow the links on the Settings page.

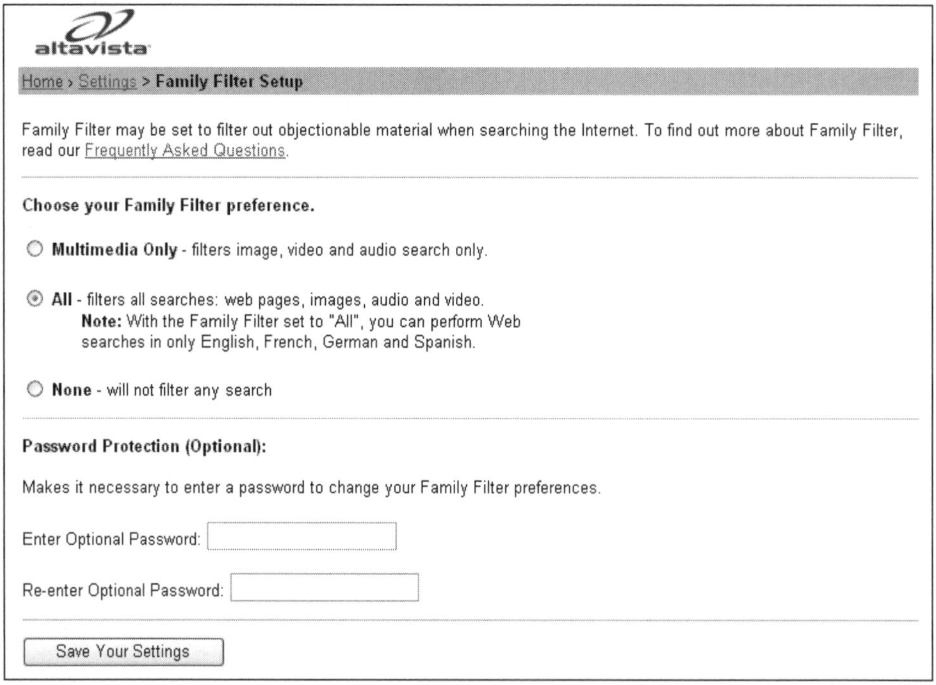

altavista

Home > Settings > **Family Filter Setup**

Family Filter may be set to filter out objectionable material when searching the Internet. To find out more about Family Filter, read our Frequently Asked Questions.

Choose your Family Filter preference.

○ **Multimedia Only** - filters image, video and audio search only.

◉ **All** - filters all searches: web pages, images, audio and video.
    Note: With the Family Filter set to "All", you can perform Web searches in only English, French, German and Spanish.

○ **None** - will not filter any search

Password Protection (Optional):

Makes it necessary to enter a password to change your Family Filter preferences.

Enter Optional Password: [   ]

Re-enter Optional Password: [   ]

[Save Your Settings]

Figure 11.26 AltaVista gives you three filtering options, shown here. You can also enable password protection if you want.

Family Filter: **on**

Figure 11.27 This link on the AltaVista search form tells you that the Family Filter is set to filter *all* Web content.

4. Click the Save Your Settings button to submit your Family Filter preferences and return to the last search results page.

If you have chosen to filter all Web content, the Family Filter will be on (**Figure 11.27**). If you've chosen to filter multimedia content only, the filter will be activated only when you use one of the multimedia search forms.

✔ Tips

- AltaVista's Family Filter works only for Web pages written in English.

- The Family Filter uses *cookie* technology to save your filter settings. If you have set your Web browser to reject cookies, you'll have to reset the Family Filter each time you visit AltaVista. (For more on this topic, including how to turn on cookies if you have turned them off, return to the Family Filter Setup page and click Frequently Asked Questions.)

- Even when you access the Family Filter from the Settings page, you'll always return to the last search page (or the home page if you haven't searched for anything yet) after you save your settings, not the Settings page.

To set Display of Web Results options:

1. Click Settings on the AltaVista home page.

2. Scroll down to Display of Web Results to see the options you can change. If you want to remove any element, just click the box next to the item to eliminate the check mark (**Figure 11.28**).

   If you're not sure whether or not to exclude an item, leave it checked until you've had more experience with AltaVista. At a minimum, you'll certainly want to keep Description and URL checked. We also find that Page Size and Page Language information come in handy from time to time.

   For an explanation of each item, scroll down the page and click the Help link.

3. Once you've selected the amount of detail you want included in your search results, decide whether you want your search terms presented in bold in your search results. If you do, make sure there is a check mark in the Bold the Search Term in the Results box.

4. Use the drop-down menu to choose the number of listings you want AltaVista to display on each page. The default setting is 10, but you can increase it to as many as 50.

   The advantage to displaying more results per page is that when you're reviewing your search results, you can simply scroll down the page, instead of having to load a new page for every 10 results.

5. When you are finished setting your Display of Web Results options, click the Save Your Settings button, and AltaVista will begin using your settings immediately. To change them at any time, just repeat the steps presented here.

Figure 11.28 If there's any particular item you would prefer not to see in your results, click the box next to it to remove the check mark.

12

EXCITE

Like many successful high-tech ventures, Excite was conceived in the garage of a suburban California home. It was the brainchild of six young software developers, fueled by burritos and a strong desire to "work together and do something entrepreneurial." They launched their service in 1995 and went public a year later.

A popular Internet portal, Excite uses the top results from all the leading search engines and directory services when returning results. It supports the use of Boolean operators and nested searches for creating complex queries. It also offers some nice features for locating multimedia files and for searching and tracking news stories.

On the downside, Excite lacks many of the power-search features that Internet users have come to expect, like the ability to search Web page titles and other fields, perform case-sensitive searches, and incorporate wildcards in queries.

Good to Know

♦ Excite supports the use of Boolean operators and offers features that facilitate searches for news stories and multimedia files.

♦ Excite lacks power-search features such as field search, case-sensitivity, and wildcard options.

♦ If you don't like Excite's cluttered home page, you can personalize it or enter your queries on a page devoted to searching.

Contact Information

Excite Network, Inc
Irvington, NY
Phone: 914-591-2000
Fax: 914-591-0110
www.excite.com

EXCITE

The Excite Home Page

The first thing you'll notice when you visit the Excite home page (www.excite.com) is that it's without a doubt the most cluttered and disorganized Web page imaginable (**Figure 12.1**). Like a teenager's room, there's stuff strewn everywhere. And depending on the season, you may even find that the site has been "decorated" for Halloween, or that snowflakes are drifting across the screen.

The good news is that Excite has a page dedicated to searching, located at search.excite.com (**Figure 12.2**).

Figure 12.2 Choose search.excite.com and use Excite's search tools without the home page clutter.

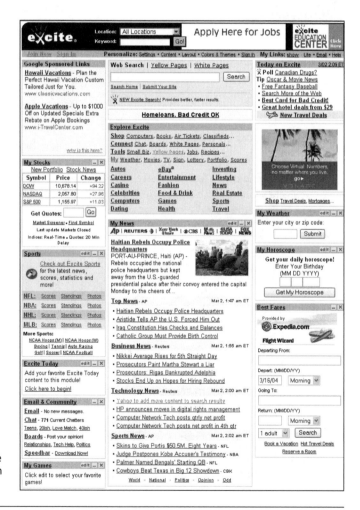

Figure 12.1 The Excite home page includes some specialized search sections, such as Explore Excite.

Figure 12.3 Excite's search form lets you specify whether you want to search the Web or another database, such as a photo archive.

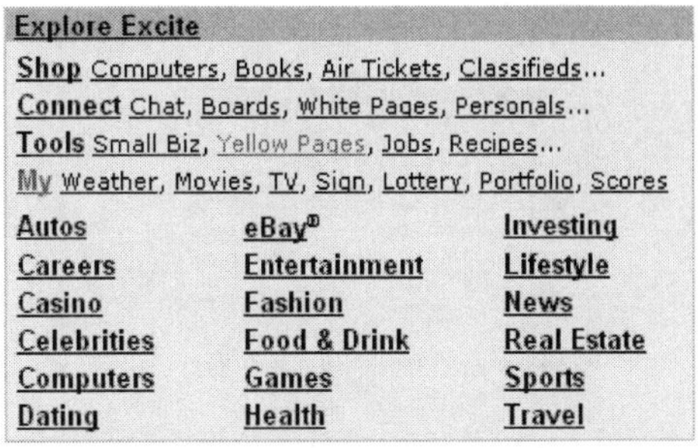

Explore Excite

Shop Computers, Books, Air Tickets, Classifieds...

Connect Chat, Boards, White Pages, Personals...

Tools Small Biz, Yellow Pages, Jobs, Recipes...

My Weather, Movies, TV, Sign, Lottery, Portfolio, Scores

Autos	eBay	Investing
Careers	Entertainment	Lifestyle
Casino	Fashion	News
Celebrities	Food & Drink	Real Estate
Computers	Games	Sports
Dating	Health	Travel

Figure 12.4 You can use Explore Excite's collection of reference tools for many common searches, such as looking up phone numbers and e-mail addresses.

Search form

Excite's search form (**Figure 12.3**) makes it easy to focus your search on a specific type of information. Just type your query in the search box and click the appropriate radio button to indicate whether you want to search the Web, the Excite directory, news articles, or photo archives.

You can search for phrases enclosed in quotation marks or use the Boolean operators AND, OR, and ANDNOT and parentheses to combine words and phrases.

Tools

If you choose to use the Excite home page as your home page, links to specialized search features are included in a section called Explore Excite. A standard feature of the Excite home page, Explore Excite (**Figure 12.4**).provides links to a number of specialized search tools—airline farefinder, searchable classified ads, concert and sporting events locator, maps and driving directions, yellow pages, people-finding tools, and more—organized by topic.

continues on next page

THE EXCITE HOME PAGE

The Explore Excite section of the Excite home page looks like a traditional Web directory, organized by topic, but it's really not. Each link takes you to a special page devoted to a single broad subject area: Autos, Business, Careers, and so on. The content varies by topic, but it typically includes pointers to the best Web sites, news headlines, specialized search tools, and (of course) advertisements for related products and services (**Figure 12.5**) Click Explore Excite's Tools link to open a basic search page, with links to Web searching, yellow and white pages, and maps (**Figure 12.6**).

Figure 12.6 The Tools link on Explore Excite opens a simpler search page.

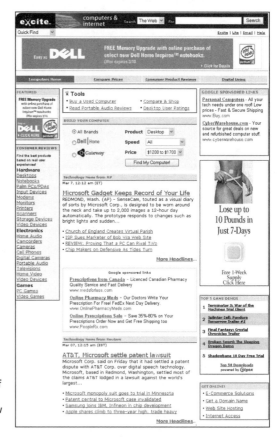

Figure 12.5 Here's an example of what you'll find if you click the Explore Excite Computers link: links to reviews, search fields to compare prices on new computers, and technology-related news stories.

✔ Tips

- Use the toolbar at the top of each page to select Quick Find to switch to a different category to search or to search the Web, the Excite directory, news articles, or photos (**Figure 12.7**).

- To use Excite's Personalize feature to create your own customized home page, click Sign In or Personalize: Settings on the home page (**Figure 12.8**) to sign in or create a free Excite account. Once you've done that, you can pick and choose the content for your page, move features around on the screen, and even change the color scheme if you're so inclined (**Figure 12.9**).

continues on next page

Select Web   Search field

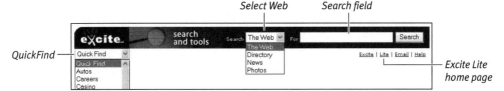

QuickFind

Excite Lite home page

Figure 12.7 The top of most Excite pages include QuickFind, to select topic directories, and a search field.

Personalize Settings   Excite Lite home page

Figure 12.8 The links for Excite's Personalize feature are below the logo on the home page. Until you sign up and log in, the Settings, Content, Layout, and Color & Themes links are inactive. To switch to the Lite version of the Excite home page, click Lite.

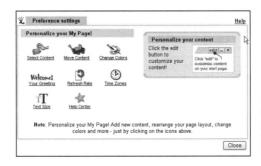

Figure 12.9 Customize the Excite home page using the options in the Preference Settings dialog box.

- If you'd rather not bother with the Personalize feature, use the Lite version of the home page (**Figure 12.10**) to reduce the home page clutter, or go to search.excite.com and enter your Excite queries from that page. It's devoted exclusively to searching.

- To make Excite your Web browser's default home page, enter these URLs in your browser's home page setup Address or Location box:

  http://www.excite.com (for the Excite home page)

  http://search.excite.com (for the Excite search page)

  If you're not sure how to access your Web browser's home page setup feature, see "Customizing Your Web Browser" in Chapter 4.

- To get back to the Excite home page from anywhere within the site, click the Excite logo that appears at the top of every page.

Figure 12.10 For an Excite portal without the clutter, use the Excite Lite home page.

Searching with Excite

Whether you use the search form on the Excite home page (www.excite.com) or the one on the page devoted exclusively to searching (search.excite.com), the process for entering a query is the same. Here are the key points to keep in mind:

◆ You can express your query as a plain-English question, one or more unique keywords, or a phrase in quotation marks.

◆ By default, Excite performs an OR search, looking for *any* of the words in your query.

◆ Excite searches are *not* case sensitive. You'll get the same results whether you use uppercase or lowercase letters or a mix of the two.

To enter a query:

1. Type a question, several unique keywords, a phrase in quotation marks, or a Boolean expression in the search form text box (**Figure 12.11**).

2. To tell Excite to search a database other than the Web, click the appropriate radio button above the search form text box. Options are Directory, News, and Photos.

Figure 12.11 Enter your search terms in the search field.

To view your search results:

1. Click the Search button (or press Enter) to submit your query.

   Your results will be presented 20 to a page, with the best matches listed first, along with a count of the total number of matches found (**Figure 12.12**).

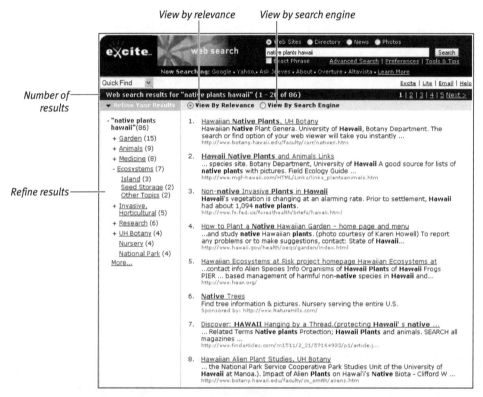

Figure 12.12 Here's an example of how Excite presents search results. The total number of matches is listed at the upper left.

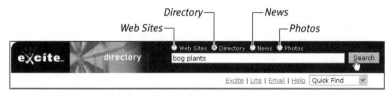

Figure 12.13 To find Web pages in the Directory with content related to your query, click the Directory link.

SEARCHING WITH EXCITE

2. The section to the left of the results suggests words or phrases you can use to refine your results. Click the plus signs (+) to expand the words; then click a word to refine the search using the selected keyword. Click the minus signs (–) to close previously expanded words.

3. To get a quick handle on your search results, try one of Excite's alternate display options:

▲ Choose View By Relevance at the top of the results page to view results based on the ones Excite thinks are most relevant.

▲ Select View By Search Engine to see the results grouped by the search engine the results come from.

4. To view any item listed on your results page, click its title link.

5. To find related items, click the Directory link (**Figure 12.13**) at the top of your search results list. Directory matches come from the Open Directory (dmoz.org) project (**Figure 12.14**).

✔ Tip

■ Use Advanced Search if you want to use Boolean operators such as AND or OR.

Figure 12.14 The Directory search shows you the categories your search words were found in. Select a category to see the results.

To refine an Excite query:

1. Try adding another search term to the words in the search field. If you want to use Boolean operators, you'll need to use the Advanced Search form.

2. Click Advanced Search (**Figure 12.15**) and re-enter your query in the form presented there (**Figure 12.16**).

   ▲ Use the predefined fields for simple Boolean searches, including searches for all of the words, the exact phrase, any of the words, or none of the words. You can use any or all of the fields in one search. For example, to search for *lilies* and the phrase *bog plants*, enter `lilies` in the All of These Words field and `bog plants` in the The Exact Phrase field (**Figure 12.17**).

   ▲ Use the Boolean terms field to write your own query, using AND, OR, and ANDNOT, along with parentheses, to create more precise queries.

   ▲ Search only for pages updated before or after certain dates, or select dates to find only pages updated between two dates.

   ▲ Use the domain filter to focus on a particular domain (`microsoft.com`) or domain type (`com`, `edu`, `gov`, and so forth) or exclude pages from a specific domain.

   ▲ To reduce the chances that the results will include sexually explicit content, turn on the adult filter.

Advanced Search

Figure 12.15 This link gives you access to Excite's Advanced Web Search page.

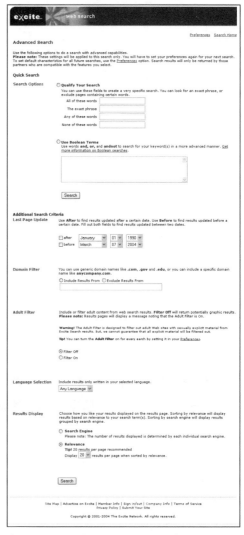

Figure 12.16 Use the Advanced Search form to restrict the search to specific domains, languages, or dates. You can also boost the number of search results per page from 20 to 40.

Figure 12.17 Enter your search words in one or more fields to refine your search.

▲ You can limit your search to Web pages written in a specific language Unlike Google, Excite has a short list of languages to choose from.

▲ You can set Excite to show between 10 and 40 search results on each page and group the results by search engine or relevance.

✔ Tips

■ For a summary of Excite search terms and how to use them, see the Excite Quick Reference (**Table 12.1**).

■ Click the Tools & Tips link to view Excite Search help..

Table 12.1

Excite Quick Reference		
FOR THIS TYPE OF SEARCH:	DO THIS:	EXAMPLES:
Plain-English Question	Simply type a phrase or question that expresses the idea or concept. Use as many words as necessary	thoroughbred racing in Kentucky Where can I find information about thoroughbred racing in Kentucky?
Phrase Search	Type the phrase enclosed in double quotation marks.	"Kentucky Derby"
AND Search (multiple words and phrases, each of which must be present)	Use AND in front of each word or phrase that must appear in the results.	racing AND "Churchill Downs"
OR Search (multiple words and phrases, one of which may be present)	Type words or phrases separated by a space or use OR between each word or phrase	Derby Preakness Derby OR Preakness
NOT Search (to exclude a word)	Type a minus sign (–) directly in front of the word or phrase you want to exclude from your results. (Note that there's no space between the minus sign and the search word or phrase.)	"horse race" –Derby
	Or use ANDNOT in front of the word or phrase you want to exclude.	"horse race" ANDNOT Derby
Case-Sensitive Search	Not available.	
Date Search	Use to find pages updated before, between, or after a specific date. Advanced Search option.	
Field Search	Not available.	
Nested Search	Use parentheses to group Boolean expressions into complex queries.	racing AND (horse OR thoroughbred)
Proximity Search	Not available.	
Wildcard Search	Not available.	

Saving a Search Query

You can create a search once and save it so that you can run it again from time to time using an Excite feature called My Searches (**Figure 12.18**).

1. You'll first have to use the Personalize feature to create a customized version of the Excite home page, as described earlier in this chapter.

2. Click Content on the Excite home page and select My Searches from the Content menu.

3. Select the type of search (Web, Directory, News, Photos), add your keywords, and then enter a name for your search (**Figure 12.19**).

4. Click Finished, and a My Searches box will appear on your personalized Excite page.

Once you've added your searches using the Edit button in the My Searches box, you can run them any time you wish simply by clicking the appropriate link.

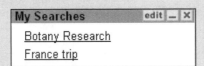

Figure 12.18 Save your popular searches on a customized Excite home page using the My Searches feature.

Figure 12.19 To create a saved search, you just need to select the search type, enter your keywords, and name your search.

Preferences

Figure 12.20 Select Preferences to change the preferences for all of your searches.

Customizing Excite

You can customize your preferences for all future searches.

Note that these settings won't apply to advanced searches. Advanced Search settings are customized each time you do an advanced search.

To configure Preferences:

1. Click the Preferences link (**Figure 12.20**) to open the Preferences page (**Figure 12.21**).

continues on next page

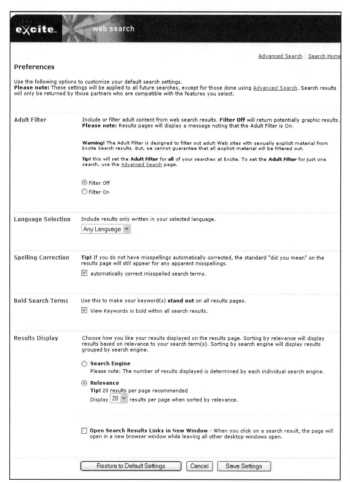

Figure 12.21 Use the Preferences page to select your language, set your adult content preferences, enable spelling correction, control the number of pages returned, and set other options.

2. Set any or all of the following preferences:

▲ Enable or disable the Adult filter.

▲ Show results only in the selected language.

▲ Automatically correct misspelled search terms.

▲ Highlight search terms using bold font.

▲ Sort results by relevance or group results by search engine.

▲ Set the number of results displayed per page; Excite can display between 10 and 40 results per page.

▲ Open each link in a new window.

3. Click Save Settings to save your preferences.

✔ Tip

■ You can restore the default settings at any time by returning to the Preferences page and clicking Restore to Default Settings.

CUSTOMIZING EXCITE

Lycos

Good to Know

- Developed in 1994 at Carnegie Mellon University, Lycos is now owned by Terra Lycos, a Spanish company that also owns HotBot and a number of other popular Web sites.

- The highly acclaimed Lycos spider is still used for building certain specialty databases, but the site is now powered by the FAST search engine.

- The Lycos Web directory comes from the Open Directory Project.

Contact Information

Lycos, Inc.
Waltham, MA
781-370-2700
www.lycos.com

One of the oldest Internet search engines, Lycos was developed in 1994 by artificial-intelligence expert Michael "Fuzzy" Mauldin at Carnegie Mellon University. The name comes from the Latin for *wolf spider*, a creature Mauldin has long admired for its tenacity in searching for and finding its prey.

Now a commercial enterprise, Lycos is owned by Terra Lycos, a Spanish conglomerate whose mission is "to be the most visited online destination in the world." In pursuit of that goal, Terra Lycos also owns and operates rival search engine HotBot (www.hotbot.com) and a number of other popular Web sites, including MatchMaker (www.matchmaker.com), Quote.com (www.quote.com), and WhoWhere? (www.whowhere.com).

Most Lycos search results come from Fast Search & Transfer (FAST), a formidable contender among the leading search technologies, with additional results supplied by Google. The Lycos Web directory, referred to as Editorial Content on many Lycos pages, is provided by the Open Directory Project (dmoz.org).

The major drawback to searching with Lycos is that you're limited to fairly basic queries. You can search for phrases by enclosing them in quotation marks and use plus and minus signs to require (+) or exclude (−) words and phrases.

Lycos

✔ Tips

■ If you're interested in Internet history, pay a visit to Michael Mauldin's Lazy Toad Ranch Web site (www.lazytd.com) and click Fuzzy's Homepage and then Professional Web Page. There, you can read the original patent for the Lycos spider and listen to several RealAudio interviews with Mauldin.

■ FAST (short for Fast Search & Transfer) was launched in 1999 by a Norwegian company. You can search FAST directly—without the Lycos interface—by going to the company's Web site at www.alltheweb.com (**Figure 13.1**). The site doesn't get much publicity because, instead of competing head-on with the leading search engines, FAST concentrates on selling its search technology to other companies.

■ For more information about the company behind Lycos—recent press releases, the management team, how to invest in the company—click About Terra Lycos at the bottom of the Lycos home page.

Figure 13.1 FAST, the search engine that powers Lycos, maintains a fairly low profile. The company uses its home page (www.alltheweb.com) to demonstrate its search technology.

The Lycos Home Page

Before doing any real searching, let's take a look at the search form on the Lycos home page (**Figure 13.2**). The key features to zero in on are the basic search form, the Advanced Search option, and the links for accessing other search-related tools.

Basic search form

The basic search form on the Lycos home page consists of a search box and a Search button for submitting your query—no drop-down menus or special options of any kind (**Figure 13.3**). This is basic searching with a capital *B*!

continues on next page

Basic search form   Specialized searches

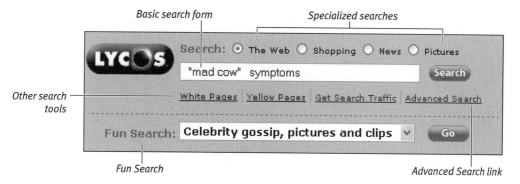

Other search tools

Fun Search   Advanced Search link

Figure 13.2 The Lycos home page includes the basic search form and links to a variety of other search-related tools. To display the Web directory, click the Websites link.

Figure 13.3 The basic search form. By default, Lycos performs an AND search, so a query like the one shown here would find pages that include both *water* and *gardening*.

Just type several words (or a phrase in quotation marks) and click Search. Lycos performs an AND search by default, looking for *all* the words and phrases that you type in the search box, so you don't even need to use plus signs.

✔ Tip

■ Are you curious about the 50 most popular search keywords? Click the Lycos 50 link to the right of the search field on the home page to open the top-50 list (**Figure 13.4**).

Figure 13.4 The Lycos 50 page lists the 50 most popular searches each day, their ranking in the previous week, and other interesting information.

Figure 13.5 Advanced Search gives you access to a number of options not available with the basic search form on the Lycos home page.

Advanced Search option

For more control over your Lycos searches, click the Advanced Search link (**Figure 13.5**). With Advanced Search, you can specify the type of search that you want to perform (AND, OR, NOT, or phrase search) and focus your search on Web page titles, the page body, or URLs. You can also limit your search by specifying search options.

For more information on Advanced Search, see "Using Advanced Search" later in this chapter.

Web directory

Like its sister company HotBot, Lycos gets its Web directory from the Open Directory Project (`dmoz.org`), a volunteer effort to catalog the Web using an approach similar to that used by Yahoo (`www.yahoo.com`). But instead of letting you browse and search the Web directory from its home page, Lycos makes you work a bit:

◆ **To browse the directory:** Type `search.lycos.com` in the browser's address bar. You can then drill down through the Web directory's 16 topic categories (**Figure 13.6**) and dozens of subcategories.

continues on next page

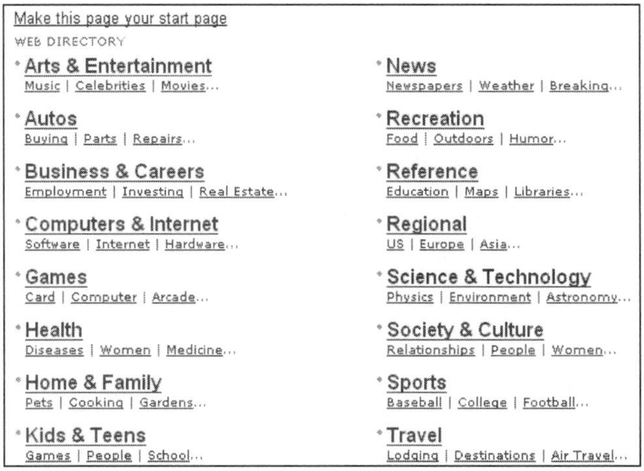

Make this page your start page
WEB DIRECTORY

Arts & Entertainment
Music | Celebrities | Movies...

Autos
Buying | Parts | Repairs...

Business & Careers
Employment | Investing | Real Estate...

Computers & Internet
Software | Internet | Hardware...

Games
Card | Computer | Arcade...

Health
Diseases | Women | Medicine...

Home & Family
Pets | Cooking | Gardens...

Kids & Teens
Games | People | School...

News
Newspapers | Weather | Breaking...

Recreation
Food | Outdoors | Humor...

Reference
Education | Maps | Libraries...

Regional
US | Europe | Asia...

Science & Technology
Physics | Environment | Astronomy...

Society & Culture
Relationships | People | Women...

Sports
Baseball | College | Football...

Travel
Lodging | Destinations | Air Travel...

Figure 13.6 The Lycos Web directory, organized into 16 major categories, is provided by the Open Directory Project.

THE LYCOS HOME PAGE

227

◆ **To search the directory using key-words used in the current search:** Choose Web Directory at the bottom of the results page (**Figure 13.7**) to see a list of results found in the directory.

◆ **To search the directory using Advanced Search:** Click Advanced Search on the Lycos home page, type a word or phrase in the search box, and use the drop-down menu to specify whether you want to do an AND, OR, or phrase search. Then select the Editorial Results radio button and click Submit Search to display results from the directory (**Figure 13.8**).

Other search tools

Like all good general-purpose search engines, Lycos offers other search tools on the home page. Along with Web searches, Lycos offers Shopping, News, and Picture searches on the basic search form; just select the appropriate radio button.

You'll also find links to White Pages and Yellow Pages as well the Fun Searches menu right below the basic search form (**Figure 13.9**).

✔ Tips

■ Lycos offers several country-specific editions of its search service, accessible from the Visit Terra Lycos Worldwide link at the bottom of the home page (**Figure 13.10**). If you live in one of the countries listed, or if you simply want to practice searching in a language other than English, give the non-U.S. versions of Lycos a try.

■ To make Lycos your default home page, follow the instructions in "Customizing Your Web Browser" in Chapter 4.

■ You can get back to the Lycos home page from anywhere in the site by clicking the Lycos logo at the top of the page.

Figure 13.7 Search HotBot or the Web directory using the links at the bottom of the results page.

Figure 13.8 Choose Editorial Results on the Advanced search page to search the Web directory.

Figure 13.9 Links for other Lycos search tools are listed above and below the search form on the Lycos home page.

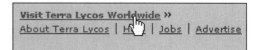

Figure 13.10 Use the link at the bottom of the Lycos home page to access country-specific versions of the search engine.

THE LYCOS HOME PAGE

Figure 13.11 Type a search like this in the basic search form, and Lycos will assume that you want to find pages that include references to all three terms. You don't have to use plus signs.

Searching with Lycos

Having learned your way around the Lycos home page, your next step is to do some searches using the basic search form. Your options here are fairly limited, but with the right choice of keywords and phrases, you may very well find what you're looking for.

If not, you can always try the Advanced Search form, which gives you more options for targeting your query. Or you can submit your search to HotBot (Lycos's sister company) or the Web directory for a second opinion.

To enter a basic search query:

1. Go to the Lycos home page (www.lycos.com) and type two or three search terms, a phrase in quotation marks, or a plain-English question in the search box (**Figure 13.11**). Lycos automatically performs an AND search, looking for *all the words* you specify. Consequently, you don't have to use plus signs in front of required search terms—"mad cow" symptoms—to require that they be included in your search results You'll get the same results with or without them.

2. To do an OR search, looking for *any of the words* you type in the search box, enclose the words in parentheses—("mad cow" BSE)—for example, to find Web pages that include references to either mad cow or BSE (the acronym for the disease's official medical name). This technique isn't documented by Lycos, but it works!

3. To exclude a word or phrase from your results, type a minus sign (–) directly in front of the word or phrase; for example, enter "mad cow" -humor to avoid turning up a lot of joke pages in your search.

✔ Tips

■ As with most search engines, it's a good idea to use two or three search terms and to be as specific as possible. To find information on how to identify mushrooms that are safe to eat, for example, don't just type mushrooms in the search box. Instead, try mushrooms edible poisonous. If you don't find what you're looking for in the first couple of pages, refine your query with Advanced Search or try another search engine.

■ Lycos searches, both basic and advanced, are *not* case sensitive. You'll get the same results whether you use uppercase, lowercase, or a combination.

■ Unlike some search engines that ignore common words (often referred to as stopwords) in phrases, Lycos will look for *every* word you include in a phrase search.

To view your search results:

1. Click Search to submit your query. Sponsored results are listed first, followed by the first 10 Web results (**Figure 13.12**).

2. Scan the Web page title and description (**Figure 13.13**) for results that appear on the first couple of pages of the Web site.

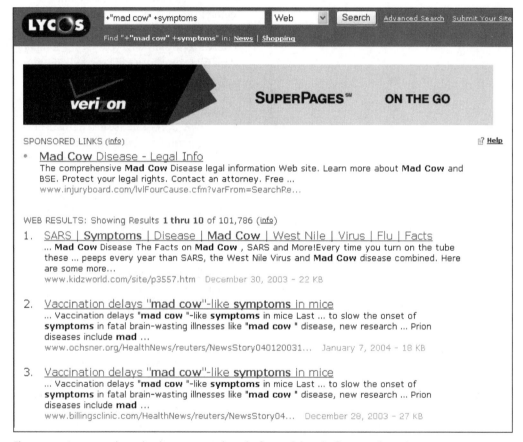

Figure 13.12 Lycos search results show sponsored results first and then the first 10 web results.

Figure 13.13 Individual entries on the search results page include the Web page title (underlined), a brief description, the Web address, and the date the page was last updated.

Figure 13.14 A follow-up to our search for *mad cow symptoms*, telling Lycos to search the original results for pages that also include the word *BSE*. You can also refine a search by selecting among the Narrow Your Search links or getting a second opinion from HotBot or the Web directory.

3. Lycos gives you the option of performing a follow-on search, or set search, focusing on the results of your original query. With the results still displayed, type a word or phrase in the search box. You can leave or delete what's already there—you'll get the same results either way. Then select Search Within These Results (**Figure 13.14**) and click Search to submit your query.

4. If your follow-on search doesn't return the results you want, you can submit your same query to HotBot or the Web directory by clicking either link after Need a Second Opinion? at the bottom of the search results page. Also, often Lycos will offer to narrow your search by adding one or more keywords to your query. Click the link to see if the suggestions Lycos offers return the results you are looking for.

✔ Tips

■ As you may recall from the discussion of field searches in Chapter 2, one excellent way to refine a search is to look for words in the *titles* of Web pages. For example, if you get too many irrelevant results from a search for `mad cow symptoms`, you could do a follow-on search of just those results by typing `title:"mad cow"` in the search box. Then select Search Within These Results and click Search for a more precisely focused set of results. Additional field-search options are available on the Lycos Advanced Search form, covered in the next section of this chapter.

■ Unfortunately, Lycos doesn't give you any control over how your search results are displayed. You can't change the number of results per page, for example, or modify the order in which they are listed.

continues on next page

■ For a summary of Lycos search terms and
syntax, see the Lycos Quick Reference
(**Table 13.1**). To access the Lycos help
information, click the Help link found
on each page.

Table 13.1

Lycos Quick Reference		
FOR THIS TYPE OF SEARCH:	DO THIS:	EXAMPLES:
Plain-English Question	Simply type a phrase or question that expresses the idea or concept, using as many words as necessary.	`Are oyster mushrooms poisonous?`
Phrase Search	Enclose the phrase in double quotation marks.	`"edible mushrooms"`
AND Search (multiple words and phrases, each of which *must* be present)	Type words or phrases separated by a space, without any special punctuation. By default, Lycos searches for *all* the words in your query, so even though plus signs (+) are allowed, you'll get the same results without them.	`"oyster mushrooms" recipes` `+"oyster mushrooms" +recipes`
	The two examples shown here would return identical results: Web pages that contain both the phrase *oyster mushrooms* and the word *recipes*.	
OR Search (multiple words and phrases, any *one* of which may be present)	Enclose the words or phrases in parentheses. The example would find Web pages that include references to either *edible mushrooms* or *mycology*.	`("edible mushrooms" mycology)`
NOT Search (exclude a word or phrase)	Use a minus sign (–) in front of a word or phrase you want to exclude from your results.	`mushrooms -recipes`
Case-Sensitive Search	Not available.	
Date Search	Not available.	
Field Search	To search titles of Web page documents, type `title:` directly in front of a word or phrase. (Note that there's no space between the colon and the search term.)	`title:mushrooms` `title:"mushroom gardening"`
	For URL, site, and referring URL field searches, use Advanced Search.	
Nested Search	Not available.	
Proximity Search	Not available.	
Wildcard Search	Not available.	

Using Advanced Search

The first thing you need to know about the Lycos Advanced Search form (**Figure 13.15**) is that it's really not all that advanced.

Nevertheless, Advanced Search includes several features that you may find yourself needing from time to time that are not offered on the Lycos basic search form:

continues on next page

Figure 13.15 The Advanced Search form, while not really all that advanced, provides several features not available when you search from the Lycos home page.

♦ **Word Filters:** Use the drop-down menus to specify that you want to perform an AND (all of the words), OR (any of the words), NOT (none of the words), or phrase search and to focus your search on Web page titles, the page body, or URLs (**Figure 13.16**). You can also find Web pages that link to a particular site.

♦ **URL/Site:** Include or exclude results from specific sites or domains.

♦ **Language:** Search for Web pages in specific languages.

♦ **Adult Filter:** Filter out potentially offensive results.

♦ **Catalog:** Choose Lycos to search the Web or choose Editorial Results to search the Lycos directory.

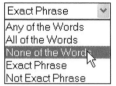

Figure 13.16 The Advanced Search form defaults to an AND search, but you can choose to include any, all, or none of the words or select a phrase search using this drop-down menu.

✔ Tip

■ After you do an advanced search, the fields you used in the search are listed at the top and bottom of the results page, allowing you to refine the search without going back to the Advanced Search Filters page (**Figure 13.17**). Click the Edit button to open the full Advanced Search Filters page.

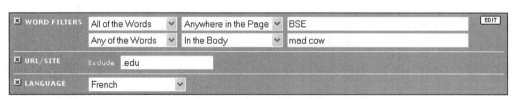

Figure 13.17 Refine your advanced search using the fields on the results page.

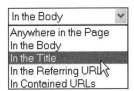

Figure 13.18 You can choose where in the page to search for your keywords.

To look for words in Web page titles, URLs, or domain names:

1. On the Advanced Search Filters page, use the form presented in the Word Filter section (**Figure 13.18**) to narrow your focus by typing a search word and choosing In the Title, In the Referring URL, or In the Contained URL.

2. Enter a URL or site name in the URL/Site search box to include or exclude sites from your search.

3. Click Submit Search.

Here are some examples:

▲ **Title:** If you're looking for information about a particular California wine called Sequoia Grove, type "Sequoia Grove" in the Word Filter search box. Type California wines in the second Word Filter search box, Then select In the Title and click Submit Search.

By limiting your search to Web sites that include the phrase *California wines* in their titles, you're much more likely to find sites that *feature* (as opposed to sites that simply *mention*) wines produced in California.

▲ **URL:** To limit your search for Sequoia Grove to the Wine.com Web site, type "Sequoia Grove" in the Word Filter search box and wine.com in the URL/Site section's Only Include search box. Click Submit Search to submit your query.

▲ **Host/Domain:** To find education sites dealing with French wines, type "French wines" in the Word Filter search box and edu in the URL/Site's Only Include box. Submit your query by clicking Submit Search. (For a list of other Internet domains, see Appendix B).

✔ Tip

■ For best results, avoid using quotation marks and other punctuation when searching titles, URLs, or URL/sites.

To limit a search by language:

1. On the Advanced Search Filters page, click Language to display the list of languages that Lycos supports (**Figure 13.19**). Select the language that you want to use.

2. Type your query in the search box.

3. Click Submit Search.

   For example, type "Chianti" in the search form, select Italian from the languages menu, and click Submit Search. Your search results will be limited to Web pages presented in Italian.

To find Web pages that link to a specific site:

1. On the Advanced Search Filters page, in the Word Filters box, type the URL for the site you want to search for links to (**Figure 13.20**) and choose In the Referring URL.

2. Click Submit Search.

   For example, if you're a fan of *The Wall Street Journal's* Wine site and want to find Web sites that link to it, with the hope of discovering some new sites that may be of interest to you as well, type wine.wsj.com in the Word Filter box, select In the Referring URL, and click Submit Search.

✔ Tips

- If your search results include a lot of links from within the Web site that you entered in the URL/Site box, type the *same* URL in the Exclude box and run the search again.

- Webmasters and Web site creators often use link referrals as a rough measure of a site's popularity. Try searching for sites that link to your own Web site if you have one.

Figure 13.19 You can limit your results to pages written in a specific language— English or two dozen other choices—by selecting the appropriate language from the list.

Figure 13.20 Choose In the Referring URL to find sites that link to a specified site.

HotBot

HotBot was launched in 1996 as a joint venture between Wired Digital (creators of *Wired* magazine) and Inktomi, a company that makes high-end computer workstations. Inktomi's role was to create the search engine software for HotBot—most notably *Slurp*, the spider responsible for crawling the Web and assembling documents into a searchable database.

Now owned by Terra Lycos (which also operates the Lycos search engine), HotBot is popular with Web searchers who appreciate the ease and speed with which it allows people to search the Web. But it doesn't get nearly as much traffic (or press attention) as search sites Google and Yahoo. That's a shame, because for all of its speed and sophistication, HotBot is also an excellent search engine for inexperienced searchers.

Keep in mind that HotBot's main focus is its lightning-fast search capability. For sheer speed, comprehensiveness, and ease of use, HotBot is a real winner.

✔ Tip

■ The name *Inktomi* (pronounced "**INK**-teh-me") comes from a Lakota Indian legend about a resourceful spider known for its ability to defeat its enemies through wit and cunning.

Good to Know

◆ HotBot rivals AltaVista in the breadth and sophistication of its search offerings, including search customization features.

◆ Launched in 1996 by Wired Digital, HotBot was acquired in 1998 by the company that owns and operates the Lycos search engine.

Contact Information

Terra Lycos
Waltham, MA
Phone: 781-370-2700
Fax: 781-370-3412
www.hotbot.com

HotBot

The HotBot Home Page

Unlike the home pages of many of its rivals, the HotBot home page (**Figure 14.1**), with its distinctive lime-green and navy-blue color scheme, is designed for searching.

The basic interface is simple, but you can enable custom Web filters, adding the features you use most to the home page.

Search form

Using the HotBot search form couldn't be easier, whether you're an accomplished search professional or a first-timer. For the professionals, the form allows the use of plus and minus signs to include (+) or exclude (–) words and phrases, as well as the Boolean operators AND, OR, and NOT. For less experienced searchers, simply typing several unique keywords (or even a question in plain English) typically produces excellent results.

If the results aren't what you expected, or if you just want to compare the results with Google or Ask Jeeves, either search engine is just one click away (**Figure 14.2**).

✔ Tips

- For instructions on making HotBot your default home page, click Help. Or follow the instructions in "Customizing Your Web Browser" in Chapter 4.

- You can return to the HotBot home page at any time by clicking the HotBot logo at the top of the page.

Figure 14.1 The HotBot home page is simple and clean, even with the blue-and-green color scheme.

Figure 14.2 Use HotBot to search HotBot, Google, and Ask Jeeves.

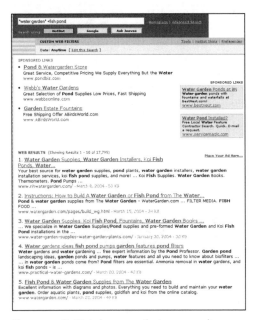

Figure 14.3 Typing a few unique keywords in the HotBot search form is the first step in performing a search.

Figure 14.4 HotBot shows you the top 10 results below sponsored listings.

Figure 14.5 Click Edit This Search to refine your search query using the Advanced Search page.

Searching with HotBot

Now let's do some actual searching and see how HotBot presents the results.

To enter a HotBot query:

◆ Go to the HotBot home page (www.hotbot.com) and type several unique keywords, a phrase in quotation marks, or a combination of words and phrases in the search form (**Figure 14.3**). You can use plus and minus signs to require (+) and exclude (–) search terms.

To refine a HotBot query:

◆ By default, HotBot performs an AND search, looking for Web pages that contain all the words in your query (**Figure 14.4**). To change that and other settings, click Edit This Search (**Figure 14.5**).

HotBot takes you to the Advanced Search page, where you can specify a variety of options to refine your search. For details, see "Advanced Search Options" later in this chapter.

To view your search results:

1. Once you've entered your query, click Search Using HotBot to submit it.

   By default, your results will be presented 10 to a page, along with the total number of matches found (**Figure 14.6**). As you may recall, these results come from the Inktomi database.

   Each listing will include what HotBot calls "full descriptions"—Web page title, one to four lines of text, date created or modified, and URL (**Figure 14.7**).

2. If you want more results, click the Google or Ask Jeeves button to automatically send the query to the Google or Ask Jeeves search engine for a second opinion (**Figure 14.8**).

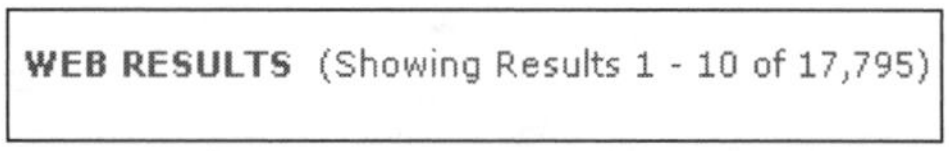

WEB RESULTS (Showing Results 1 - 10 of 17,795)

Figure 14.6 HotBot tells you how many results your search found.

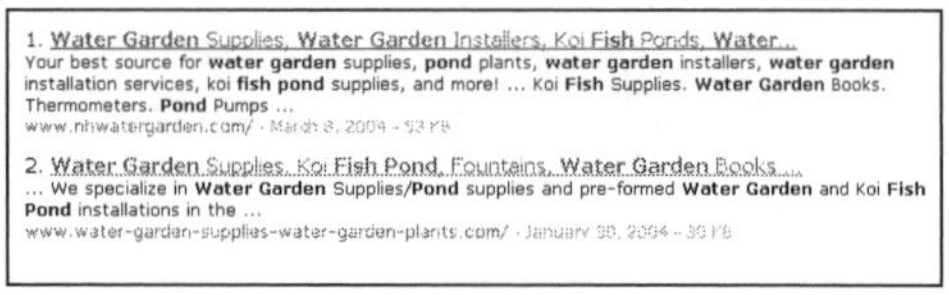

1. Water Garden Supplies, Water Garden Installers, Koi Fish Ponds, Water...
Your best source for **water garden** supplies, **pond** plants, **water garden** installers, **water garden** installation services, koi **fish pond** supplies, and more! ... Koi **Fish** Supplies. **Water Garden** Books. Thermometers. **Pond** Pumps ...
www.nhwatergarden.com/ - March 8, 2004 - 53 KB

2. Water Garden Supplies, Koi Fish Pond, Fountains, Water Garden Books ...
... We specialize in **Water Garden** Supplies/**Pond** supplies and pre-formed **Water Garden** and Koi **Fish Pond** installations in the ...
www.water-garden-supplies-water-garden-plants.com/ - January 30, 2004 - 39 KB

Figure 14.7 By default, HotBot includes the title, a short description, the URL, and the date the page was created in the results. You can change this on the HotBot Result Preferences page.

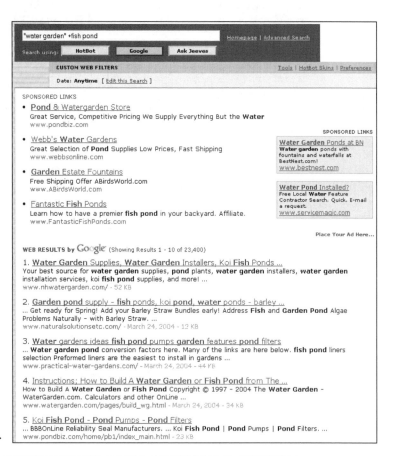

Figure 14.8 If the results from HotBot don't get you what you want, click the Google or Ask Jeeves button.

Figure 14.8 If the results from HotBot don't get you what you want, click the Google or Ask Jeeves button.

Domain/Site
add to homepage

Figure 14.9 Click the Add to Homepage link to add an Advanced Search option to HotBot's home page.

✔ Tips

- For best results with HotBot, use at least two or three search terms and be as specific as possible.

- You can add any of the Advanced Search options to the HotBot home page by clicking Add to Homepage (**Figure 14.9**) on the Advanced Search page.

To change your result preferences:

1. To change your results settings, click Preferences at the top of the search page and then Result Prefs (**Figure 14.10**).

continues on next page

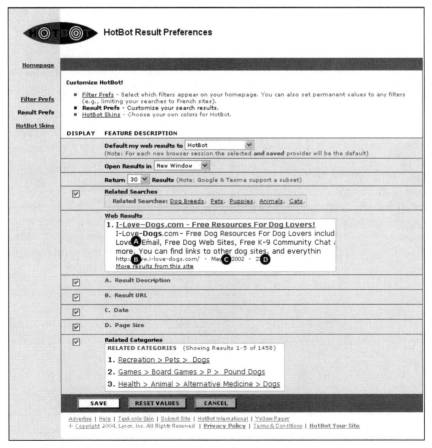

Figure 14.10 Use the results preferences to control how the results are displayed on the page.

2. Select the options you want to use. You can *do any of the following:*

▲ Choose the default search engine to use.

▲ Open results in a new window. Use this option to open multiple browser windows and to avoid going back to the results and losing your place.

▲ Display more results per page by increasing the number in the Return *x* Results field (up to 100).

▲ Show related searches on the results page.

▲ Control the amount of detail presented for each listing by changing the Web Results settings to show (or hide) Result Description, Result URL, Date, and Page Size information.

▲ Show related categories, when available. Even with this enabled, you won't see categories with every search.

3. Click Save to save these settings.

✔ **Tip**

■ To limit your results to Web pages written in English, choose English from the Advanced Search Language menu (see "Advanced Search Options" later in this chapter).

Custom Web Filters and Advanced Search

You probably noticed that the Custom Web filter and Edit This Search use the same form as Advanced Search. So is there a difference between these options?

Custom Web filters are your search preferences. These settings are saved to a cookie and persist between searches. If you set the first Word Filters option to Exact Phrase, In the Body, it remains on that setting until you change it.

Selections made in an advanced search apply only to the current search. The search fields are reset to the default after the results are returned. If you choose Advanced Search after doing a search, the search fields are cleared.

When you need to refine a search, choose Edit This Search, not Advanced Search. Your original search words are carried over to the Advanced Search form.

Advanced Search Options

HotBot has a limited set of custom search options. You can refine your current search results by clicking Edit This Search, or you can click Advanced Search to set up advanced options before you begin searching. In either case, HotBot takes you to its Advanced Search page (**Figure 14.11**).

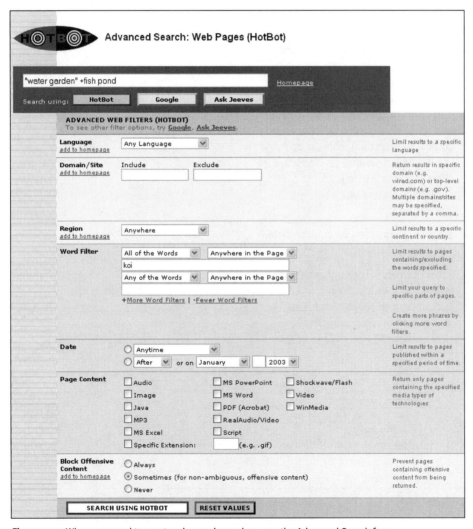

Figure 14.11 When you need to create advanced searches, use the Advanced Search form.

To set Advanced Search options:

1. Click Advanced Search on the HotBot home page and type your query in the search form.

   You can also click Edit This Search on any search results page to refine your current query with advanced options.

2. *Set any of the following options:*

   ▲ **Language:** Display only pages written in a specific language.

   ▲ **Domain/Site:** Include or exclude specific domains or sites in your search (**Figure 14.12**). This option lets you focus your search on a particular continent, country, domain name, or type of domain (com, edu, gov, and so on). To target a particular country, you'll need the country's two-letter Internet code (cl for Chile, es for Spain, and so on). For a list, see Appendix B.

   ▲ **Region:** Return results from a specific region or continent.

   ▲ **Word Filter:** Select any of the Boolean options in the Word Filter section and select the field that you want that operator to apply to (**Figure 14.13**):

Figure 14.12 Include or exclude domains or sites in your searches.

Figure 14.13 Change the Word Filter option so HotBot performs the type of search you prefer.

ADVANCED SEARCH OPTIONS

All of the Words: The default setting. This performs an AND search.

Any of the Words: Similar to a Boolean OR search.

None of the Words: Similar to a Boolean NOT search.

Exact Phrase: You don't need to enclose the phrase in quotation marks if you use this option. You'll typically get the same results with or without quotation marks.

Not Exact Phrase: This is a NOT search on a phrase.

In the Body: Look for your search terms in the body of Web pages.

In the Title: Look for your search terms in the titles of Web pages.

In the Referring URL: Look for your search terms in the URLs of Web pages.

In Contained URLs: Find Web pages that include hyperlinks to a specific URL—a technique often used by Web site creators to get a measure of their sites' popularity. To work properly, your search must include the Web site's *complete* URL. For example, to find Web pages that link to Microsoft, you need to type http://www.microsoft.com in the HotBot search form.

▲ **Date:** Show pages updated before or after a specific date (**Figure 14.14**).

continues on next page

Figure 14.14 Search for pages created before or after a date. Here we're looking for pages created after January 1, 2003.

▲ **Page Content:** Show only pages containing specific file types, such as multimedia files or Java applets. You can also look for a specific file extension (GIF, JPEG, TIFF, and so on). You can select multiple file types if you like (**Figure 14.15**).

▲ **Block Offensive Content:** Choose whether to include potentially offensive content in the results.

3. Click Search Using HotBot when you are ready to begin your search.

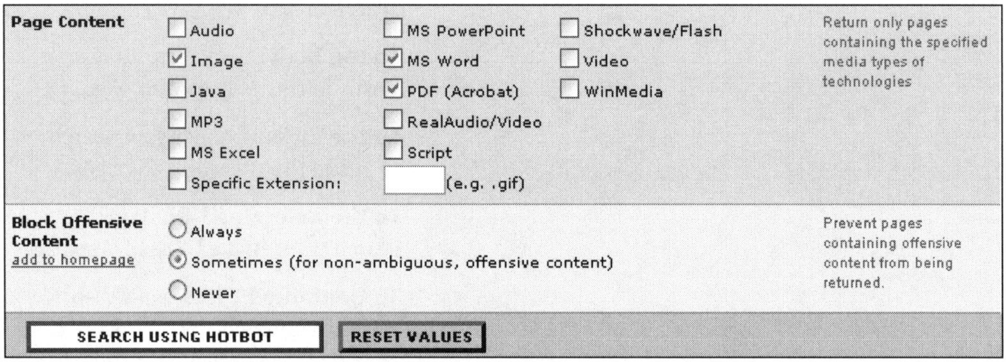

Figure 14.15 Choose one or more file types you want to search for.

Figure 14.16 You can use meta words in the search field instead of creating an advanced search.

Field searching with meta words

You can incorporate one or more of HotBot's field-search terms, called *meta words*, right into your queries.

For example, instead of using the Word Filter menu's In the Title option to search for the phrase *Jeep Grand Cherokee* in the titles of Web pages, you can type `title:"Jeep Grand Cherokee"` in the HotBot search form (**Figure 14.16**).

Similarly, you can use the `domain:` field-search term to look for specific domain names or types of domains, and `linkdomain:` to find Web pages that link to specific sites. You can even combine these two field-search terms to look for, say, education (`edu`) domains that link to a particular Web site.

✔ Tips

■ For the most part, HotBot's meta words duplicate the search capabilities provided on the main search form and the Advanced Search page. Unless you're a power searcher, you'll probably find it easier to use the point-and-click approach rather than incorporating meta words into Boolean expressions.

■ For additional search tips and techniques, click Help on the HotBot home page. You'll also find a summary of HotBot search features and syntax in the HotBot Quick Reference (**Table 14.1**).

■ For a summary of meta words, along with search examples, see the HotBot Meta Words Quick Reference (**Table 14.2**).

Table 14.1

HotBot Quick Reference	
FOR THIS TYPE OF SEARCH:	DO THIS:
Plain-English Question	Simply type the question in the search form and select All of the Words from the search form's Word Filter menu.
Phrase Search	Type the phrase with or without quotation marks and select Exact Phrase on the Word Filter menu.
	To look for multiple phrases or for a phrase and a single word, put the phrase in quotation marks and select All of the Words from the Word Filter menu.
AND Search (multiple words and phrases, each of which *must* be present)	Type words and/or phrases and select All of the Words from the Word Filter menu. You can type a plus sign (+) in front of each word or phrase, but it's not really necessary with an All of the Words search.
	You can also combine words and phrases with AND and select Boolean Phrase from the Word Filter menu.
OR Search (multiple words and phrases, any one of which may be present)	Type words or phrases separated by spaces and select Any of the Words from the Word Filter menu.
	Alternatively, combine words and phrases with OR and choose Boolean Phrase from the Word Filter menu.
NOT Search (to exclude a word or phrase)	Type a minus sign (–) in front of a word or phrase you want to exclude from the results. Alternatively, use NOT in front of the word or phrase and specify Boolean Phrase.
Date Search	Use the Date menu on the Advanced Search form to select a time frame (one week to two years).
Field Search (Web page titles)	Choose In the Title from the Word Filter menu on the HotBot home page to specify that you want to search the page title.
	Alternatively, you can use the HotBot meta word `title:` in your query. (See Table 14.2 for examples.)
Field Search (geography, domain, or domain type)	Use the HotBot meta word `domain:`. For example, enter `domain:jp` to look for sites in Japan. Enter `domain:com` to look for commercial sites in North America. For more examples, see Table 14.2.
	Alternatively, you can click Advanced Search and use the Location/Domain section to focus your search on a particular geographic region, country, domain, or domain type (`com`, `edu`, `gov`, and so on).
Field Search	Use the Page Content section to search for specific file types, including image, video, MP3, or JavaScript files.
	Alternatively, you can use `feature:` meta words in your queries on the HotBot home page to find plug-ins, embedded scripts, Java applets, audio and video files, and so on. (See Table 14.2 for a complete list.)

Table 14.2

HotBot Meta Words Quick Reference	
META WORD FORMAT:	**WHAT IT DOES:**
title:*word or phrase*	Searches Web page titles for the word or phrase you specify: for example, title:Edmund's or title:"car guides".
domain:*name*	Restricts searches to the specified domain name. Domains can be specified up to three levels: for example, domain:com, domain:ford.com, and domain:www.ford.com.
linkdomain:*name*	Restricts searches to pages containing links to the domain you specify. For example, linkdomain:edmunds.com finds pages that point to the Edmund's Car Guides Web site.
feature:acrobat	Searches for Adobe Acrobat files.
feature:applet	Searches for pages with embedded Java applets.
feature:activex	Detects ActiveX controls or layouts.
feature:audio	Searches for audio formats.
feature:embed	Searches for plug-ins.
feature:flash	Searches for Macromedia Flash plug-in HTML.
feature:form	Searches for forms in HTML documents.
feature:frame	Searches for frames in HTML documents.
feature:image	Searches for image files (GIF, JPEG, and so on).
feature:script	Searches for embedded scripts.
feature:shockwave	Searches for Macromedia Shockwave files.
feature:table	Searches for tables in HTML documents.
feature:video	Searches for video formats.
feature:vrml	Searches for VRML files.
scriptlanguage:javascript	Searches for pages containing JavaScript. (Note that lowercase is required for the term *javascript*.)
scriptlanguage:vbscript	Searches for pages containing VBScript. (Note that lowercase is required for the term *vbscript*.)

ADVANCED SEARCH OPTIONS

Customizing HotBot

You can tailor the HotBot search form to your particular style of searching. You can pick from a list of search options to select the settings you use most often; HotBot will then use your chosen settings automatically whenever you perform a HotBot search. You can also set any of these search options so that they appear under the search box on the HotBot home page.

If you decide to make HotBot your primary (or backup) search engine, you'll definitely want to take advantage of its search-form customization features. They're easy to set up and will save you time in the long run.

If you decide to make HotBot your primary search engine, you'll also want to install the HotBot Desktop toolbar for Internet Explorer.

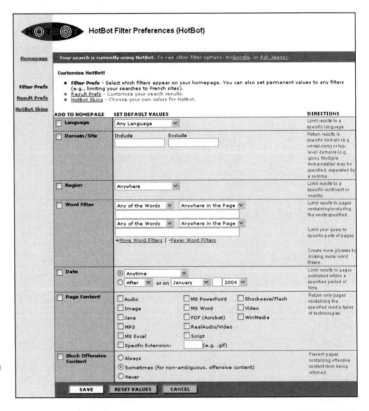

Figure 14.17 Set your search defaults using HotBot Filter Preferences.

To customize HotBot's search form:

1. Go to the HotBot home page (www.hotbot.com) and click Custom Web Filters [Add] to access the HotBot Filters Preferences page (**Figure 14.17**).

   Helpful tips on what each setting does appear to the right of each option.

2. Search options currently used on the HotBot home page have check marks next to them. To add or remove an option, click the box to make the check mark appear or disappear.

3. Use the drop-down menu next to each option to change its default setting. For example, if you typically want search results to include pages that contain any of your search words, set the menu to Any of the Words, to make that the default. Similarly, if you want to avoid pages written in foreign languages, set the Language menu to English.

4. Adding a Word Filter option (**Figure 14.18**) to the search form lets you easily specify words or phrases that must, should, or must not appear in your search results.

continues on next page

Figure 14.18 Use Word Filter to create AND and OR queries.

CUSTOMIZING HOTBOT

5. Once you've made all your changes, click Save; then go back to the HotBot home page, where you'll find your customized search settings all ready for your next search (**Figure 14.19**).

6. To change your default settings at any time, just click the Preferences link to return to the HotBot Filter Preferences page, make your new selections, and click Save. To restore HotBot's original settings, click Reset Values on the HotBot Filter Preferences page.

✔ Tip

■ HotBot's customization feature uses *cookie* technology to remember your settings. If you've disabled cookies in your Web browser, you'll need to enable them if you want your settings saved.

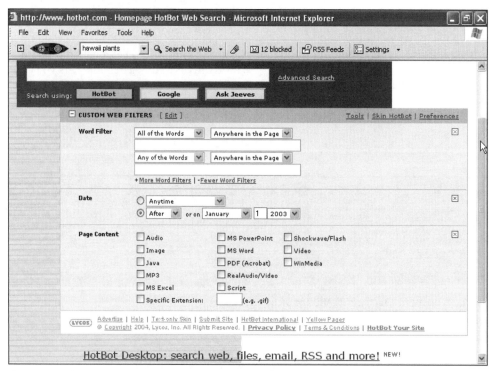

Figure 14.19 When you add custom Web filters, as was done here, you can perform advanced searches from the home page.

Adding a HotBot toolbar

HotBot offers two toolbars: the Deskbar, which is added to your Windows taskbar, and the HotBot Desktop toolbar, which is a toolbar for Internet Explorer (**Figure 14.20**). The taskbar version is convenient since you can use it without opening the browser, but it doesn't work very well. The Internet Explorer works very well and adds a task pane to Internet Explorer, which can come in handy.

To use the HotBot Desktop toolbar:

1. On the HotBot home page, click the Tools link to open the Tools page, which has links for downloading both toolbars.

2. Download and install the toolbar of your choice. You can install both, but we recommend installing only the IE toolbar version.

3. Enter your search words in the search field and click the Search button.

continues on next page

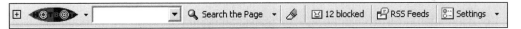

Figure 14.20 if you plan to use HotBot as your default search engine, install the HotBot Desktop toolbar.

CUSTOMIZING HOTBOT

4. You can also *do any of the following* from the HotBot Desktop toolbar:

▲ Click the plus sign (+) to open the HotBot search pane (**Figure 14.21**).

▲ Click the HotBot icon to return to HotBot.com, or click the arrow to select the Advanced Search or Tools page.

▲ Click the Search the Web button, or click the arrow to search other areas, including files and e-mail on your computer.

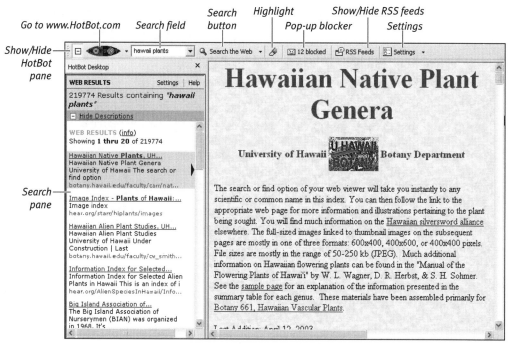

Figure 14.21 in addition to the toolbar, HotBot installs a search pane. Hide and show it using the plus (+) and minus (–) signs on the toolbar.

▲ Click the Highlight button to high-light your search words on the page (**Figure 14.22**).

▲ Like all IE toolbar add-ons, the HotBot Desktop toolbar includes a pop-up blocker. It also includes an RSS reader. Click these buttons to activate these features.

▲ Configure the toolbar settings using the Settings button.

✔ Tips

■ Enter a word or words in the search field and choose Search This Site from the search button's drop-down menu to high-light your search words on the current page. If you've entered multiple keywords, they will be highlighted in different colors.

■ RSS, the acronym for Really Simple Syndication, is a popular new file format used by news sites to replace e-mail news-letters and bloggers. After you subscribe to an RSS feed, the RSS reader goes out and fetches these specially formatted files and displays them in your browser.

Figure 14.22 Click the Highlight button to find your search words on Web pages. Use it instead of Edit > Find to locate words on any Web page.

PART 3

SPECIALIZED SEARCH ENGINES

Search Engines for Special Purposes

In Part 2, we introduced you to the most popular search engines and showed you how to use them to maximum advantage. In our view, you could pick any two of these engines, learn their ins and outs, and rely on them almost exclusively whenever you need to find information on the Web.

There *are* other search engines, however, that are designed for special purposes. They can't be used for general Internet searches, but when you need certain kinds of information, they should be your first stop.

In this part of the book, we tell you about the specialized search engines and the features they provide. We cover these topics:

- **Searching newsgroups**
- **Locating mailing lists**
- **Finding people**
- **Finding businesses**
- **Other search tools**

The chapters on searching newsgroups and locating mailing lists show you how to search and use two of the oldest collaborative features on the Internet: Usenet newsgroups and mailing lists. The Internet is a great replacement for White Pages and Yellow Pages directories published by phone companies, and we show you how to find people and businesses using some of the best online directories available.

The last chapter in this part lists some of the best specialized search sites, from Allmusic.com and CDNOW for music, to Amazon.com for books, to the Centers for Disease Control and Prevention for health issues, to the United States Postal Service for zip code lookups.

✔ **Tip**

■ If you haven't done so already, be sure to read the chapters on search basics in Part 1 of this book. The next chapters include references to search techniques and terminology that are explained in more detail in Part 1.

SEARCHING
NEWSGROUPS

Google™
Groups

The World Wide Web gets most of the press coverage, but for many people, Usenet newsgroups are the best thing about the Internet. Think of them as electronic word-of mouth—millions of people from all over the world sharing information, ideas, and personal experiences. Some 46,000 newsgroups are out there, each devoted to a specific topic. And unlike Web sites, nobody owns or controls newsgroups, so people are free to say anything they wish—rants, raves, and tirades included.

You have to take a lot of what you find in newsgroups with a grain of salt, of course. But the fact is, newsgroups can be an excellent source of information—especially if you use Google Groups to find the really good stuff. Google Groups also makes it relatively easy for you to avoid the junk-mail postings—generally known as *spam*—that have made reading some newsgroups a less-than-positive experience.

continues on next page

What You Can Search

◆ Usenet newsgroup archives, from posts just hours old to posts dating back to May 1981.

Contact Information

Google, Inc.
Mountain View, CA
Phone: 650-623-4000
Fax: 650-618-1499
groups.google.com

Google Groups gives you complete access to the full range of Google's newsgroup databases and search capabilities, including the following:

◆ **Newsgroup archives:** Google Groups has the largest collection of indexed, archived Usenet newsgroup postings available anywhere. The search form on the Google Groups home page (**Figure 15.1**) allows you to search the newsgroup database back to May 12, 1981.

Search form

Advanced Groups Search

Newsgroup directory

Figure 15.1 The Google Groups home page includes a basic search form and newsgroup directory.

◆ **Advanced searching:** Google Groups is *optimized* for searching newsgroups. You can do a quick search on a couple of keywords. But for even better results, and to avoid being swamped with irrelevant results, use the Advanced Groups Search page.

◆ **Query language:** The Google Groups query language is quite sophisticated and well documented and allows all the standard types of searches (AND, OR, NOT, and phrase searching).

In short, the Google Groups Web site is superb, and for serious newsgroup searching, it just can't be beat.

✔ Tips

■ *Usenet* (short for Usenet Network) is a program that was created in 1979 to help foster communication and the exchange of ideas among people interested in the UNIX operating system. The program was designed to use the Internet to automatically transmit news about UNIX. That's why, to this day, the features Usenet offers are called *newsgroups*. But these days, of course, news about the UNIX operating system is found in only a tiny fraction of the 46,000 or so newsgroups in existence.

■ The predecessor of Google Groups was a service called Deja News, founded in 1995—the name is a pun on the phrase *déjà vu*, that odd sensation we all get from time to time of having heard or seen something before. Google purchased Deja News in 2001.

■ If you'd like to know more about Internet history, terminology, and slang, look for the *Internet Glossary and Quick Reference Guide*, published by AMACOM.

Understanding Newsgroup Names

The Google Groups site (`groups.Google.com`) is so well designed and easy to use that you'll have newsgroup searching mastered in no time. But before you plunge in, you need to understand the terminology associated with Usenet newsgroups.

The names of specific newsgroups (or discussions) don't make much sense until you understand the concept of *newsgroup hierarchies*—the system used on the Internet to organize the groups into general areas, topics, and subtopics. The most popular top-level newsgroup hierarchies are `alt`, `biz`, `comp`, `misc`, `news`, `rec`, `sci`, and `soc`. These are described in **Table 15.1**.

Specific topics and subtopics under these main areas are designated by the addition of a period (or dot) and an identifying word: for example, `misc.health` (pronounced "miss-dot-health"), `misc.health.arthritis`, and so forth.

One of the best ways to get a handle on Usenet newsgroup names and hierarchies is to spend a few minutes browsing newsgroups.

Table 15.1

Popular Newsgroup Hierarchies	
alt	Alternative newsgroups—everything from sexy stuff to the truly offbeat.
biz	Business-related newsgroups that welcome advertising and marketing messages.
comp	Computer-related newsgroups.
misc	A grab-bag category, including the popular `misc.jobs` and `misc.forsale` sites.
news	Groups concerned with the Usenet network (not current affairs, as you might think).
rec	Recreation and hobbies.
sci	Science-related newsgroups.
soc	Groups devoted to social issues, often related to a particular culture.

Figure 15.2 Google Groups's newsgroup directory lets you explore newsgroups by *hierarchy*, the system used on the Net to name and organize discussion groups.

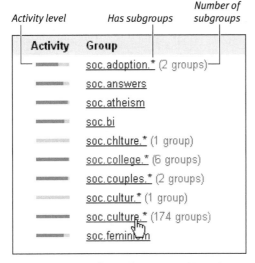

Figure 15.3 The soc (society) newsgroup hierarchy includes soc.culture, which, according to information to the right of the group name, is further broken down into 174 newsgroups.

Figure 15.4 As you're browsing newsgroups with Google Groups, you can always stop and search the category you're exploring.

To browse newsgroups:

1. Click one of the top-level newsgroup hierarchies (**Figure 15.2**) on the Google Groups home page.

2. Continue working your way down through the resulting pages until you find the specific newsgroup that you're looking for. At each point along the way, groups with additional subgroups are identified with an asterisk (*) followed by the number of subgroups in that group (**Figure 15.3**).

   The activity level of each group is shown in a bar to the left of the group name. If the bar is gray, the group is not active at all; if the bar is completely green, the group is very active.

3. You can stop at any point and do a keyword search of a specific group or the entire Google Groups database (**Figure 15.4**).

✔ Tips

- In addition to browsing newsgroups, you can use Google Groups to post messages and subscribe to newsgroups. See "Posting to Newsgroups" later in this chapter.

- For more on Usenet newsgroup hierarchies, see Appendix C.

Searching Newsgroups

Browsing newsgroups is okay for starters, but Google Groups's real power lies in its newsgroup search capabilities. Your best bet is to skip the form on the Google Groups home page, which is likely to produce too much information to be very useful. Instead, use the Advanced Groups Search form for your Google Groups newsgroup searches.

Advanced Groups Search
Preferences
Groups Help

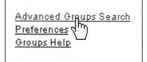

Figure 15.5 Most of the time, you'll want to use this link on the Google Groups home page to go directly to Advanced Groups Search.

To search with Advanced Groups Search:

1. Click Advanced Groups Search (**Figure 15.5**) on the Google Groups home page to access the Advanced Groups Search form (**Figure 15.6**).

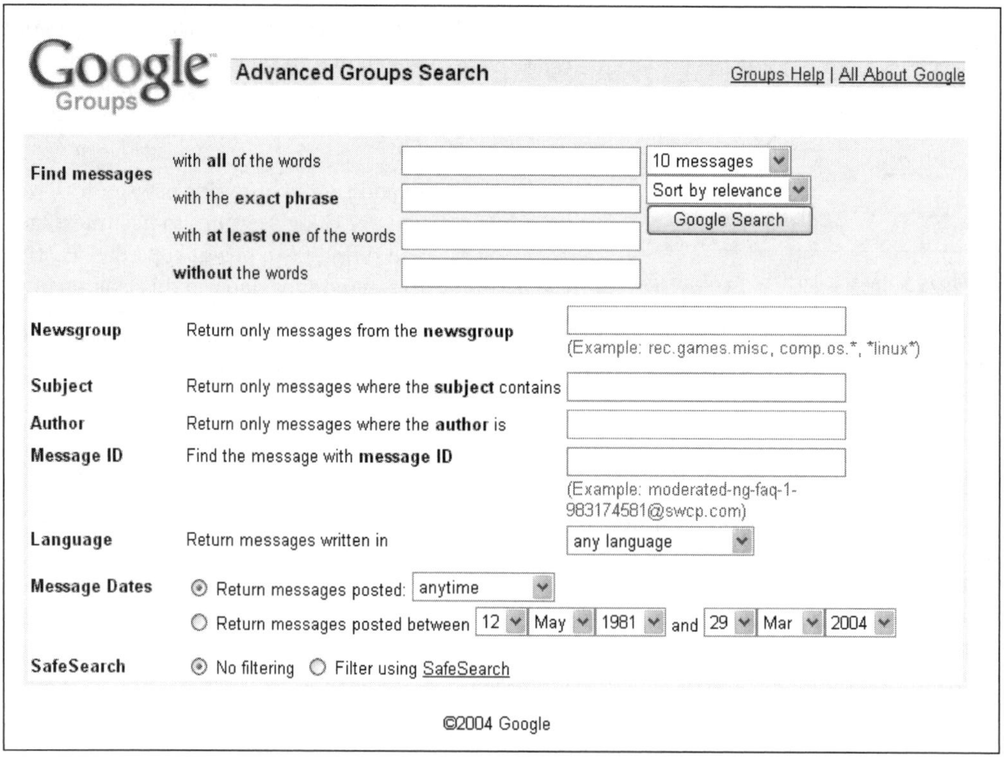
Google
Groups
Advanced Groups Search
Groups Help | All About Google
Find messages
with all of the words
with the exact phrase
with at least one of the words
without the words
10 messages
Sort by relevance
Google Search
Newsgroup
Return only messages from the newsgroup
(Example: rec.games.misc, comp.os.*, *linux*)
Subject
Return only messages where the subject contains
Author
Return only messages where the author is
Message ID
Find the message with message ID
(Example: moderated-ng-faq-1-983174581@swcp.com)
Language
Return messages written in
any language
Message Dates
Return messages posted: anytime
Return messages posted between 12 May 1981 and 29 Mar 2004
SafeSearch
No filtering
Filter using SafeSearch
©2004 Google

Figure 15.6 The Advanced Groups Search form is easy to use and gives you a great deal of control over your newsgroup searches.

2. Type your search terms in the text boxes, choosing to search for all of the words, an exact phrase, any of the specified words, or none of the specified words (**Figure 15.7**).

Advanced Groups Search also lets you specify the number of search results displayed per page (as one of these values: 10, 20, 30, 50, or 100). And you can sort the results by relevance (how well a site matches your search terms) or date posted.

3. Because the Google Groups archives are so vast, you may sometimes want to limit your search to a specific newsgroup or hierarchy (**Figure 15.8**).

4. If you want, specify a field search. You can search the Subject and Author fields of newsgroup messages simply by typing search terms in the spaces provided on the Advanced Groups Search form (**Figure 15.9**).

continues on next page

Find messages	with **all** of the words	internet explorer error	10 messages
	with the **exact phrase**		Sort by relevance
	with **at least one** of the words		Google Search
	without the words		

Figure 15.7 Enter words in the fields to tell Google Groups what kind of search you want. Here, we're doing an AND search, looking for all of the words. You can use any or all of the fields.

| Newsgroup | Return only messages from the **newsgroup** | comp.os.ms-windows* |
| | | (Example: rec.games.misc, comp.os.*, *linux*) |

Figure 15.8 Use the Newsgroup field to limit your search a specific newsgroup.

| Subject | Return only messages where the **subject** contains | |
| Author | Return only messages where the **author** is | |

Figure 15.9 Use these fields to search by subject or author.

5. If you know the message ID, you can enter it on the form to find the message. Since you need to know the message ID before you can search for it, you'll only use this option when someone gives you the ID, which can be found in the message header.

6. You can limit your results to a specific language or set the Language option to Any for the widest possible search.

7. You can search for messages posted within a specified range of dates going back to May 1981.

8. To filter out potentially offensive content, choose Filter Using SafeSearch.

9. Once you've made all your search selections, click the Google Search button to submit your query.

   Google Groups returns the results (**Figure 15.10**).

Figure 15.10 Here's an example of how Google Groups presents newsgroup search results.

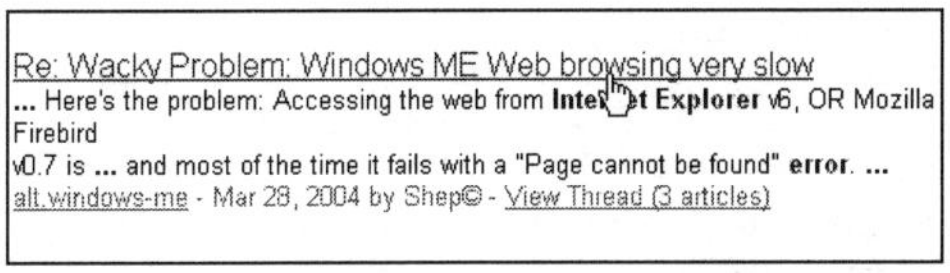

Re: Wacky Problem: Windows ME Web browsing very slow
... Here's the problem: Accessing the web from Internet Explorer v6, OR Mozilla Firebird
v0.7 is ... and most of the time it fails with a "Page cannot be found" error. ...
alt.windows-me - Mar 28, 2004 by Shep© - View Thread (3 articles)

Figure 15.11 Click the subject link to view the message.

To use the search results:

1. To view the complete text of any message (**Figure 15.11**), click its subject link.

2. Once you're on a message page, you can scroll back and forth through other messages, use the Complete Thread link to view the complete *message thread* (the original message and all subsequent replies), and post messages of your own (**Figure 15.12**).

continues on next page

Figure 15.12 When you display a specific message, your search terms are presented in bold and highlighted to make them easy to spot.

3. You can click the author's name link (**Figure 15.13**) to learn about a person's other newsgroup interests and activities. Though by no means foolproof, checking a person's posting history can help you assess the reliability of a source.

From: Shep© (nospam@nospam.net)
Subject: Re-Wacky Problem: Windows ME Web browsing very slow
Newsgroups: alt.windows-me, comp.os.ms-windows.networking
Date: 2004-03-28 03:32:57 PST

Figure 15.13 Clicking an author's name shows you the person's *posting history*—the specific newsgroups in which the person participates and the number of messages posted.

✔ Tips

■ Google Groups supports phrase searching; the Boolean operators AND, OR, and NOT, and field searches. For details, see the Google Groups Quick Reference (**Table 15.2**).

■ Searches are *not* case-sensitive, so you can type search terms in uppercase or lowercase, or a combination, and you'll get the same results.

■ Don't expect to find images, program listings, and other encoded binary files among Google Groups postings. They're simply too large and can't be easily indexed.

■ To access Google Groups's help information, click Groups Help on the Google Groups home page.

Table 15.2

Google Groups Quick Reference

FOR THIS TYPE OF SEARCH:	DO THIS:	EXAMPLES:
Plain-English Question	Not recommended. Use a phrase or AND search instead.	
Phrase Search	Type the phrase as a sequence of words surrounded by double quotation marks.	`"forensic medicine"`
AND Search (multiple words and phrases, each of which must be present)	Simply type the words or phrases separated by a space.	`cholesterol exercise`
OR Search (multiple words and phrases, any one of which may be present)	Use OR or	(pipe symbol) to connect two or more words or phrases. Both examples would find newsgroup postings that mention either *fitness* or *nutrition*.	`fitness OR nutrition` `fitness	nutrition`
NOT Search (exclude a word or phrase)	Use a minus sign (–) in front of a word or phrase you want to exclude from your results. To look for postings about vitamins but not herbal vitamins, for example, you might want to exclude *herbal*	`vitamins -herbal`
Case-Sensitive Search	Not available.	
Field Search	Use the Advanced Groups Search form for fill-in-the-blank searching of newsgroup author, subject, and newsgroup name fields.	

	Alternatively, you can use the following field-search operators on the search form itself:
	Author: *author*:
	Subject: *insubject*:
	Group name: *group*:
		`author:bjones@nih.edu`
		`insubject:"lyme disease"`
		`group:sci.med.diseases`

Nested Search	Use parentheses to group search expressions into more complex queries. The example would find postings that mention *clinical study* or *clinical trial*.	`clinical (study OR trial)`
Proximity Search	Not supported.	
Wildcard Search	Not supported.	

Posting to Newsgroups

Google Groups makes it easy for you to reply to newsgroup posts or to post new messages. Keep in mind that you aren't just posting to a group or forum on Google's server; your message will be sent to thousands of newsgroup servers worldwide.

Before you can post a message, you need to register with Google Groups. This is easy—Google just needs a valid e-mail address and a password (**Figure 15.14**). You'll need to confirm your membership by following the instructions you receive in an e-mail message that Google will send to you. Once you've confirmed, you can log in and post new messages or reply to others'.

✔ Tip

■ If you are posting a question to a newsgroup because you have a problem and need help, search Google and Google Groups before posting. You may find the answer before you ask the question.

Figure 15.14 Before you can post a message, you need to create a Google account. If you already have a Google account, click Sign in Here.

To create a new post:

1. Browse to the group you want to post to or use search to find a relevant group. Choose the group wisely and don't post the same message to more than two or three groups. It's bad netiquette to post to multiple groups.

2. Click the Post a New Message to [*Newsgroup*] link (**Figure 15.15**) to open the Compose Your Message form.

continues on next page

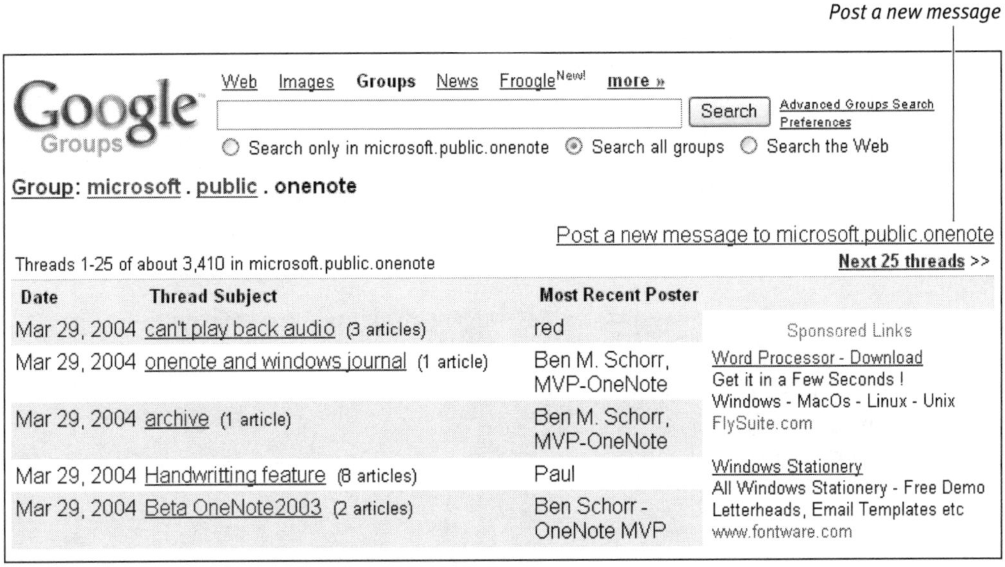

Post a new message

Figure 15.15 Locate a newsgroup that interests you; then click the Post a New Message to [*Newsgroup*] link, where [*Newsgroup*] is the name of the newsgroup.

POSTING TO NEWSGROUPS

3. Enter an informative subject. Don't enter *Help!* or other common but unhelpful words in the subject (**Figure 15.16**).

4. Explain your problem and ask the question. Give enough information to explain the problem, but don't make your entry too long—aim for 300 words or less.

5. Preview your message before posting. Some groups are really fussy about proper spelling and grammar, so you may want to write your message in Word and spell check it and then copy and paste into the form.

6. Click Post Message (**Figure 15.17**); your message will be posted to news servers worldwide within minutes.

Figure 15.17 Once you are satisfied with the message, click Post Message.

Figure 15.16 Enter a descriptive subject and write your message; then preview your message.

POSTING TO NEWSGROUPS

Figure 15.18 To post a reply, click Post a Follow-up to This Message, found at the end of each posting.

To reply to a post:

1. Click the Post a Follow-up to This Message link found at the bottom of each posting (**Figure 15.18**).

2. The Compose Your Message form opens with the message you are replying to quoted in the message box (**Figure 15.19**). Trim the unimportant text from the quote and add your reply.

3. Preview the message; then click Post Message.

Figure 15.19 Google quotes the original message in the message box; enter your comments and then preview and post the message.

Newsgroup Safety

Newsgroups are potentially the least safe area of the Internet. Some newsgroup users live to flame and harass other users, especially if they are new to the group. E-mail address collecting spiders scan newsgroups constantly for addresses to add to their lists of addresses for sale. Viruses and Trojan horses are often posted to newsgroups to help them spread faster.

As dangerous as newsgroups are, it's easy to protect yourself.

◆ Always read approximately the last two weeks worth of messages before posting. This helps you learn the posting style of the regulars and how they act. Learn who acts like bullies so you can avoid arguing with them.

◆ Never post with your real e-mail address,. Use a Hotmail or Yahoo e-mail address to keep spam and viruses out of your inbox.

 You may have noticed that some people "munge" (add extra words to) their address with letters or words in all capitals, like this: dp@poremNOSPAMsky.com. A spammer's automated mailing system won't remove the extra words, and any message it sends will be undeliverable, but anyone who wants to reply directly can easily figure out the real address. Others use completely fake addresses such as nospam@nospam.net.

◆ Whether you use your real name or an alias as your display name is up to you. I use my real name (and a special address I use only to post to newsgroups), but others use aliases that don't readily identify themselves. Whatever you choose to do, always using the same display name and e-mail address helps others know it's you.

◆ Don't flame or harass people and don't post private or personal information. Not only are your posts traceable, even with a fake address and display name; they are also sent to servers around the world and archived for all time.

◆ Ignore mean people, especially if you are new to a group. Learn when to stop arguing with people who think they are always right, even when they aren't. Remember: The messages are archived forever, and you don't want to look like a fool five years from now.

◆ If you post a problem and ask for help at a newsgroup, search both Google and Google Groups to verify any solutions you receive before using them. Also search for the person suggesting the solution to see if he or she is trustworthy.

LOCATING MAILING LISTS

Internet mailing lists consist of groups of people who regularly exchange e-mail on a subject that interests them. As with newsgroups, there are tens of thousands of mailing lists covering every conceivable topic. The vast majority of them are private—university professors discussing scholarly subjects, clubs and associations communicating with their members, families doing genealogical research or planning reunions. But there are plenty of general-interest mailing lists that welcome subscribers. The trick is to find them.

There are three very popular mailing list hosts: Yahoo Groups, LSoft, and Topica.

Topica (pronounced "TOP-i-kuh") has a database of over 70,000 individual mailing lists, LSoft boasts nearly 70,000 public lists, while Yahoo Groups blows both away with over 300,000 lists.

With so many lists to choose from, finding the "right" list to join looks like a daunting task. It doesn't have to be.

Begin by searching for a list using keywords; then look at the number of subscribers. Too few subscribers often means very little traffic and even fewer expert members—especially important for technical lists. Too many subscribers may mean hundreds of messages a day to your mailbox.

What You Can Search

◆ Directory of over 300,000 mailing lists

◆ Message archives for public lists and lists to which you subscribe

Contact Information

Yahoo!
Sunnyvale, CA
Phone: 408-349-3300
Fax: 408-349-3301
groups.yahoo.com

continues on next page

How many subscribers is too few or too many is difficult to answer, since it depends on the topic of the list. Good technical lists should have at least 500 members, preferably 1000 to 2000, while lists supporting a specific physical condition or disease may be more supportive with fewer than 100 members.

Once you find a list that sounds interesting, you can click a link to subscribe (or to request more information if it's a members-only group for which you might qualify). From that point on, you'll receive all the group's postings automatically by e-mail.

Mailing lists aren't as freewheeling and interactive as newsgroups, but they are often more personal and can result in long-term friendships. It takes some effort to locate and subscribe to the right ones, but once you find the right list, you'll feel like part of a community, especially if you're active in the list.

Mailing lists also aren't nearly as likely as newsgroups to be polluted with advertisements and get-rich-quick solicitations, because many list owners go to the trouble of making sure that such junk never reaches your mailbox. There's also the fact that people who have taken the time to seek out and subscribe to a particular mailing list are likely to be genuinely (perhaps passionately) interested in the subject, so members can be an incredible information resource.

✔ Tips

■ Mailing lists vary widely in what they offer and how they operate. Some maintain searchable archives. Some give you the option of reading digests instead of complete messages. Some lists are quite interactive, while others are designed primarily to distribute a newsletter or magazine and do little to encourage interaction with or among members.

■ Many mailing lists have a message archive available for nonmembers to browse. Reading some of the messages is the best way of determining whether a mailing list will be interesting and worthwhile for you.

■ There are other widely used and respected mailing-list directories available on the Web. Though not as comprehensive, they're worth knowing about, if only to get a different perspective on the mailing-list phenomenon:

Freelists: www.freelists.org

MSN Groups: groups.msn.com

Tile.Net: tile.net/lists

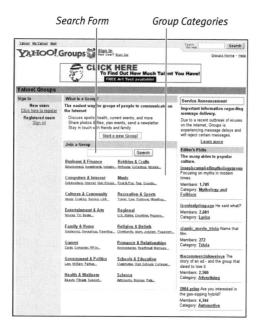

Figure 16.1 The Yahoo Groups home page includes a search form and a directory of mailing lists organized into several broad topics.

Searching for Mailing Lists

Before you can join a mailing list, you need to find one. Because Yahoo Groups has so many groups, we'll search there.

The Yahoo Groups home page (**Figure 16.1**) gives you two ways of locating Internet mailing lists (or *groups* as they are called at Yahoo):

◆ The groups are organized like a directory, and you can click one of several broad categories or subcategories—such as Business & Finance or the subcategories of Employment, Investments, or Industry—to display a special page devoted to mailing lists on that topic.

◆ You can use the search form to do a keyword search of all the mailing lists in the Yahoo Groups database.

Mailing List Services

◆ Yahoo Groups (`groups.yahoo.com`) lists over 300,000 public mailing lists, some with public archives. You do not need to join Yahoo Groups to read lists with public archives or to subscribe by e-mail to a list. This site also offers group features, including file storage, a calendar, and a database.

◆ LSoft (`/www.lsoft.com/lists/`) has nearly 70,000 publicly accessible lists, many with online archives available to nonmembers.

◆ Topica (`www.topica.com`) has some 70,000 free mailing lists, and many have online archives you can read without joining the list (but you will need to join Topica).

◆ If you want to start your own mailing list, you can set one up in minutes at Topica or Yahoo Groups. In fact, this is one of the reasons Yahoo Groups has so many lists with 25 or fewer subscribers.

◆ LSoft doesn't offer a free list hosting service. However, LSoft has a free version of its list server software available for noncommercial use, which you can use if you have a server.

◆ MSN Groups and freelists.org offer free hosting services as well.

To search for mailing lists:

1. Go to the Yahoo Groups home page at www.yahoogroups.com.

2. To browse for mailing lists by subject, click one of the topics or subtopics in the List Directory (**Figure 16.2**).

3. To do a search, type one or more keywords (or a phrase in quotation marks) in the Join a Group search form.

   Searches are *not* case sensitive, so you can use uppercase or lowercase letters, and you'll get the same results.

4. Click Search to submit your query and view your results (**Figure 16.3**).

   Category matches, if any, will be presented first, followed by mailing list matches. Short descriptions, number of members, and archive status are listed with the group name.

Figure 16.2 Browse the categories or use Search to find a category.

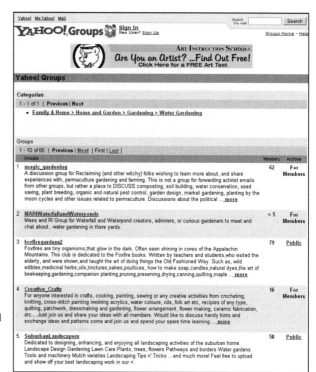

Figure 16.3 Search results are presented like this, with matching categories followed by matching lists. Groups with readable archives are public and have clickable links. The search results also list the number of members.

5. Click the name of the mailing list to go to the group's home page. Prepared by the list owner, the description typically includes a description of the list (**Figure 16.4**) and details on how to subscribe, unsubscribe, communicate with the list owner, and access other features such as archives and digests. You can also look at a monthly view of the group's activity. Use this to gauge the activity, especially for groups with a members-only archive.

continues on next page

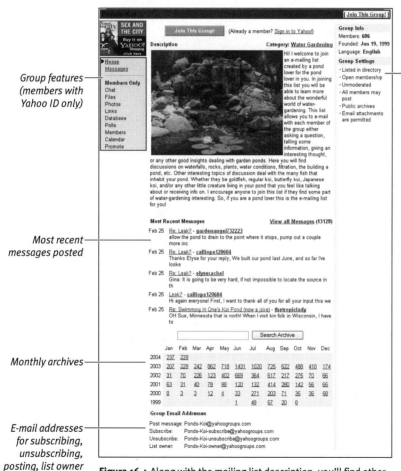

Group features (members with Yahoo ID only)

Group settings

Most recent messages posted

Monthly archives

E-mail addresses for subscribing, unsubscribing, posting, list owner

Figure 16.4 Along with the mailing list description, you'll find other useful information, such as the availability of a message archive, number of subscribers, and message volume.

6. In many cases, you can subscribe to a list simply by clicking the appropriate button or link (**Figure 16.5**). If the group has public archives, you can read the group information online without joining the group.

7. If you are a member of Yahoo (and you are if you ever signed up for a Yahoo e-mail address), sign in with your Yahoo ID and password. After signing in, you can have messages sent to any e-mail address you own.

If you don't have a Yahoo ID and don't want to create one, subscribe by e-mail using the subscription address at the bottom of the page. Note that you may not have access to some list features unless you have a Yahoo ID.

✔ Tip

■ Mailing lists almost always have a special e-mail address for subscribing and unsubscribing. (When you use that address, your request is handled automatically, without any intervention on the part of the list's owner.) Don't make the classic new-user mistake of sending a subscription-related message to the address designated for posting messages to the mailing list (**Figure 16.6**).

Figure 16.5 Yahoo Groups makes it easy to join a mailing list.

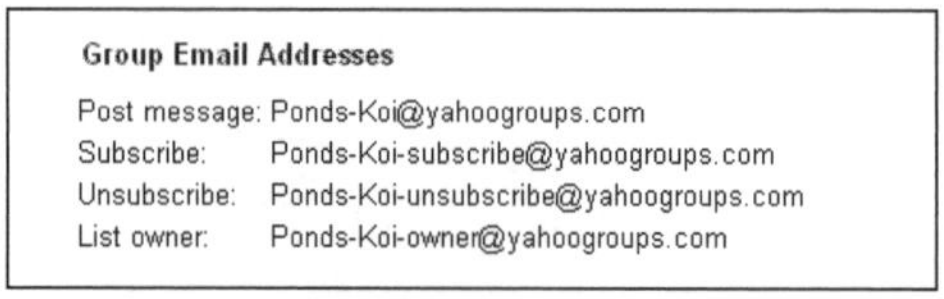

Group Email Addresses

Post message: Ponds-Koi@yahoogroups.com
Subscribe: Ponds-Koi-subscribe@yahoogroups.com
Unsubscribe: Ponds-Koi-unsubscribe@yahoogroups.com
List owner: Ponds-Koi-owner@yahoogroups.com

Figure 16.6 Be sure to pay careful attention to the address used for *joining* versus *posting to* a mailing list. Other list subscribers won't take kindly to receiving your subscription request in their mailboxes.

Are You a Lurker?

On average, about 10 percent of the members are active on any given list, posting the majority of the messages or answering most of the questions. Some of the remaining members are active enough that list members recognize their names, but the vast majority, as many as 75 percent, read the messages but never post to the list. We call these mailing list wallflowers *lurkers*.

While a list with too many active members will flood your mailbox, one with too few active members soon dies. Participation is a great way to make friends (or enemies), and in many cases, the friendship continues offline.

Figure 16.7 If you can't find a group, start your own.

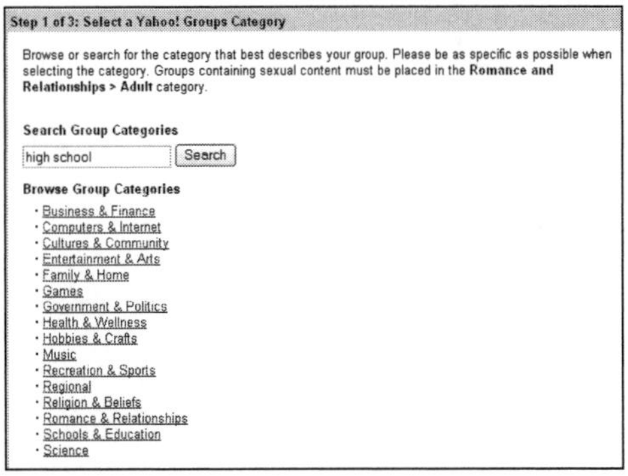

Figure 16.8 Select a category from the directory or search for a category.

Browse Group Categories

Top > Schools & Education > K-12 > High Schools > By Region > U.S. States > **Tennessee**   Place my group in *Tennessee*

Figure 16.9 Once you find an appropriate category, click the link to place your category in it.

Creating a Mailing list

If you can't find a mailing list for the topic you want to discuss, or if you want a private list for family, clubs, or alumni, you can easily create one.

To create your own group:

1. Sign in to Yahoo Groups and click Start a Group on the Yahoo Groups home page. If you don't have a Yahoo ID, you'll need to create one to create a group.

2. Click Start a New Group! on the Yahoo Groups home page (**Figure 16.7**).

3. Choose a category for your group. Use Search to bring up existing categories, using a keyword for the type of list you are creating (**Figure 16.8**). For example, if you are creating a group for your high school class reunion, enter `high school`; then choose more specialized categories.

4. Click `Place my Group in` *category* to create your group (**Figure 16.9**).

continues on next page

CREATING A MAILING LIST

5. Enter a short but descriptive name for your group (up to about 30 letters is good), an e-mail address, and a description (**Figure 16.10**).

6. Choose an e-mail address from your profile (**Figure 16.11**).

Congratulations! You've just created your first mailing list (**Figure 16.12**).

7. You can customize your settings and make your list private, if desired. Then all that's left to do is invite members.

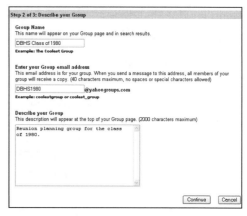

Figure 16.10 Enter a title, e-mail address, and group description for your group.

Figure 16.11 Choose an e-mail address and Yahoo profile to use as the list owner and enter the verification code. Click Continue to create your group.

Figure 16.12 All that's left to do is customize the group settings and invite members to join your group.

FINDING PEOPLE

The Internet is one big electronic address book, and if you know where to look, you can find almost anyone's street address, phone number, or e-mail address. While Google, Yahoo, and the other search engines covered earlier include address and phone number searches, other search engines are used only for finding people.

With as little as a name and a city or state, you can usually find street addresses and phone numbers. In some cases, it's very easy to find addresses and phone numbers online. In other cases, you'll need to search databases, and you still may come up short.

Web sites specializing in *people-finding* tools consistently rank among the Internet's 100 most frequently visited sites. Here are several excellent directory sites:

AnyWho	www.anywho.com
InfoSpace	www.infospace.com
SuperPages	www.superpages.com
Switchboard	www.switchboard.com
WhitePages	www.whitepages.com
WhoWhere?	www.whowhere.com
Yahoo! **People Search**	people.yahoo.com

What You Can Search

- ◆ Worldwide e-mail directory

- ◆ Telephone directory for residential and business listings in the United States, Canada, and Europe

- ◆ Reverse lookup directories (phone, address, e-mail, and area code)

Contact Information

InfoSpace, Inc.
Bellevue, WA
Phone: 425-201-6100
Fax: 425-201-6150
E-mail: information@infospace.com
www.infospace.com

continues on next page

The best way to judge the quality of any people-search site is by searching for people whose addresses and phone numbers you already know: yourself, friends, and family.

Don't be too disappointed if you come up empty handed at any of these search sites. They often contain old addresses and phone numbers. E-mail addresses are even less reliable and often available only if the person updated his or her records to include it.

✔ Tips

■ People-finding sites are often referred to as *white pages* because their databases typically include residential telephone numbers and street addresses—just like you find in your local telephone directory white pages. The difference is that you can search for anyone, anywhere in the United States.

■ When we say "anyone, anywhere," we mean it quite literally. You can use these sites to find parents, grandparents, neighbors, and friends who have never so much as touched a computer keyboard, let alone gone online.

■ Because they allow you to cast such a wide net, white pages are terrific for locating former classmates, tracking down long-lost military buddies, and doing genealogical research. Yahoo! People Search (`people.yahoo.com`) is attempting to make the process even easier by allowing you to add descriptive keywords when you add or update your listing.

■ Learn to use at least a couple of white pages Web sites. Like all search engines, each site has strengths and weaknesses. A site that's great for looking up phone numbers might not have e-mail addresses, while a site that is a great resource for e-mail addresses may not have street addresses.

■ Don't underestimate the power of using Google or any of the other general-purpose search engines to locate e-mail addresses. Use the person's name as the search keyword. You'll find several current e-mail addresses for me in any of the general-purpose search engines, but only outdated addresses in any of the people-search databases.

■ Some of the people-finder sites give a limited set of free data, often just the name and city, hoping to sell you the rest of the information. Don't fall for it; try a different site instead.

Finding E-mail Addresses

When you want to find an e-mail address, InfoSpace is the place to start. It has the largest address database, in part because it's partnered with MSN to provide directory searches to Hotmail and MSN members, and as a result, it has a large percentage of Hotmail addresses.

There are just a few things you need to know to take full advantage of InfoSpace's people-finding features. Start by going to the InfoSpace home page (www.infospace.com), where you'll find a menu of directory options (**Figure 17.1**).

Figure 17.1 The InfoSpace home page includes a set of people-finding tools.

Canadian and UK searches

To search for e-mail addresses:

1. Click Email Search on the InfoSpace home page to display the Email Search form (**Figure 17.2**). For relatively unusual names, try completing just the Last Name field. For common names like Smith or Jones, fill in the City, State/Province, and Country fields as well, using the drop-down menus to make your selections.

2. Click Search to submit your query. If InfoSpace finds a match, that information will be presented (**Figure 17.3**). If it comes up empty, you'll be given the opportunity to refine your search.

3. If a follow-up search is unsuccessful, try another directory site or even a general-purpose search engine such as Google.

✔ Tips

■ Unlike its competitors, InfoSpace doesn't actually provide you with e-mail addresses at its Web site. Instead, you're given a clickable link that you can use to send a message to a person you've located in the e-mail directory. The recipient can then decide whether or not to reveal his or her e-mail address by responding to your message.

■ It's usually best to start with a name-only search. If you get too many hits, complete additional fields one at a time. If your search returns nothing, try a variation on the person's first name (Margaret instead of Meg, for example). Or use a single letter in the First Name field (E to find Ed or Edward or Edwin).

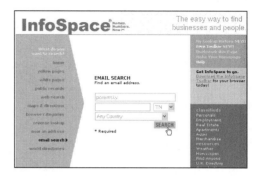

Figure 17.2 Here's the InfoSpace search form for locating e-mail addresses worldwide.

Figure 17.3 Results of an e-mail search are presented in this format. Instead of giving you the actual e-mail address, InfoSpace provides a link you can click to send the person a message.

■ If you're not sure of the spelling of a last name, make your best guess and then try a couple of variations. Unfortunately, InfoSpace doesn't support truncation or the use of wildcards in the Last Name field. So a search for Meyer will find listings for that name only, and you'll have to do a second search to look for Meyers.

■ InfoSpace offers a feature called Reverse Lookup that allows you to search for the *owner* of an e-mail address. You can also use Reverse Lookup to find all the people in the InfoSpace directory who work at a particular company. For example, a Reverse Lookup search for @microsoft.com would bring up the names of all the Microsoft employees in the directory. To use this feature, just click Reverse Lookup on the InfoSpace home page and choose Email Lookup.

■ You'll find a summary of InfoSpace search features in the InfoSpace Quick Reference (**Table 18.1**).

Table 18.1

InfoSpace Quick Reference	
FOR THIS TYPE OF SEARCH:	DO THIS:
E-mail Address Search (Worldwide)	Click Email Search on the InfoSpace home page to display the search form. Start by completing just the Last Name and First Name fields.
	To narrow a search, complete additional fields one at a time, in this order: Country, State/Province, City.
	To broaden a search, try a partial entry in the First Name field. Searching for **A** in the First Name field and Fletcher in the Last Name field would find listings for *Albert, Al,* and *A. S. Fletcher.*
Phone Number and Address Search	Click White Pages on the InfoSpace home page to display the search form. Start by completing the Last Name, First Name, and State fields.
	To narrow a search, complete the City field.
	To broaden a search, try a partial entry in the First Name field. Searching for Jo Anderson would find listings for *Joe Anderson* as well as *Joseph Anderson.*
	Another way to broaden a search that includes a City field is to select the Search Metro Area option.
Reverse Lookup	Click Reverse Lookup on the InfoSpace home page and enter phone and fax numbers, street addresses, e-mail addresses, and area codes.

Finding Phone Numbers and Addresses

While you may often fail to find an e-mail address for someone whom you know has an e-mail address, finding street addresses and phone numbers is usually easier.

Several of the directory services are excellent choices for looking up addresses and phone numbers. Some of the directory services link the address to online maps or do "neighbor searches," which return the names, addresses, and phone numbers of other residents on the street. Others link to vCards (virtual address cards), allowing you to add a contact to Outlook or other programs that support vCards.

The best solution: Use the InfoSpace Phone & Address Search feature. If the person lives in the United States, Canada, or Europe, chances are you can find both an address (including zip code for U.S. addresses) and telephone number.

To search for phone numbers and addresses:

1. From the InfoSpace home page (www.infospace.com), click White Pages.

2. Enter the person's name in the spaces provided on the White Pages Search form (**Figure 17.4**). It's generally a good idea to start with a broad search, completing just the Last Name, First Name, and State/Province fields. If the name you're looking for is quite common, you might want to take your best guess at completing the City field as well.

Figure 17.4 The White Pages Search form lets you look for residential phone numbers and addresses in the United States.

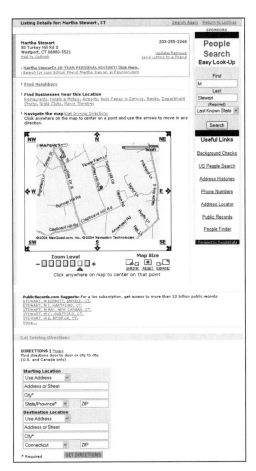

Figure 17.5 The search results include street address, city, state, zip code, phone number, and links for getting maps and driving directions.

Figure 17.6 Click this link to find all the other residents of a particular street—your own or someone else's!

3. Click Search to display your results (**Figure 17.5**). If InfoSpace locates multiple entries in its database, you'll be presented with a list of all the matches. For details on a specific listing, just click the name.

4. If you get an exceptionally large number of hits, you can go back and narrow the search. (Try adding a city, for example, if you haven't already.)

5. If you get too few hits (or none at all), check your spelling. Or try typing just an initial in the First Name field.

   For United States searches that include a City field, you might also try selecting the Search Metro Area option on the White Pages Search form, so that your search will be expanded to include the outlying suburbs for a major metropolitan area.

✔ Tips

■ InfoSpace gets home addresses and telephone numbers from companies that compile the information published in regional phone books. The InfoSpace database is updated about four times a year. If the person you're looking for has moved recently, it may take several months or so for the new information to make its way into the InfoSpace database.

■ Keep in mind that many people list themselves in the phone book with a first initial instead of a full name. If your search for, say, Janet Parker is unsuccessful, try searching for J Parker.

■ Once you've located a specific address that's of interest, you can use InfoSpace's Find Neighbors feature (**Figure 17.6**), on the search results page, to get the names, addresses, and phone numbers of all the other residents on that street.

To do reverse lookups of phone numbers and addresses:

1. Click Reverse Lookup on the InfoSpace home page and select Phone Number Lookup (**Figure 17.7**).

2. Use the Reverse Phone Number form (**Figure 17.8**) to find out who a particular phone number belongs to. You can even search for a partial number as long as you know the area code and first few digits.

3. To find out who lives at a certain address, use the Address Lookup form (**Figure 17.9**). Fill in the House Number, Street Name, and City fields and select a state from the drop-down menu.

✔ Tips

- The one caveat when using the Reverse Lookup Address Lookup form is that you may have to go through a couple of iterations to get the right entry in the Street Name field. The search software isn't very sophisticated and requires that you use "standard postal abbreviations." Consequently, if you type, say, River Road in the Street Name field, you won't find listings for *River Rd* and will have to try again using River Rd (no period).

- InfoSpace's Reverse Lookup Phone Number Lookup form allows you to search for partial numbers only if you know the area code. If that's the part of the phone number you *don't* know, try AnyWho (www.anywho.com). Its Reverse Lookup feature lets you look for phone numbers that begin or end with certain numbers.

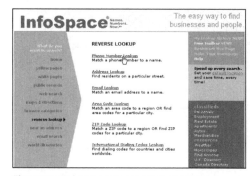

Figure 17.7 Select Reverse Lookup to do reverse lookups based on phone numbers, addresses, zip code, or area codes.

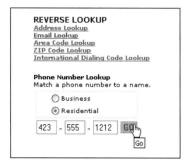

Figure 17.8 Reverse lookup of phone numbers is a neat feature. You can even search on partial phone numbers.

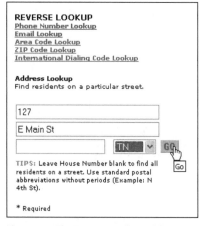

Figure 17.9 The Reverse Lookup Address Lookup form lets you search for the name and phone number of the residents of a particular street address.

Choosing a Directory Service

The following is a list of popular directory services and their features:

- AnyWho (www.anywho.com), powered by AT&T's directory service, is useful for U.S. address and phone numbers. It includes reverse phone number lookup, business lookup, find neighbors, and map and directions features.

- InfoSpace (www.infospace.com) includes worldwide business directories, along with address, phone number, and e-mail address lookups. It includes options to add addresses to Outlook and send e-mail to yourself or a friend.

- SuperPages (www.superpages.com) provides the address and phone number lookups for Verizon. Like a traditional phone book, Superpages has white and yellow pages along with city guides. It has find neighbors and map and directions features.

- Switchboard (www.switchboard.com) is a good resource for finding people and businesses, both addresses and phone numbers. Reverse lookups accept less than 10-digits. It also maps addresses.

- WhitePages.com (www.whitepages.com) provides address and reverse phone lookup. It includes carrier lookup, allowing you to identify cellular numbers. Other features include zip code and area code lookup for the United States and Canada. The site can save contacts to Outlook and map addresses.

- WhoWhere? (www.whowhere.com) offers people and business searches. The interface is less intuitive than others', and the site uses one form for all types of address lookup.

- Yahoo! People Search (people.yahoo.com) provides e-mail address, street address, and phone lookups. It can save contacts to Outlook and map addresses and get driving directions. It does not offer reverse phone number lookups.

FINDING BUSINESSES

18

Switchboard.com

You can use virtually any Web search engine to find information on businesses like Barnes & Noble, Disney, Federal Express, and Microsoft. Product announcements, catalogs, press releases, stock quotes, earnings reports—all these (and more) are available on the World Wide Web.

But what about the vast numbers of businesses, large and small, that have yet to establish a presence on the Web? The fact is, most companies, like most people, are *not* online.

And what if the information you're looking for is pretty straightforward—you want a street address or phone number so that you can visit the company or call to ask a specific question? Surprisingly, many business Web sites don't even include this information, or they bury it so deep that it's almost impossible to find.

What You Can Search

◆ Directory of U.S. businesses and individuals searchable by name and type of business

◆ Database of maps and driving directions

◆ Reverse phone number lookup

For situations like these, what you need is an online *yellow pages directory*. The one we'll focus on here is Switchboard. It's well designed, easy to use, and extremely fast.

continues on next page

Contact Information

Switchboard, Incorporated
Westboro, MA
Phone: 508-898-8000
E-mail: webmaster@Switchboard.com
www.Switchboard.com

With Switchboard, you can search for businesses by name or type—a standard feature of all the major yellow pages directories. Look for, say, `Italian restaurants` or `dry cleaners`, and Switchboard will present you with a list that includes the name, address, and phone number.

Another Switchboard feature you'll appreciate is the ability to set up a *search profile*. Fill out a simple form with your home and work addresses and tell Switchboard to store the information. From then on, whenever you do a search, you can automatically look for businesses that are "Near My Home" or "Near My Work." No need to worry about specifying multiple cities, zip codes, or area codes. Switchboard will present the results in order by distance, with the closest ones listed first.

Good as Switchboard is, you may from time to time have to check another yellow pages directory, either because the site is down or overloaded, or because you need to do a type of search that Switchboard doesn't offer. On those occasions, try one of these sites:

AnyWho   `www.anywho.com`

Citysearch   `www.citysearch.com`

InfoSpace   `www.infospace.com`

SmartPages   `www.smartpages.com`

SuperPages   `www.superpages.com`

Yahoo! Yellow Pages   `yp.yahoo.com`

✔ Tip

- AnyWho is the home of the AT&T Toll-Free Directory.

Finding a Web Site's Contact Information

As we've said, many business Web sites don't include a phone number or street address, either purposely or because it simply hasn't occurred to them that people might want to reach them that way. Furthermore, some companies operate on the Web using an entirely different business name from the one that's listed in print and online yellow pages directories. But that doesn't mean you can't track them down.

One way to do so is to consult the Whois database maintained by Network Solutions. Just go to the Network Solutions Web site (`www.networksolutions.com`), click Whois Lookup, and enter the *domain name* (for example, `xrefer.com` or `westward.net`) for the Web site that you're interested in finding out about.

The Whois database will provide you with the name of the company that owns the domain name, along with the mailing address, phone number, and often even a contact person.

Finding Businesses with Switchboard

To look for businesses with Switchboard, go to the Switchboard home page at www.switchboard.com (**Figure 18.1**).

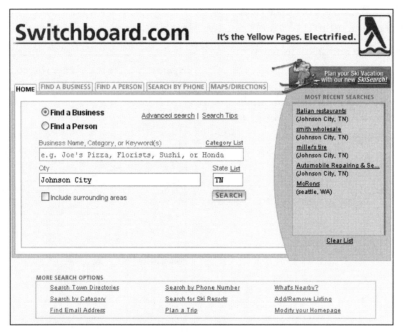

Figure 18.1 The Switchboard home page lets you search for businesses by category or by company name.

To search for businesses:

1. Enter the type of business or a specific business name and city and state in the space provided on the search form (**Figure 18.2**). Then check the Include Surrounding Areas check box to tell Switchboard that you want to search regionally, and choose a distance from the city center, up to 100 miles away.

2. Click the Search button to display your results.

   If you included surrounding areas in your search and Switchboard finds multiple listings, they'll be presented in order by distance (**Figure 18.3**).

Figure 18.2 To see results from a region, choose Include Surrounding Areas and select a distance to search within.

Figure 18.3 When Switchboard finds more than one matching business, matches are ordered by distance from the city center.

Figure 18.4 If an exact match isn't found, Switchboard displays matching categories for you to select from.

Figure 18.5 Here's a sample Switchboard search result. Choose from the links below the listing to get maps or driving directions or find nearby businesses.

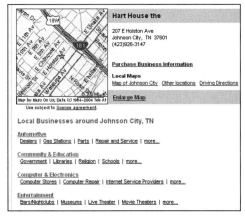

Figure 18.6 Selecting What's Nearby includes a map and business categories.

When you use categories or keywords, or if Switchboard can't find a business by the name you entered, you'll be presented with a category list to choose from. (**Figure 18.4**) Select a category to display the listings.

3. Click links below the search results for more information, such as a map and driving directions (**Figure 18.5**). Click What's Nearby to view a map and search for a list of restaurants or tourist attractions close to the selected business (**Figure 18.6**).

continues on next page

4. Choose Narrow Your Search to select businesses that offer specific services (**Figure 18.7**).

5. To do a new search, enter new keywords or a business name in the Search For field that appears at the top of the page (**Figure 18.8**). You can also use the menu buttons to choose other options available at the site—getting maps and driving directions without doing a search, finding a person, and browsing a directory of businesses organized by town.

✔ Tips

■ You can browse businesses by category (**Figure 18.9**) by selecting Category List on the Switchboard home page.

■ A list of your most recent searches is shown to the right of the search form.

■ Search from the Home tab and select the Find a Business or Find a Person radio button, or choose the Find a Business or Find a Person tab. The searches are the same either way.

■ Switchboard always performs an AND search, looking for business listings that match *all the words* in your query. (There's no way to do an OR search.) Searches are *not* case sensitive, so you can type your queries using uppercase, lowercase, or a combination, and you'll get the same results.

■ If you want to look for a particular type of business but aren't sure what search terms to use, start with a single, very general term like pets or roofing or travel. Switchboard will then present you with a list of business categories that you can choose from to focus your query.

Figure 18.7 Narrow your search to businesses offering specific services.

Figure 18.8 Use the search field at the top of the page or select a button to begin a new search.

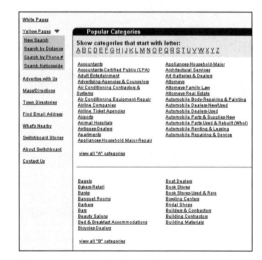

Figure 18.9 Browse businesses by category.

Figure 18.10 Choose Find a Person to search for a small business owner if the business isn't listed in the yellow pages.

- To show up in a yellow pages directory, companies must have a *business listing* with the telephone company. Many home-based businesses choose not to pay the higher rates for such listings, so you won't find them in the yellow pages. Instead, do a Switchboard Find a Person search (**Figure 18.10**). Look for the business owner's name rather than the company name.

- For a summary of Switchboard search features, see the Switchboard Quick Reference (**Table 18.1**). To find out about new features that may have been added, click the Help link that appears at the top of all Switchboard pages.

FINDING BUSINESSES WITH SWITCHBOARD

Table 18.1

Switchboard Quick Reference*	
FOR THIS TYPE OF SEARCH:	**DO THIS:**
Business Name Search	To search for a specific business, enter its name (or one or two unique words) in the search form text box.
	Select Include Surrounding Area and select the distance to include, up to 100 miles.
Business Category Search	To search for all the businesses in a particular category, type one or two unique words in the search form text box.
Point-to-Point Search	Click the Directions link that appears below every listing in your Switchboard search.
	To get maps and driving directions without searching, select the Maps/Directions tab on the Switchboard home page.

Note: Switchboard always performs an AND search, looking for all the words in your query. (There's no way to do an OR search.) Also, Switchboard ignores case.

OTHER SEARCH TOOLS FROM A TO Z

19

You've seen what a breeze it can be to use highly specialized search engines like InfoSpace (www.infospace.com) and Switchboard (www.switchboard.com). Because they're each designed for a single, relatively narrow task—looking for people and businesses in white pages and yellow pages directories similar to those used by telephone companies—the search forms are simple, and there's very little complexity to master. Just fill in the blanks and away you go.

For the most part, that's what you'll find with the 32 special-purpose search engines profiled in this chapter. Each is designed to handle searching for a particular *type* of information really well—whether it's the latest book by a favorite author or Microsoft's Technical Support phone numbers or your Aunt Harriet's zip code. Many offer help pages and search tips, but for most of them, you won't need to learn any special search rules and commands. In our experience, about the only thing that's difficult about special-purpose search engines is remembering to use them.

continues on next page

Where to Find Specialized Search Engines

When you need a special-purpose search engine for a subject not covered in this chapter, try one of these sites:

Search Engine Guide
www.searchengineguide.com

Search Engine Watch
www.searchenginewatch.com/links

That being the case, what we'll focus on here is where to find these special-purpose sites and the subject matter or type of information you can search with each one. Read the descriptions and visit some or all of the sites. Then add the ones you think you might use on a regular basis to your Web browser's Bookmarks or Favorites list. That way, you can get to them easily whenever you need them.

Allmusic.com

www.allmusic.com

If you're looking for information about your favorite artist, you can search the All Music Guide (AMG) by artist, songs, album, or genre.

Did you ever wonder how many artists recorded Pete Townshend's "Pinball Wizard"? Do you know the names of all the bands Eric Clapton was a member of? It takes just a couple of clicks at allmusic.com to find the answers to these questions and more.

✔ Tip

■ Other sites owned by AMG are All Classical Guide (`allclassical.com`), All Movie Guide (`allmovie.com`), and All Game Guide (`allgame.com`).

Amazon.com

amazon.com.

www.amazon.com

Amazon.com's mission is to sell books, and they do a superb job of that from their Web site, also known as "Earth's Biggest Bookstore." But the Web site (`www.amazon.com`) is worth learning about even if you have no intention of ever placing a book order. Imagine being able to search a database of some 2.5 million books by author, title, subject, ISBN, or publisher. You can produce a master list of all the books by a favorite author, for example, or search for every book with the word *chocolate* in the title.

You can also tap into a rich collection of reader reviews, current bestseller lists, author interviews, and book reviews from *The New York Times*, NPR, Oprah, and elsewhere.

If there's a book you're looking for that's not in the Amazon.com database (either because it's out of print or not yet published), let Amazon know and they'll try to find it for you.

✔ Tips

- You can do a quick search for books from the Amazon.com home page. But for more precise queries, click Books and then Advanced Search and use the form that allows you to specify author, title, subject, and so on.

- Barnes & Noble (`www.bn.com`) and Borders (`www.borders.com`) also offer searchable databases of current books. For used and out-of-print titles, try Alibris (`www.alibris.com`) or Bibliofind (`www.bibliofind.com`).

CDNOW

Never miss a beat.™

www.cdnow.com

Now partnered with Amazon.com, CDNOW (`www.cdnow.com`) is in the business of selling things—in this case, CDs and videos. To do so, they offer a searchable database of more than 500,000 CDs and VHS/DVD movies. You can look for a particular artist, album title, song title, record label, video title, or actor or director.

The CDNOW site also includes Top 20 lists, buyer's guides, sound clips, biographies, and entertainment news.

Centers for Disease Control and Prevention

www.cdc.com

There's enough medical and health-related information on the Internet to make your heart race and your head spin. So it's no wonder that the Web site operated by the Centers for Disease Control and Prevention (CDC) has become such a popular destination for people seeking reliable and timely information about healthcare issues.

You can do a keyword search of the entire CDC database or limit your query to the health department for a particular state. Other highlights of the CDC Web site (www.cdc.gov) include the following:

◆ **A-Z Index:** A directory of fact sheets on specific diseases and medical conditions.

◆ **Publications & Products:** Download CDC publications or read online.

◆ **Health & Safety:** Information on many topics from birth defects to traveler's health and workplace safety.

◆ **Data & Statistics:** Statistical data for health-related issues, including birth and death records, children's growth charts, and research on aging .

✔ Tip

■ Other reliable sources often cited by medical professionals include Health A to Z (www.healthatoz.com), Healthfinder (www.healthfinder.gov), and the National Library of Medicine (www.nlm.nih.gov). All three of these sites provide access to Medline, a highly respected database of medical literature, with abstracts and article summaries from *The New England Journal of Medicine, Journal of the American Medical Association*, and elsewhere.

Citysearch

www.citysearch.com

Visit Citysearch (www.citysearch.com) when visiting an unfamiliar city to find restaurants, attractions, shopping, and businesses. Use it at home to find businesses near your home or workplace.

Think of Citysearch, a division of TicketMaster, as an online yellow pages, providing local search services with up-to-date information on businesses, from restaurants and retail stores to travel and professional services for thousands of towns and cities nationwide.

◆ Search for specific types of restaurants, such as Mexican or Asian, or search by cuisine, price, or ambience.

◆ Use Citysearch to check movie show times and local concerts and events.

◆ Users can add reviews and rate local businesses.

CNET Shareware.com

SHAREWARE.com
search for shareware programs & free software

www.shareware.com

CNET Shareware.com is a "virtual software library" that let's you search a catalog of 250,000 shareware programs of all types—games, utilities, screensavers, word processor add-ons, fonts, and so forth. (Shareware is "software on the honor system." Try the program for a designated period—usually 30 days—and then register and pay for it if you decide to keep it on your system.) The programs themselves are located in shareware archives and corporate sites throughout the Internet, but they can be downloaded directly from Shareware.com (www.shareware.com).

A related CNET search service called Download.com is also offered on the Shareware.com home page. The names are confusing at first, since, as we've said, you can both search for and download shareware from Shareware.com. So what's Download.com? It's a searchable catalog of demos, drivers, and patches offered by the creators of *commercial* (rather than shareware) programs.

✔ Tips

■ For best results, use Shareware.com's drop-down menu to specify your computer platform (Windows, Linux, Macintosh, Palm, Windows CE, and so on).

■ You can use double quotation marks to search for phrases (`"download accelerator"`) and plus and minus signs to include (+) or exclude (–) search terms.

■ Searching Shareware.com and downloading software are the easy parts. The hard part is identifying the really good stuff.

Consumer World

www.consumerworld.com

Consumer World (`www.consumerworld.org`) is a master site for consumer-related information. Created in 1995 by consumer advocate and educator Edgar Dworsky, the site provides links to over 2,000 consumer resources available on the Internet (categorized for easy browsing), as well as a search form you can use to zero in on a specific topic.

Consumer agencies, product reviews, and buyer's guides from *Consumer Reports* and other sources, travel bargains and airline farefinders, the best credit card deals, health insurance options, tips for reducing junk mail—you'll find information on these and more with a Consumer World search.

✔ Tips

- Searching online for product reviews and buyer's guides is a lot easier than storing all those back issues of *Consumer Reports* and paging through them when you're ready to make a purchase decision.

- If you're a *Consumer Reports* subscriber, you might want to consider signing up for the searchable online version of the magazine, which gives you access to the current issue and four years of back issues. The annual fee is $19 for magazine subscribers ($26 for nonsubscribers). For more information, go to Consumer Reports Online at `www.consumerreports.org`.

DineSite Guide to Local Dining

DineSite.com
World-class Guides to Local Dining.

www.dinesite.com

How's this for a neat idea: collect reviews, menus, and prices for hundreds of the best restaurants all over the United States and make them available (and searchable) on the Web. That's what DineSite (`www.dinesite.com`) offers for some 12,000 metro areas across the United States.

You can search for restaurants in a given area by location, type of cuisine, price, or "amenities" (things like wheelchair access, parking, special menus, smoking rules, entertainment, outdoor dining, and so forth). You can also specify that you want to see listings only for restaurants whose write-ups include menus.

✔ Tips

- Take the time to look up your favorite restaurants and post reviews. If your favorite restaurant isn't listed, add it.

- For a second opinion on a restaurant's food, decor, service, and price, consult the popular *Zagat Surveys*, available online at Zagat.com (`www.zagat.com`). Both the Web site and the familiar pocket-sized burgundy guides are the creation of Nina and Tim Zagat—whose name, the Web site helpfully explains, is pronounced "za-GAT" (rhymes with "the cat").

Edmund's Automobile Buyer's Guides

www.edmunds.com

Edmund's Guides are required reading for anyone in the market for a new or used car. This Web site (www.edmunds.com) lets you search online for the following information, and more, whenever you need it:

- Reviews by make and model
- Road test reports
- Dealer prices
- Used car and truck prices
- Loan and lease quotes

It's actually a directory rather than a search engine, but the site is so well designed and organized that you really won't mind.

Encyclopedia Britannica

www.britannica.com

If you love the *Encyclopedia Britannica*, you'll be pleased to know that the full text of this venerable reference work is now available—and searchable—online.

Britannica.com, located on the Web at www.britannica.com, offers monthly ($9.99) and yearly ($59.95) subscriptions. You can search for free and read excerpts from articles, but you need a paid subscription to read full articles. The site gives you complete access to the *Britannica* database, along with original commentary, special multimedia presentations, and a searchable and browsable directory of outstanding Web sites, selected by *Britannica* editors to supplement your database searches.

✔ Tips

- You can use plus and minus signs in your *Encyclopedia Britannica* queries to include (+) or exclude (–) words and phrases. To search for a phrase, enclose the words in double quotation marks.

- You can use Boolean operators AND, OR, NOT, and ADJ (to look for two words adjacent to each other).

- Encarta (encarta.msn.com) offers two levels of service: free, which provides a limited number of full articles, and premium, which includes over 60,000 articles for $4.95 a month. Encarta is also included in the MSN Premium service.

- Bartleby.com (www.bartleby.com) provides free access to the *Columbia Encyclopedia* and hundreds of other books and resources.

Epicurious Food

www.eat.epicurious.com

Created by Condé Nast, the publisher of *Gourmet* and *Bon Appétit* magazines, Epicurious (`www.eat.epicurious.com`) is a cook's and food-lover's delight. You'll find complete menus, practical cooking tips and techniques, and cookbook reviews and recommendations. But the best part about the site is its Recipe File, a searchable database of more than 16,000 recipes that have appeared in *Gourmet* and *Bon Appétit*.

If you're a subscriber to one or both magazines, you'll appreciate not having to root through the recycle pile to find a recipe you forgot to clip out. Just search the database, using one or two keywords to identify the type of recipe and a unique ingredient: `eggplant and appetizer`, for example. Chances are, you'll find it.

✔ Tip

- Recipes from Martha Stewart's magazine and television show are also available online at `www.marthastewart.com`.

Expedia Travel Information

www.expedia.com

In the not so distant past, the best way to book an airline flight or plan a vacation was through a travel agent. Those days are over for most people online. Booking flights over the Internet is the easiest and often the cheapest way to book flights. One of the fastest and most reliable places to compare prices and schedules is Microsoft's Expedia travel Web site (`www.expedia.com`).

You can also use Expedia to check the status of a specific flight, search for hotels and "specialty lodgings" (apartments, country inns, and bed-and-breakfast accommodations), and locate the best car-rental deals. There's also a handy currency converter so that you can check the exchange rate just prior to leaving for a foreign country.

✔ Tips

- Sign up for Expedia's Fare Tracker service, and they'll send you an e-mail message each week alerting you to the best fares for up to three travel destinations.

- Travelocity (`www.travelocity.com`) or Orbitz (`www.orbitz.com`) are other good choices for travel information. They are similar to Expedia and offer most of the same services, including airline fare-finder and fare-tracker features.

FedEx Package Tracking

www.fedex.com

If you use overnight courier services on a regular basis, the FedEx Web site (www.fedex.com) is one you should definitely get to know. It can be a real timesaver when the FedEx phone lines are jammed, or any time you want to get a question answered quickly.

With FedEx Package Tracking, you can search the company's shipping database by airbill number to find out exactly when your shipment was delivered and who signed for it. The Drop-off Locator, another searchable database, will help you identify the nearest self-service and staffed FedEx locations and the cutoff times for dropping off your package.

✔ Tip

■ Airborne (www.airborne.com), UPS (www.ups.com), and the U.S. Postal Service (www.usps.com) also offer online package tracking services.

FindLaw Legal Resources

FindLaw.

www.findlaw.com

FindLaw (www.findlaw.com) is one of the premier sites for doing legal research on the Web. You can browse the site's legal resources directory, which is organized by topic, or use one of several FindLaw search services:

◆ **LawCrawler**, to find cases, codes, and regulations at legal sites throughout the Internet.

◆ **Supreme Court Center**, for Supreme Court decisions dating back to 1893.

◆ **Find a Lawyer**, to locate a lawyer or law firm by name, practice, or city/state.

◆ **Forms**, for over 8,000 federal and state court forms and sample agreements for small businesses.

◆ **Legal News**, for current news articles on a specific subject.

◆ **Library**, for background information in articles written by top attorneys, bar associations, and government agencies.

✔ Tips

■ To display FindLaw resources geared to your particular interests, click the appropriate link in the navigation bar at the top of the home page (Legal Professionals, Students, Business, or Public).

■ For best results, be sure to click Help at the bottom of the home page and get to know the material presented there. The search tips and advice provided in FindLaw Help and LawCrawler Information are likely to prove especially useful.

FirstGov

www.firstgov.com

An official Web site of the United States government, FirstGov (`www.firstgov.gov`) is designed to give you one-stop access to all local, state, and federal government resources that are available online. The site offers three ways for locating information:

◆ Search by keyword using the FirstGov search form.

◆ Browse the FirstGov subject directory, which is organized into topics like Agriculture and Food, Federal Benefits and Grants, and Money and Taxes.

◆ Click the link for a specific branch of the U.S. government: Executive, Legislative, or Judicial.

✔ Tips

■ FirstGov doesn't currently offer much in the way of search tips and help information, except to say that, in choosing your search terms, you should "try to be as exact as possible."

■ Give the search form a try, but if you don't find what you're looking for after a couple of queries, use the subject directory or the links for branches of government. If it's congressional activities you're interested in, for example, click Legislative Branch, and you'll find information about the United States Senate and House of Representatives, the Congressional Budget Office, and the Library of Congress. Then click Library of Congress, and you'll find a link for Thomas Legislative Information. Named in honor of Thomas Jefferson, this site (`thomas.loc.gov`) gives you access to the full text of the *Congressional Record*, all legislation currently under consideration by Congress, and historical documents such as the Declaration of Independence and the Constitution.

HighBeam Research

www.highbeam.com

Formerly the Electric Library, HighBeam Research (www.highbeam.com) is an incredible research tool. It gives you access to a searchable archive containing more than 28 million documents from over 2600 sources, some dating back 20 years. The sources include more than 150 full-text newspapers, 800 magazines, 2000 classic books, 2 international news wires, and countless maps, photographs, and TV and radio transcripts.

You can pose a question in plain English and launch a search of the entire eLibrary database, or focus on one or more types of sources (newspapers, magazines, books, pictures, maps, or transcripts).

This is a subscription service with two levels of membership: a free Basic membership, which lets you search and preview articles, or Full membership, which gives you access to complete articles for $19.95 a month or $99.95 a year. You can sign up for a seven-day free trial at the HighBeam Research Web site.

✔ Tips

- For search tips and details on the specific sources that are included in a HighBeam Research search, go to the home page and click Customer Support and then Using HighBeam eLibrary.

- To locate online English-language media outlets worldwide, try the free service called NewsDirectory. Located at www.newsdirectory.com, this site organizes more than 14,500 news sources into a searchable directory.

Information Please Almanacs

www.infoplease.com

Sometimes all you need is a quick fact or a bit of trivia—the latest population figures from the United States Census, for example, or Oprah Winfrey's birthday. When that's the case, visit Infoplease (www.infoplease.com), a free online reference site that gives you access to data from the various *Information Please* almanacs as well as material from *The Columbia Electronic Encyclopedia*, a dictionary provided by Random House, and a database of biographical information.

✔ Tip

- There's also a special kids' version of Infoplease called Fact Monster (www.factmonster.com), where school students can not only search but also ask questions and get help with homework assignments.

Internet Movie Database

www.imdb.com

"Where have I seen that actor before?" If you've ever left a movie theater puzzling over that question, you need the Internet Movie Database (IMDb). With information on over 150,000 movies and hundreds of thousands of actors, actresses, and crew members, IMDb (`www.imdb.com`) is the single best film resource we've encountered on the Web.

You can search IMDb for a specific actor or actress (or crew member) for a brief biography and a complete list of other movie credits. Or you can search by movie title to find out when a particular film was made and who was involved in the production—director, cast, and crew.

There's lots more besides, and the site is now owned by online bookseller Amazon.com, so it's sure to get better and better.

✔ Tip

- For advanced search options, such as finding the names of all the movies in which, say, Lauren Bacall and Humphrey Bogart appear together, click More Searches on the IMDb home page and then click People Working Together.

MapQuest

www.mapquest.com

MapQuest (`www.mapquest.com`) specializes in worldwide maps and driving directions between any two places in the United States. The maps won't replace your trusted road atlas or the large, fold-out variety you keep in the glove compartment of your car. But the point-to-point driving directions, including estimated mileage, are a neat feature.

Based on our experience, you'll still want to consult your favorite map or road atlas to verify the suggested route, but in general, MapQuest is pretty reliable. Give it a try before your next road trip.

✔ Tips

- If you use MapQuest often, the site has a browser toolbar you can install in Internet Explorer.

- Other map sites include MapPoint (`www.mappoint.com`) and Yahoo Maps (`maps.yahoo.com`).

MelissaData

www.melissadata.com

Geared toward direct marketers, MelissaData (`www.melissadata.com/lookups/`) has interesting demographic data available to anyone free of charge. Look up the number of home sales and average selling price, or income tax information, including average gross incomes, number of returns, average refunds, filing status, and age, in your zip code.

You can also find information on nonprofit organizations by zip code, including address, revenue, and assets.

Individuals who donated $200 or more to federal political campaigns are listed by zip code.

✔ Tips

- Would you like to see an aerial view of your neighborhood? Choose US Address Lookup and enter your street address and zip code.

- Detailed reports are available for purchase.

Microsoft Product Support Services

support.microsoft.com

If you've ever tried calling a major software company for technical support, you know how frustrating it can be to get even the simplest question answered. You either get a busy signal right from the start, or you work your way intently through the company's voice-mail menu system, only to be put on hold.

Microsoft does a better job than most at handling technical support calls, but they also supplement their phone operation with an outstanding product-support Web site, located at `support.microsoft.com`.

The site gives you access to the Microsoft Knowledge Base—the place to look for answers to questions about any Microsoft product. Other searchable databases offered at the site include Frequently Asked Questions, Download Center (for service releases, patches, and updates), and Microsoft Newsgroups.

✔ Tip

- If all else fails and you simply have to talk to a real person, click Phone Numbers to access a directory of Microsoft technical support numbers and service options, organized by product.

Monster Career Center

content.monster.com

Originally known as the Monster Board, Monster.com is the Internet's most popular job-hunting site. But in addition to its gigantic searchable database of job openings and resume postings, the site's Career Center (content.monster.com) offers one of the best collections of job-hunting and career-development resources on the Net.

You'll find sound advice on writing cover letters and resumes, the latest salary surveys from the U. S. Department of Labor's Bureau of Labor Statistics and other sources, relocation tools and calculators, and a searchable database of company information.

✔ Tip

■ The Bureau of Labor Statistics Web site (www.bls.gov) is another excellent place to look for career information and salary data. Among other things, you can search the latest edition of *The Occupational Outlook Handbook*, one of the most comprehensive sources of information on a wide range of occupations. Updated every two years, *Handbook* entries for specific occupations typically include descriptions of job activities, working conditions, education and training requirements, projected earnings, and job prospects.

New York Times Book Reviews

Books

The New York Times

www.nytimes.com/pages/books

One of several "*New York Times* on the Web" features, the Book Review site (www.nytimes.com/pages/books/) gives you access to all the book reviews, book news, and author interviews that have appeared in *The New York Times* since 1980, searchable by title, author, or keyword. You can also browse the current issue of *The New York Times Book Review*, which is supplemented by Web-only features like author interviews, complete first chapters of selected books, and expanded versions of the hardcover and paperback bestseller lists (30 titles instead of 15).

✔ Tip

■ For best results when looking for a book title or an author's name at the *New York Times* Web site, enclose the words in double quotation marks: "Ship of Gold" or "Gary Kinder".

Parent Soup

www.parentsoup.com

Whether you're awaiting the birth of your first child or packing the last one off to college, you're sure to have questions and concerns, and iVillage's Parent Soup Web site (www.parentsoup.com) may just have the answers.

Parent Soup's database includes thousands of articles on all aspects of parenting, from very specific concerns (like how to deal with the current body-piercing craze) to more general issues like baby-proofing your house and financing your child's college education.

Other popular features at the site include the following:

- The Baby Name Finder
- Pregnancy and first-year calendars
- Child and senior care directories

Peterson's Education & Career Center

www.petersons.com

Brought to you by the publishers of *Peterson's Guide to Four-Year Colleges* and dozens of other well-known education and career guides, the Peterson's site (www.petersons.com) makes much of that same information available online in searchable form.

There are separate databases for private secondary schools, colleges and universities, graduate programs, study abroad, camps and summer programs, and executive education and training.

✔ Tip

- If you've found the right school but need help figuring out how to pay for it, visit the FinAid Web site (www.finaid.org), where you can search for scholarships, fellowships, and loans.

Project Gutenberg E-Texts

www.gutenberg.net

Project Gutenberg was started 30 years ago by Michael Hart at the University of Illinois. His objective was to make all of the world's great works of literature available online so that students and researchers could study them at no cost. Volunteers from all over the world do the typing, and the project survives solely on donations.

Today, the Project Gutenberg archive (www.gutenberg.net) includes more than 3,000 works, all of which are in the public domain, so no laws are being broken. You can search the archive for the complete text of *Aesop's Fables*, *Alice in Wonderland*, the Bill of Rights, the Book of Mormon, and the King James Bible, to name just a few examples. The project is also slowly expanding to include musical scores and important images (like the original Tenniel illustrations for *Alice in Wonderland* and an MPEG file of the moon landing).

Of course, only the most dedicated and under-funded scholars would choose to read *Moby Dick* on their computer screens. The real advantage to having great works of literature available online is that they can be down-loaded to your computer and then *searched* using any word processor.

✔ Tip

- For those occasions when all you need is a quick quote (rather than the full text) from one of the literary classics, try Bartleby.com (www.bartleby.com).

Tax Forms and Information

www.1040.com

Have you ever sat down to work on your taxes, only to find that you're missing one vital form? It's probably an obscure one, too—one that's not likely to be available at the post office or library, even if they're still open when you make your discovery.

Thanks to 1040.com (www.1040.com), a service of Drake Software, you need never face this problem again. You can download federal and state tax forms, along with all the relevant instructions and publications, at any time of the day or night.

✔ Tips

- You'll need Adobe Acrobat Reader to view and print the forms that you get from 1040.com. If you don't have that program on your system already, you can download it for free at many Web sites, including 1040.com.

- The Internal Revenue Service Web site (www.irs.gov) offers tax forms, too, of course. But 1040.com is easier to use and often faster than the official government site.

Travelocity

www.travelocity.com

When you are planning a vacation or a business trip, try Travelocity (www.travelocity.com). While many people use it only to book flights and hotel rooms, you can also look for cruises and last-minute vacation deals.

Select Guides & Advice to learn about destinations. Travelocity also offers travel advice and reviews posted by other travelers.

With a Travelocity account (free), you can send travel updates, including flight status alerts and gate notifications, to your phone, fax, PDA, or pager. When you use Travelocity to track the lowest fares to your favorite destinations, you'll receive an e-mail when fares drop.

✔ Tip

- Store your frequent flyer, car rental, and hotel preferred guest numbers with your account.

TV Guide Online

www.tvguide.com

Television listings and the Internet were simply made for each other, so we're happy to report that *TV Guide* has done an excellent job with its Web site (www.tvguide.com). With the magazine, the only way to find the channels and times is to laboriously page through each day's listings. But with the *TV Guide* Web site, finding what you want is a snap!

The first time you visit the site and click TV Listings, you'll be asked to enter your zip code and type of service (cable, broadcast, or satellite). From then on, whenever you visit the site and use any of the search functions, your local area listings will be presented automatically.

✔ Tip

- The *TV Guide* Web site uses *cookies* to remember your zip code information. If you've disabled cookies in your Web browser, you'll have to enter your zip code information each time you visit the site.

UPS Package Tracking

www.ups.com

Not to be outdone by FedEx, rival United Parcel Service (UPS) also offers Package Tracking and Drop-off Locator features at its Web site (www.ups.com).

For Package Tracking, you simply enter the UPS tracking number, and you'll be presented with a detailed report on the status of your shipment. The Drop-off Locator helps you find the nearest place (often your neighborhood grocery or office-supply store) that will accept packages for shipping by UPS.

✔ Tips

■ UPS tracking numbers are typically quite long, and it's easy to make a mistake when typing them in the search form. If you were sent the tracking number in an e-mail message, use your program's Copy and Paste features to enter the number in the UPS search form instead of typing it yourself.

■ Create a My UPS account, and you can create and print shipping labels online.

Wall Street Journal Online

www.wsj.com

Don't cancel your subscription to the traditional paper version of *The Wall Street Journal* that's delivered in time to enjoy with your morning coffee or carry with you on the train for your commute to work. But if you'd like to be able to search for articles that have appeared in the *Journal* during the past 30 days, spring for an extra $39 per year ($79 for nonsubscribers) for access to the online edition, available on the Net at www.wsj.com.

✔ Tip

■ Subscribers to the online edition of *The Wall Street Journal* are also given access to the Dow Jones News/Retrieval Publications Library—more than 6,000 newspapers, news wires, magazines, trade and business journals, transcripts, and newsletters going back 20 years. You can search this database as part of your online subscription, but you'll be billed individually for any articles you choose to view and print (or save to disk)—articles are as little as $1.25 each.

Zip Code Lookups

www.usps.com

The United States Postal Service (USPS)
is the target of lots of criticism and jokes,
but here's an example of something they're
really doing right: a convenient, easy-to-use,
zip code locator. Just go to the Web site
(www.usps.com), click Find ZIP Codes, and
enter a street address, city, and state. Almost
instantly, the system tells you the nine-digit
ZIP+4 code for that location.

When you think about the time and effort
required to travel to the post office and thumb
through that big fat zip code directory there,
you know this tool is a wonderful innova-
tion—and a great example to leave you with
as we end this chapter (and this part of the
book) on special-purpose search engines.

✔ Tips

- To save keystrokes when you want to
  visit the USPS Web site, you can just type
  usps in your Web browser's Address or
  Location box.

- In addition to zip codes, you can get
  postal-rate information, order stamps,
  and track packages at the USPS Web site.

- Visit the USPS site to print prepaid shipping labels for Express or Priority Mail
  packages (www.usps.com/send).

SEARCH ENGINES QUICK REFERENCE

For each search engine covered in this book, we've assembled the most important commands and other essential information into one or more Quick Reference guides. How do you do an AND search with AltaVista or Google? Are Yahoo queries case sensitive? What Boolean operators are allowed with Lycos? This is the information we have always wanted to have at hand for our own online searches but could never find all in one place.

The Quick Reference guides appear throughout the book in the individual search engine chapters. But we've collected them all in this appendix, arranged in alphabetical order by search engine name, to make them easier to find. If you're like us, you'll be turning to these pages often as you explore the Web with your favoritie search engines.

AltaVista www.altavista.com

AltaVista Basic Search Quick Reference

FOR THIS TYPE OF SEARCH:	DO THIS:	EXAMPLES:
Plain-English Question	Simply type the question in the search form text box. Use as many words as necessary.	What is the date of the Battle of Trafalgar?
Phrase Search	Type the phrase as a sequence of words surrounded by double quotation marks.	"Battle of Trafalgar"
AND Search (multiple words and phrases, each of which must be present)	Use a plus sign (+) in front of each word or phrase that must appear in the results.	+London + "art museum"
OR Search (multiple words and phrases, any one of which may be present)	Type words or phrases separated by spaces, without any special notation.	Stratford Shakespeare
NOT Search (exclude a word or phrase)	Use a minus sign (–) in front of a word or phrase you want to exclude from the results.	+python –monty
Case-Sensitive Search	Use lowercase to find any combination of uppercase and lowercase letters. Use capital letters (initial caps or a combination of uppercase and lowercase) to force an exact match of your search term. The first example would match *Bath* (but not *bath* or *BATH*). The second example would match *BATH* only.	Bath BATH
Date Search	Not available on the Basic Search form. Use Advanced Search	
Field Search	Type the field-search keyword in lowercase, followed by a colon and your search word or phrase.	title:"Victoria and Albert Museum" host:cambridge.edu domain:com
Nested Search	Not available on the Basic Search form. Use Advanced Search.	
Proximity Search	Not available on the Basic Search form. Use Advanced Search.	
Wildcard Search	Use an asterisk (*) at the end of or within a word, along with at least three letters at the beginning of the search term.	Brit* col*r

AltaVista www.altavista.com

AltaVista Advanced Search Quick Reference

FOR THIS TYPE OF SEARCH:	DO THIS:	EXAMPLES:
Plain-English Question	Not recommended on Advanced Web Search form. Use Basic Search instead.	
Phrase Search	Just type the phrase in the search box (*without* quotation marks). AltaVista interprets as a phrase any words that appear together without a search operator between them.	Tower of London
AND Search (multiple words and phrases, each of which must be present)	Use AND between words or phrases to specify that both must be present in the results.	Oxford AND Cambridge
OR Search (multiple words and phrases, any one of which may be present)	Use OR between words or phrases to specify that you want to find references to either or both terms.	Oxford OR Cambridge
NOT Search (exclude a word or phrase)	Use AND NOT in front of the word or phrase you want to exclude from the query.	Oxford AND NOT Cambridge
Case-Sensitive Search	Use lowercase to find any *combination* of uppercase and lowercase letters. Use capital letters (initial caps or a combination of uppercase and lowercase) to force an *exact match* of your search term, as shown in the example.	Round Table
Date Search	Type the range of dates you want to search in the From and To boxes, using the format *DD/MM/YY*. The example would search for dates between January 1, 2001, and December 3, 2001 (not March 12, 2001).	From: 01/01/01 To: 03/12/01
Field Search	Type field-search keyword in lowercase, immediately followed by a colon and your search word or phrase.	title:Castle Howard domain:com host:cambridge.edu
Nested Search	Use parentheses to group search expressions into more complex queries. The example would find *Queen Mother* as well as *Queen Mum*.	Queen (Mother OR Mum)
Proximity Search	Use NEAR to find words or phrases that appear within 10 words of each other. The example would find *bed and breakfast* as well as *bed & breakfast* and *breakfast in bed*.	bed NEAR breakfast.
Wildcard Search	Enter an asterisk (*) at the end of or within a word and at least three letters at the beginning of the search term.	bicycl* col*r

AltaVista www.altavista.com

AltaVista Field Search Quick Reference		
SEARCH TERM:	**DESCRIPTION:**	**EXAMPLES:**
anchor:	Searches for Web pages that contain the specified hyperlink.	anchor:"free product samples"
applet:	Searches for Java applets. If you don't know the name of the applet, try combining an applet wildcard search with some other search term.	applet:beeper +applet:* +Java
domain:	Searches Web addresses for a specific domain (com, edu, gov, net, and so on) or two-letter Internet country code. (See Appendix B for a complete list.)	domain:edu domain:uk
host:	Searches just the host name portion of Web addresses.	host:beatlefest.com host:oxford.edu host:BBC
image:	Searches Web pages for the file names of images that match your search term.	image:ringo.gif image:*.gif
like:	Searches for Web pages similar to (or related in some way to) the specified URL.	like:www.beatle.net
link:	Searches for hypertext links (URLs) embedded in a Web page.	link:www.songlyrics.com
text:	Searches for text in the body of the Web page.	text:"Strawberry Fields"
title:	Limits the search to the part of the Web page that the author labeled as the title.	title:"John Lennon"
url:	Searches for text in complete Web addresses (URLs).	url:beatles.html

AOL Search *search.aol.com*

AOL Search Quick Reference		
FOR THIS TYPE OF SEARCH:	DO THIS:	EXAMPLES:
Plain-English Question	Type a question that expresses the idea or concept, using as many words as necessary.	`Does Norm Abram have a Web site`
Phrase Search	Type the phrase enclosed in double quotation marks or use phrase connectors.	`"New Yankee Workshop"` or `brother-in-law`
AND Search (multiple words and phrases, each of which must be present)	Type words or phrases separated by a space. You can also use the Boolean operator AND (uppercase or lowercase) to connect two or more search terms or put plus signs (+) directly in front of required search terms. All three examples will produce the same results.	`"paint shaver" clapboard` `"paint shaver" AND clapboard` `+"paint shaver" +clapboard`
OR Search (multiple words and phrases, *any* one of which may be present)	Use the Boolean operator OR (uppercase or lowercase) to combine words and phrases.	`woodworking OR cabinetry`
NOT Search (exclude a word or phrase)	Use a minus sign (–) to exclude a word or phrase.	`"custom windows" -software`
Case-Sensitive Search	Not available.	
Date Search	Advanced Search option.	
Field Search	Advanced Search option.	

Ask Jeeves www.ask.com

Ask Jeeves Quick Reference

FOR THIS TYPE OF SEARCH:	DO THIS:	EXAMPLES:
Word or Phrase Search	Type the phrase enclosed in quotation marks or use punctuation marks to separate words.	`"detroit tigers"` or `detroit.tigers`
AND Search (multiple words and phrases, each of which must be present)	The default search type; AND is not required.	`Asia business`
OR Search (multiple words and phrases, any one of which may be present)	Use OR to connect two or more words or phrases, either one of which may appear in the guide's title or keywords.	`justice OR judicial`
Wildcard Search	Not supported.	
Nested Search	Use parentheses to group search expressions into more complex queries. The example would find references to *art museum* and *art gallery*.	`art (museum OR gallery)`
Weather	Get local weather forecasts. Enter `weather` and the city name or zip code in the search form, in either order.	`weather Austin` or `37601 weather`
Stock Quotes and Information	Enter the stock symbol or company name and stock	`quote. Msft stock quote`
Famous People	Enter the person's name to get pictures, bibliographical information, and related links a famous people.	`Abe Lincoln`
Weights and Measures	Enter a phrase or question about weights or measures to open the weights and measures converter. Time, data, weight, length, area, volume, and temperature conversions are supported.	`how many feet in a mile`

Excite www.excite.com

Excite Quick Reference

FOR THIS TYPE OF SEARCH:	DO THIS:	EXAMPLES:
Plain-English Question	Simply type a phrase or question that expresses the idea or concept. Use as many words as necessary	thoroughbred racing in Kentucky Where can I find information about thoroughbred racing in Kentucky?
Phrase Search	Type the phrase enclosed in double quotation marks.	"Kentucky Derby"
AND Search (multiple words and phrases, each of which must be present)	Use AND in front of each word or phrase that must appear in the results.	racing AND "Churchill Downs"
OR Search (multiple words and phrases, one of which may be present)	Type words or phrases separated by a space or use OR between each word or phrase	Derby Preakness Derby OR Preakness
NOT Search (to exclude a word)	Type a minus sign (–) directly in front of the word or phrase you want to exclude from your results. (Note that there's no space between the minus sign and the search word or phrase.)	"horse race" –Derby
	Or use ANDNOT in front of the word or phrase you want to exclude.	"horse race" ANDNOT Derby
Case-Sensitive Search	Not available.	
Date Search	Use to find pages updated before, between, or after a specific date. (Advanced Search option)	
Field Search	Not available.	
Nested Search	Use parentheses to group Boolean expressions into complex queries.	racing AND (horse OR thoroughbred)
Proximity Search	Not available.	
Wildcard Search	Not available.	

Google www.google.com

Google Quick Reference

FOR THIS TYPE OF SEARCH:	DO THIS:	EXAMPLES:
Plain-English Question	Simply type a phrase or question that expresses the idea or concept, using as many words as necessary.	`Who invented the steam engine?`
Phrase Search	Type the phrase surrounded by double quotation marks (common words will be ignored, even with quotation marks).	`"industrial revolution"`

AND Search (multiple words and phrases, each of which must be present)	Type the words (or phrases in quotation marks) separated by a space, without any special punctuation. Use a plus sign (+) only if one of the words in your query is a very common word (or *stopword*).	`Edison "light bulb"`
		
		`+about guides history`

OR Search (multiple words and phrases, any one of which may be present)	Type words or phrases (no quotation marks allowed) separated by OR (full caps required).	`phonograph OR speaking machine`
NOT Search (to exclude a word or phrase)	Use a minus sign (–) directly in front of the word or phrase you want to exclude.	`Lincoln -"town car"`
Synonym Search	Use a tilde (~) in front of the search word to include synonyms in the search.	`~food` returns recipes and nutrition information.
Case-Sensitive Search	Not available.	
Date Search	Advanced search option; choose from within the last three months, six months, or year.	
Field Search	Type the field-search term followed by a colon and the search word or phrase. Note that there is no space after the colon. (For fill-in-the-blanks field searching, use Advanced Search.)	
	Titles. Use `allintitle:` or `intitle:` with one or more search words. The first example would look for *both* words in page titles; the second would look for *either* word.	`allintitle:inventions inventors` `intitle:inventions inventors`
	URLs. Use `allinurl:` or `inurl:` with one or more words to find in the URL. The first example you want would look for *both* words; the second would look up *either* word.	`allinurl:pdf 1099` `inurl:patents trademarks`
	Domains. Use `site:` followed by a domain name or type (com, edu, gov, and so on) along with the search word or phrase you want to find at that site or domain type.	`site:nationalgeographic.com inventions` `site:gov patents`
	The first example would find pages at the National Geographic Web site that include the word *inventions*. The second would find government (gov) Web sites that include the word *patents*.	
	Links. Use `link:` with a specific Web address to find all pages that link to that address. The example would find pages that link to the U.S. Patent and Trademark Office. You *cannot* combine a `link:` search term with another search word or phrase.	`link:www.uspto.gov`
Numeric Range	Type the lower number, followed by three periods and the higher number. Don't use spaces between the numbers or periods. Leave either number off to do an open-ended search.	`20...30 ...100 1000...`
Nested Search	Not available.	
Proximity Search	Not available.	
Wildcard Search	Not available.	

Google www.google.com

Google Specialty Search Formats and Keywords

FOR THIS TYPE OF SEARCH:	USE THIS FORMAT:	EXAMPLES:
Address Lookup	Enter the last name and the city and state or zip code. Punctuation and case are ignored.	smith jackson tn
Airline Flight Information	Enter the flight number.	ua11 or usair 782
Airport Weather and Delays	Enter the airport code followed by the word *airport*.	jfk airport
Business Search	Enter the business type and the city. The state is optional but should be used for smaller cities.	pizza cleveland
Calculator	Enter an equation or natural-language query.	3.6 miles in km or 5*5+23
FAA Airplane Registration Numbers	Enter the plane's number, usually found on a plane's tail.	n199ua
FCC Equipment IDs	Put the word *fcc* before the equipment ID and include spaces or dashes. Not case sensitive.	fcc B4Z-34009-PIR
FedEx Tracking Numbers	Enter the tracking number.	999999999999
Map Addresses	Enter the street and the city and state or zip code. Punctuation and case are ignored.	124 main johnson city tn
Patent Numbers	Put the word *patent* before the patent number.	patent 5123123
Telephone Area Codes	Enter the three-digit area code.	650
Telephone Numbers (reverse lookup)	Enter the 10-digit number. You can also use the traditional format, with parentheses or hyphens, but the format with periods will not work.	4235551212 or (423) 555-1212 or 423-555-1212 are acceptable; 423.555.1212 won't work.
UPC Codes	Enter the number without spaces or dashes; be sure to include the first and last numbers.	073333531084
UPS Tracking Numbers	Enter the tracking number.	1Z9999W999999999
USPS Tracking Numbers	Enter the number as received from USPS, including spaces.	1234 1234 1234 1234 1234 1234 12
Vehicle ID Numbers (VINs)	Enter the number as written.	1AAAAA999A9AA99999

Google Groups groups.google.com

Google Groups Quick Reference

FOR THIS TYPE OF SEARCH:	DO THIS:	EXAMPLES:
Plain-English Question	Not recommended. Use a phrase or AND search instead.	
Phrase Search	Type the phrase as a sequence of words surrounded by double quotation marks.	"forensic medicine"
AND Search (multiplewords and phrases, each of which must be present)	Simply type the words or phrases separated by a space.	cholesterol exercise
OR Search (multiple words and phrases, any one of which may be present)	Use OR or | (pipe symbol) to connect two or more words or phrases. Both examples would find newsgroup postings that mention either *fitness* or *nutrition*.	fitness OR nutrition fitness | nutrition
NOT Search (exclude a word or phrase)	Use a minus sign (–) in front of a word or phrase you want to exclude from your results. To look for postings about vitamins but not herbal vitamins, for example, you might want to exclude *herbal*	vitamins -herbal
Case-Sensitive Search	Not available.	
Field Search	Use the Advanced Groups Search form for fill-in-the-blank searching of newsgroup author, subject, and newsgroup name fields.	
	Alternatively, you can use the following field-search operators on the search form itself:	
	Author: *author:*	author:bjones@nih.edu
	Subject: *insubject:*	insubject:"lyme disease"
	Group name: *group:*	group:sci.med.diseases
Nested Search	Use parentheses to group search expressions into more complex queries. The example would find postings that mention *clinical study* or *clinical trial*.	clinical (study OR trial)
Proximity Search	Not supported.	
Wildcard Search	Not supported.	

HotBot www.hotbot.com

HotBot Quick Reference	
FOR THIS TYPE OF SEARCH:	DO THIS:
Plain-English Question	Simply type the question in the search form and select All of the Words from the search form's Word Filter menu.
Phrase Search	Type the phrase with or without quotation marks and select Exact Phrase on the Word Filter menu.
	To look for multiple phrases or for a phrase and a single word, put the phrase in quotation marks and select All of the Words from the Word Filter menu.
AND Search (multiple words and phrases, each of which must be present)	Type words and/or phrases and select All of the Words from the Word Filter menu. You can type a plus sign (+) in front of each word or phrase, but it's not really necessary with an All of the Words search.
	You can also combine words and phrases with AND and select Boolean Phrase from the Word Filter menu.
OR Search (multiple words and phrases, any one of which may be present)	Type words or phrases separated by spaces and select Any of the Words from the Word Filter menu. Alternatively, combine words and phrases with OR and choose Boolean Phrase from the Word Filter menu.
NOT Search (to exclude a word or phrase)	Type a minus sign (–) in front of a word or phrase you want to exclude from the results. Alternatively, use NOT in front of the word or phrase and specify Boolean Phrase.
Date Search	Use the Date menu on the Advanced Search form to select a time frame (one week to two years).
Field Search (Web page titles)	Choose In the Title from the Word Filter menu on the HotBot home page to specify that you want to search the page title.
	Alternatively, you can use the HotBot meta word `title:` in your query.
Field Search (geography, domain, or domain type)	Use the HotBot meta word `domain:`. For example, enter `domain:jp` to look for sites in Japan. Enter `domain:com` to look for commercial sites in North America.
	Alternatively, you can click Advanced Search and use the Location/Domain section to focus your search on a particular geographic region, country, domain, or domain type (`com`, `edu`, `gov`, and so on).
Field Search	Use the Page Content section to search for specific file types, including image, video, MP3, or JavaScript files.
	Alternatively, you can use `feature:` meta words in your queries on the HotBot home page to find plug-ins, embedded scripts, Java applets, audio and video files, and so on.

HotBot www.hotbot.com

HotBot Meta Words Quick Reference	
META WORD FORMAT:	WHAT IT DOES:
title:*word or phrase*	Searches Web page titles for the word or phrase you specify: for example, title:Edmund's or title:"car guides".
domain:*name*	Restricts searches to the specified domain name. Domains can be specified up to three levels: for example, domain:com, domain:ford.com, and domain:www.ford.com.
linkdomain:*name*	Restricts searches to pages containing links to the domain you specify. For example, linkdomain:edmunds.com finds pages that point to the Edmund's Car Guides Web site.
feature:acrobat	Searches for Adobe Acrobat files.
feature:applet	Searches for pages with embedded Java applets.
feature:activex	Detects ActiveX controls or layouts.
feature:audio	Searches for audio formats.
feature:embed	Searches for plug-ins.
feature:flash	Searches for Macromedia Flash plug-in HTML.
feature:form	Searches for forms in HTML documents.
feature:frame	Searches for frames in HTML documents.
feature:image	Searches for image files (GIF, JPEG, and so on).
feature:script	Searches for embedded scripts.
feature:shockwave	Searches for Macromedia Shockwave files.
feature:table	Searches for tables in HTML documents.
feature:video	Searches for video formats.
feature:vrml	Searches for VRML files.
scriptlanguage:javascript	Searches for pages containing JavaScript. (Note that lowercase is required for the term *javascript*.)
scriptlanguage:vbscript	Searches for pages containing VBScript. (Note that lowercase is required for the term *vbscript*.)

InfoSpace www.infospace.com

InfoSpace Quick Reference

FOR THIS TYPE OF SEARCH:	DO THIS:
E-mail Address Search (Worldwide)	Click Email Search on the InfoSpace home page to display the search form. Start by completing just the Last Name and First Name fields.
	To narrow a search, complete additional fields one at a time, in this order: Country, State/Province, City.
	To broaden a search, try a partial entry in the First Name field. Searching for A in the First Name field and Fletcher in the Last Name field would find listings for *Albert, Al,* and *A. S. Fletcher.*
Phone Number and Address Search	Click White Pages on the InfoSpace home page to display the search form. Start by completing the Last Name, First Name, and State fields.
	To narrow a search, complete the City field.
	To broaden a search, try a partial entry in the First Name field. Searching for Jo Anderson would find listings for *Joe Anderson* as well as *Joseph Anderson.*
	Another way to broaden a search that includes a City field is to select the Search Metro Area option.
Reverse Lookup	Click Reverse Lookup on the InfoSpace home page and enter phone and fax numbers, street addresses, e-mail addresses, and area codes.

Lycos www.lycos.com

Lycos Quick Reference		
FOR THIS TYPE OF SEARCH:	DO THIS:	EXAMPLES:
Plain-English Question	Simply type a phrase or question that expresses the idea or concept, using as many words as necessary.	Are oyster mushrooms poisonous?
Phrase Search	Enclose the phrase in double quotation marks.	"edible mushrooms"
AND Search (multiple words and phrases, each of which must be present)	Type words or phrases separated by a space, without any special punctuation. By default, Lycos searches for *all* the words in your query, so even though plus signs (+) are allowed, you'll get the same results without them. The two examples shown here would return identical results: Web pages that contain both the phrase *oyster mushrooms* and the word *recipes*.	"oyster mushrooms" recipes +"oyster mushrooms" +recipes
OR Search (multiple words and phrases, any *one* of which may be present)	Enclose the words or phrases in parentheses. The example would find Web pages that include references to either *edible mushrooms* or *mycology*.	("edible mushrooms" mycology)
NOT Search (exclude a word or phrase)	Use a minus sign (–) in front of a word or phrase you want to exclude from your results.	mushrooms -recipes
Case-Sensitive Search	Not available.	
Date Search	Not available.	
Field Search	To search titles of Web page documents, type title: directly in front of a word or phrase. (Note that there's no space between the colon and the search term.) For URL, site, and referring URL field searches, use Advanced Search.	title:mushrooms title:"mushroom gardening"
Nested Search	Not available.	
Proximity Search	Not available.	
Wildcard Search	Not available.	

MSN Search search.msn.com

MSN Search Basic Search Quick Reference

FOR THIS TYPE OF SEARCH:	DO THIS:	EXAMPLES:
Plain-English Question	Simply type a question that expresses the idea or concept, using as many words as necessary.	What's the best place for cross-country skiing in Minnesota?
Phrase Search	Type the phrase enclosed in double quotation marks.	"Gunflint Lodge"
AND Search (multiple words and phrases, each of which must be present)	Type words or phrases separated by a space. MSN Search automatically searches for *all* the words, so plus signs (+) aren't necessary.	skiing snowboarding
OR Search (multiple words and phrases, any one of which may be present)	Not available. Use Advanced Search.	
NOT Search	Use a minus sign (–) directly in front of the word or phrase you want to exclude from your results. (Note that there's no space between the minus sign and the search word.)	skiing -downhill
Case-Sensitive Search	Not available.	
Date Search	Not available. Use Advanced Search.	
Field Search	Not available. Use Advanced Search.	
Nested Search	Not available. Use Advanced Search.	
Proximity Search	Not available.	
Wildcard Search	Not available. Use Advanced Search.	

MSN Search search.msn.com

MSN Search Advanced Search Quick Reference		
FOR THIS TYPE OF SEARCH:	DO THIS:	EXAMPLES:
Plain-English Question	Type a question that expresses the idea or concept and choose All the Words on the Find menu.	When was the Mir space station launched"?
Phrase Search	Type the phrase without any special punctuation and choose The Exact Phrase on the Find menu.	Hubble space telescope
AND Search (multiple words and phrases, each of which must be present)	Type words or phrases separated by a space and choose All the Words on the Find menu. Alternatively, you can combine words and phrases with the Boolean operator AND (full caps required) and choose Boolean Phrase on the Find menu.	"space camp" scholarships "space camp" AND scholarships
OR Search (multiple words and phrases, any one of which may be present)	Type words or phrases separated by a space and choose Any of the Words on Find menu. Alternatively, you can combine words and phrases with the Boolean operator OR (full caps required) and choose Boolean Phrase on the Find menu.	NASA "space program" NASA OR "space program"
NOT Search (to exclude a word or phrase)	Use the Boolean operator AND NOT (full caps required) with the word or phrase you want to exclude and choose Boolean Phrase on Find menu.	shuttle AND NOT challenger
Case-Sensitive Search	Not available.	
Field Search	Three types of field searches are possible:	
	Titles. Type search words or phrases in the search box and choose Words in Title on the Find menu.	astronaut hall of fame
	Links. Type the complete URL (including http://) in the search box and choose Links to URL on the Find menu.	http://www.astronaut.org
	Domain. Use the Domain text box on the form to limit your search to a domain type (com, edu, gov, org, and so on) or to a specific domain.	Domain: nasa.gov Domain: com
Nested Search	Combine search terms with Boolean operators and parentheses and choose Boolean Phrase from the Find menu.	(NASA OR "space program") AND budget AND 2001
Proximity Search	Not available.	
Wildcard Search	Use the Enable Stemming option to automatically search for both *root* words and *variations*. With stemming enabled, a search for *budget* would also find references to *budgets*, *budgetary*, and *budgeting*.	budget

Switchboard www.switchboard.com

Switchboard Quick Reference*	
FOR THIS TYPE OF SEARCH:	DO THIS:
Business Name Search	To search for a specific business, enter its name (or one or two unique words) in the search form text box.
	Select Include Surrounding Area and select the distance to include, up to 100 miles.
Business Category Search	To search for all the businesses in a particular category, type one or two unique words in the search form text box.
Point-to-Point Search	Click the Directions link that appears below every listing in your Switchboard search.
	To get maps and driving directions without searching, select the Maps/Directions tab on the Switchboard home page.

Note: Switchboard always performs an AND search, looking for all the words in your query. (There's no way to do an OR search.) Also, Switchboard ignores case.

Yahoo www.yahoo.com

Yahoo Quick Reference

FOR THIS TYPE OF SEARCH:	DO THIS:	EXAMPLES:
Plain-English Question	Not recommended.	
Phrase Search	Type the phrase as a sequence of words surrounded by double quotation marks.	`"Russian lacquer boxes"`
AND Search (multiple words and phrases, each of which must be present)	Use a plus sign (+) in front of a word or phrase that *must* appear in the results.	`+antiques +Victorian`
OR Search (multiple words and phrases, *any* one of which may be present)	Type words or phrases separated by a space, without any special notation.	`eggs "Carl Faberge"`
NOT Search (to exclude a word or phrase)	Use a minus sign (–) in front of a word or phrase you want to exclude from your results. To find software Easter eggs, for example, you might want to exclude the word *Fabergé*.	`"Easter eggs" -Faberge`
Case-Sensitive Search	Not available.	
Date Search	Not available. However, you *can* search for categories and Web sites that have been added to the Yahoo directory within a certain time frame.	
	To do that, click Advanced Search on the Yahoo home page and use the drop-down menu to select a time frame.	
Field Search	To search titles of Web page documents, enter `intitle:` directly in front of a word or phrase.	`intitle:"oriental rugs"`
	To search Web page URLs, enter `inurl:` directly in front of the word you want to find.	`inurl:carpeting`
	To search within a domain, enter `site:` directly in front of the domain you want to search.	`site:microsoft.com`
	To limit a search to a particular host, enter `hostname:` in front of the domain.	`hostname:office.microsoft.com`
	To search for multiple words in fields, use multiple search terms with plus signs (+).	`+inurl:oriental +inurl:rug`
	To not include a keyword in the results, use a minus sign (–) before the field name.	`intitle:oriental -intitle:rugs` or `Xbox -site:microsoft.com`
	To search for documents or other sites that are linked to a site, use `link:`	`link:http://www.microsoft.com`
Nested Search	Not available.	
Proximity Search	Not available.	

Yahoo www.yahoo.com

Yahoo Special Search Shortcuts

To find:	Do this:	Examples:
Airport Information (with links to the latest conditions, links to maps, directions, local weather, and airport terminal maps where available)	Enter an airport name or airport code.	`hartsfield airport` or `atl airport`
Book Search	Enter the book's ISBN.	`032122373X`
Definitions (from the American Heritage® Dictionary and a link to additional meanings and related information, including pronunciation and etymology)	Enter `define` followed by any English word.	`define rampage`
FAA Registration Numbers.	Enter the aircraft registration number, usually found on the tail of an airplane.	`n3601p`
FedEx Tracking	Enter `fedex` plus the tracking number.	`fedex 12345678`
Flight Tracker	Enter an airline name or code and flight number.	`American airlines 22` or `aa 22`
Hotel Search (location and links to a detailed description of the property, including a map showing the property's location in relation to various points of interest, and a calendar to check availability)	Enter the type of accommodation and location desired.	`dallas hotels` or `Asheville bed and breakfast`
Maps and Driving Directions	Enter a street address, city, and state or the keyword `map` and a location.	`55 e broadway new york` or `map chicago`
News	Enter the keyword `news` and any topic news currently in	`election the news.`
Patents	Enter `patent` and any U.S. patent number.	`patent 1234567`
Sports: College (scores and information about games in progress)	Enter a college or team name, the name of the sport, and the keyword `scores`.	`duke basketball scores`
Sports: Professional (scores and information about games in progress)	Enter a team name and the keyword `scores`.	`dodger scores`
Stock Quotes (including latest price, intraday chart, news headlines, and links to additional financial information)	Enter `Quote` and the ticker symbol.	`quote msft`
Traffic Reports	Enter the location followed by the keyword `traffic`.	`Chicago traffic`
UPC Bar Codes (with links to product information)	Enter the UPC bar code.	`01795106435`
UPS Tracking	Enter the tracking code.	`1Z40EW620354504737`
USPS Tracking	Enter `usps` and the tracking number.	`usps 1234 1234 1234 1234`
Vehicle Identification Number (VIN)	Enter the 17-character VIN.	`ZFFYT53A510122721`
Weather (current conditions)	Enter `weather` and a location.	`weather houston`
Yellow Pages Search	Enter a business category and a city or a business name in a city.	`starbucks omaha` or `restaurants in denver`

INTERNET DOMAINS AND COUNTRY CODES

Many search engines let you look for Web sites based on Internet *domains* and *country* codes. Searching by domain allows you to focus your search on a particular *type* of organization: commercial, education, government, and so on. Searching by country code makes it possible to zero in on (or avoid) sites that originate in a specific country.

To help you take full advantage of domain and country-code search options, this appendix includes three tables (**Tables B.1**, **B.2**, and **B.3**):

◆ **Country Codes (alphabetical by country)**

◆ **Country Codes (alphabetical by code)**

◆ **Top-Level Domains (TLDs):** Includes the seven original TLDs as well as those added in 2001.

Even if you never have occasion to do a country-code or domain search, this information may come in handy from time to time, simply for deciphering an e-mail or Web site address. Internet domains are pretty obvious, but you'll find that country codes aren't always easy to guess: AU, for example, is Australia (not Austria, which is AT).

Table B.1

Country Codes (alphabetical by country)					
Afghanistan	AF	Chad	TD	Gibraltar	GI
Albania	AL	Chile	CL	Greece	GR
Algeria	DZ	China	CN	Greenland	GL
American Samoa	AS	Christmas Island	CX	Grenada	GD
Andorra	AD	Cocos (Keeling) Islands	CC	Guadeloupe	GP
Angola	AO	Colombia	CO	Guam	GU
Anguilla	AI	Comoros	KM	Guatemala	GT
Antarctica	AQ	Congo	CG	Guinea	GN
Antigua/Barbuda	AG	Congo, Dem. Republic of	CD	Guinea-Bissau	GW
Argentina	AR	Cook Islands	CK	Guyana	GY
Armenia	AM	Costa Rica	CR	Haiti	HT
Aruba	AW	Cote D'Ivoire	CI	Heard Island/ McDonald Islands	HM
Australia	AU	Croatia	HR	Holy See (Vatican)	VA
Austria	AT	Cuba	CU	Honduras	HN
Azerbaijan	AZ	Cyprus	CY	Hong Kong	HK
Bahamas	BS	Czech Republic	CZ	Hungary	HU
Bahrain	BH	Denmark	DK	Iceland	IS
Bangladesh	BD	Djibouti	DJ	India	IN
Barbados	BB	Dominica	DM	Indonesia	ID
Belarus	BY	Dominican Republic	DO	Iran	IR
Belgium	BE	East Timor	TP	Iraq	IQ
Belize	BZ	Ecuador	EC	Ireland	IE
Benin	BJ	Egypt	EG	Israel	IL
Bermuda	BM	El Salvador	SV	Italy	IT
Bhutan	BT	Equatorial Guinea	GQ	Ivory Coast	CI
Bolivia	BO	Eritrea	ER	Jamaica	JM
Bosnia-Herzegovina	BA	Estonia	EE	Japan	JP
Botswana	BW	Ethiopia	ET	Jordan	JO
Bouvet Island	BV	Falkland Islands (Malvinas)	FK	Kazakstan	KZ
Brazil	BR	Faroe Islands	FO	Kenya	KE
British Indian Ocean Territory	IO	Fiji	FJ	Kiribati	KI
Brunei Darussalam	BN	Finland	FI	Korea (North)	KP
Bulgaria	BG	France	FR	Korea (South)	KR
Burkina Faso	BF	French Guiana	GF	Kuwait	KW
Burundi	BI	French Polynesia	PF	Kyrgyzstan	KG
Cambodia	KH	French Southern Territories	TF	Laos	LA
Cameroon	CM	Gabon	GA	Latvia	LV
Canada	CA	Gambia	GM	Lebanon	LB
Cape Verde	CV	Georgia	GE	Lesotho	LS
Cayman Islands	KY	Germany	DE	Liberia	LR
Central African Republic	CF	Ghana	GH	Libyan Arab Jamahiriya	LY

Country Codes (alphabetical by country)

Country	Code	Country	Code	Country	Code
Liechtenstein	LI	Palau	PW	Sweden	SE
Lithuania	LT	Palestinian Territory	PS	Switzerland	CH
Luxembourg	LU	Panama	PA	Syrian Arab Republic	SY
Macau	MO	Papua New Guinea	PG	Taiwan	TW
Macedonia	MK	Paraguay	PY	Tajikistan	TJ
Madagascar	MG	Peru	PE	Tanzania	TZ
Malawi	MW	Philippines	PH	Thailand	TH
Malaysia	MY	Pitcairn	PN	Togo	TG
Maldives	MV	Poland	PL	Tokelau	TK
Mali	ML	Portugal	PT	Tonga	TO
Malta	MT	Puerto Rico	PR	Trinidad and Tobago	TT
Marshall Islands	MH	Qatar	QA	Tunisia	TN
Martinique	MQ	Reunion	RE	Turkey	TR
Mauritania	MR	Romania	RO	Turkmenistan	TM
Mauritius	MU	Russian Federation	RU	Turks and Caicos Islands	TC
Mayotte	YT	Rwanda	RW	Tuvalu	TV
Mexico	MX	Saint Helena	SH	Uganda	UG
Micronesia	FM	Saint Kitts and Nevis	KN	Ukraine	UA
Moldova	MD	Saint Lucia	LC	United Arab Emirates	AE
Monaco	MC	Saint Pierre and Miquelon	PM	United Kingdom	UK
Mongolia	MN	Saint Vincent and Grenadines	VC	United States	US
Montserrat	MS	Samoa	WS	U.S. Minor Outlying Islands	UM
Morocco	MA	San Marino	SM	Uruguay	UY
Mozambique	MZ	Sao Tome and Principe	ST	Uzbekistan	UZ
Myanmar	MM	Saudi Arabia	SA	Vanuatu	VU
Namibia	NA	Senegal	SN	Vatican City State	VA
Nauru	NR	Seychelles	SC	Venezuela	VE
Nepal	NP	Sierra Leone	SL	Viet Nam	VN
Netherlands	NL	Singapore	SG	Virgin Islands (British)	VG
Netherlands Antilles	AN	Slovakia	SK	Virgin Islands (U.S.)	VI
New Caledonia	NC	Slovenia	SI	Wallis and Futuna	WF
New Zealand	NZ	Solomon Islands	SB	Western Sahara	EH
Nicaragua	NI	Somalia	SO	Yemen	YE
Niger	NE	South Africa	ZA	Yugoslavia	YU
Nigeria	NG	South Georgia/ Sandwich Islands	GS	Zambia	ZM
Niue	NU	Spain	ES	Zimbabwe	ZW
Norfolk Island	NF	Sri Lanka	LK		
Northern Mariana Islands	MP	Sudan	SD		
Norway	NO	Suriname	SR		
Oman	OM	Svalbard and Jan Mayen	SJ		
Pakistan	PK	Swaziland	SZ		

INTERNET DOMAINS AND COUNTRY CODES

Table B.2

Country Codes (alphabetical by code)					
AD	Andorra	CI	Cote D'Ivoire (Ivory Coast)	GP	Guadeloupe
AE	United Arab Emirates	CK	Cook Islands	GQ	Equatorial Guinea
AF	Afghanistan	CL	Chile	GR	Greece
AG	Antigua/Barbuda	CM	Cameroon	GS	South Georgia/ Sandwich Islands
AI	Anguilla	CN	China		
AL	Albania	CO	Colombia	GT	Guatemala
AM	Armenia	CR	Costa Rica	GU	Guam
AN	Netherlands Antilles	CU	Cuba	GW	Guinea-Bissau
AO	Angola	CV	Cape Verde	GY	Guyana
AQ	Antarctica	CX	Christmas Island	HK	Hong Kong
AR	Argentina	CY	Cyprus	HM	Heard Island/ McDonald Islands
AS	American Samoa	CZ	Czech Republic		
AT	Austria	DE	Germany	HN	Honduras
AU	Australia	DJ	Djibouti	HR	Croatia
AW	Aruba	DK	Denmark	HT	Haiti
AZ	Azerbaijan	DM	Dominica	HU	Hungary
BA	Bosnia-Herzegovina	DO	Dominican Republic	ID	Indonesia
BB	Barbados	DZ	Algeria	IE	Ireland
BD	Bangladesh	EC	Ecuador	IL	Israel
BE	Belgium	EE	Estonia	IN	India
BF	Burkina Faso	EG	Egypt	IO	British Indian Ocean Territory
BG	Bulgaria	EH	Western Sahara	IQ	Iraq
BH	Bahrain	ER	Eritrea	IR	Iran
BI	Burundi	ES	Spain	IS	Iceland
BJ	Benin	ET	Ethiopia	IT	Italy
BM	Bermuda	FI	Finland	JM	Jamaica
BN	Brunei Darussalam	FJ	Fiji	JO	Jordan
BO	Bolivia	FK	Falkland Islands (Malvinas)	JP	Japan
BR	Brazil	FM	Micronesia	KE	Kenya
BS	Bahamas	FO	Faroe Islands	KG	Kyrgyzstan
BT	Bhutan	FR	France	KH	Cambodia
BV	Bouvet Island	GA	Gabon	KI	Kiribati
BW	Botswana	UK	United Kingdom	KM	Comoros
BY	Belarus	GD	Grenada	KN	Saint Kitts and Nevis
BZ	Belize	GE	Georgia	KP	Korea (North)
CA	Canada	GF	French Guiana	KR	Korea (South)
CC	Cocos (Keeling) Islands	GH	Ghana	KW	Kuwait
CD	Congo, Dem. Republic of	GI	Gibraltar	KY	Cayman Islands
CF	Central African Republic	GL	Greenland	KZ	Kazakstan
CG	Congo	GM	Gambia	LA	Laos
CH	Switzerland	GN	Guinea	LB	Lebanon
				LC	Saint Lucia

Country Codes (alphabetical by code)

Code	Country	Code	Country	Code	Country
LI	Liechtenstein	OM	Oman	TF	French Southern Territories
LK	Sri Lanka	PA	Panama	TG	Togo
LR	Liberia	PE	Peru	TH	Thailand
LS	Lesotho	PF	French Polynesia	TJ	Tajikistan
LT	Lithuania	PG	Papua New Guinea	TK	Tokelau
LU	Luxembourg	PH	Philippines	TM	Turkmenistan
LV	Latvia	PK	Pakistan	TN	Tunisia
LY	Libyan Arab Jamahiriya	PL	Poland	TO	Tonga
MA	Morocco	PM	Saint Pierre and Miquelon	TP	East Timor
MC	Monaco	PN	Pitcairn	TR	Turkey
MD	Moldova	PR	Puerto Rico	TT	Trinidad and Tobago
MG	Madagascar	PS	Palestinian Territory	TV	Tuvalu
MH	Marshall Islands	PT	Portugal	TW	Taiwan
MK	Macedonia	PW	Palau	TZ	Tanzania
ML	Mali	PY	Paraguay	UA	Ukraine
MM	Myanmar	QA	Qatar	UG	Uganda
MN	Mongolia	RE	Reunion	UM	U.S. Minor Outlying Islands
MO	Macau	RO	Romania	US	United States
MP	Northern Mariana Islands	RU	Russian Federation	UY	Uruguay
MQ	Martinique	RW	Rwanda	UZ	Uzbekistan
MR	Mauritania	SA	Saudi Arabia	VA	Vatican (Holy See)
MS	Montserrat	SB	Solomon Islands	VC	Saint Vincent and Grenadines
MT	Malta	SC	Seychelles	VE	Venezuela
MU	Mauritius	SD	Sudan	VG	Virgin Islands (British)
MV	Maldives	SE	Sweden	VI	Virgin Islands (U.S.)
MW	Malawi	SG	Singapore	VN	Viet Nam
MX	Mexico	SH	Saint Helena	VU	Vanuatu
MY	Malaysia	SI	Slovenia	WF	Wallis and Futuna
MZ	Mozambique	SJ	Svalbard and Jan Mayen	WS	Samoa
NA	Namibia	SK	Slovakia	YE	Yemen
NC	New Caledonia	SL	Sierra Leone	YT	Mayotte
NE	Niger	SM	San Marino	YU	Yugoslavia
NF	Norfolk Island	SN	Senegal	ZA	South Africa
NG	Nigeria	SO	Somalia	ZM	Zambia
NI	Nicaragua	SR	Suriname	ZW	Zimbabwe
NL	Netherlands	ST	Sao Tome and Principe		
NO	Norway	SV	El Salvador		
NP	Nepal	SY	Syrian Arab Republic		
NR	Nauru	SZ	Swaziland		
NU	Niue	TC	Turks and Caicos Islands		
NZ	New Zealand	TD	Chad		

INTERNET DOMAINS AND COUNTRY CODES

Table B.3

Top-Level Domains (TLDs)	
Common Domains (in use now)	
DOMAIN:	INTENDED FOR USE BY:
com	Commercial establishments/businesses
edu	Educational institutions
gov	Government agencies
int	International organizations
mil	U.S. military facilities
net	Internet networks like EarthLink and ComCast
org	Nonprofit organizations
Newest Top-Level Domains*	
DOMAIN:	INTENDED FOR USE BY:
aero	Airports, airlines, and related companies
biz	Commercial establishments/businesses
coop	Nonprofit cooperatives
info	Information
museum	Museums
name	Individuals
New Domains (approved for use, expected to be implemented soon)	
DOMAIN:	INTENDED FOR USE BY:
pro	Accountants, lawyers, and physicians

*Prior to the addition of these new domains, many individuals registered com, net, and org domains for personal use.

Domain Name Update

For the latest information on the availability of the new Internet top-level domains, visit the ICANN Web site at www.icann.org. ICANN, short for Internet Corporation for Assigned Names and Numbers, is the organization responsible for approving new domains.

USENET NEWSGROUP HIERARCHIES

Google Groups (`groups.google.com`) greatly simplifies the process of finding information in Usenet newsgroups. It's no longer necessary to know exactly which newsgroup deals with a particular topic. Just tell Google that you want to direct your query to newsgroups instead of the Web and let it take care of the details.

Eventually, though, you may want to employ the power-searching technique of limiting your newsgroup queries to *specific* newsgroups. Or you may simply want to know what those "alt-dot-something" names mean and how they get assigned. The key concept is newsgroup *hierarchies*.

The first part of a newsgroup name is the major topic, or *top-level* hierarchy—`alt` for the wildly popular "alternative" newsgroups, `biz` for business-related groups, `comp` for computer hardware and software, `sci` for science, and so forth. Each of these major topics is then broken down into subtopics, and those are broken down again and again as additional groups are created for discussions of greater and greater specificity.

continues on next page

For example, in the alt hierarchy, a group called alt.music might be formed to discuss music in general. Over time, some participants may decide they want to focus on a specific *type* of music, like jazz, while others prefer to discuss bluegrass. So two new groups are formed: alt.music.jazz and alt.music.bluegrass. Things can get even more specific as people decide to focus on a favorite jazz or bluegrass musician. The newsgroup name gets longer and longer as the topic of discussion becomes more and more specific.

Of the hundreds of top-level newsgroup hierarchies, the ones you are most likely to encounter are presented in **Table C.1**, along with brief descriptions.

✔ Tips

- For advice on searching Usenet newsgroups with Google Groups, see Chapter 15.

- Although Google Groups's specialty is newsgroup searches, it isn't the best place to look for a comprehensive list of newsgroup hierarchies. Instead, try one of these sites:

  Master List of Newsgroup Hierarchies: www.magma.ca/~leisen/mlnh

  Tile.Net Newsgroup Hierarchy List: tile.net/news

Table C.1

Popular Usenet Newsgroup Hierarchies	
TOPIC	DESCRIPTION
alt	Alternative newsgroups—everything from sexually oriented topics to the truly offbeat. They're called "alternative" because they don't fit neatly anywhere else. Many Usenet servers don't carry these groups.
bionet	Biology network.
bit	Articles from Bitnet LISTSERV mailing lists; used mainly by the academic community.
biz	Business-related newsgroups. This is the place for advertisements, marketing, and other commercial postings (product announcements, product reviews, demo software, and so on).
cern	Discussions relating to CERN, the European Particle Physics Lab located in Geneva, Switzerland. It was at CERN that Tim Berners-Lee developed the World Wide Web to enhance collaboration on research documents.
clari	ClariNet News, a commercial service providing UPI wire news, newspaper columns like Dave Barry, and lots more to sites that subscribe.
comp	Computer-related newsgroups. Topics of interest to computer professionals and hobbyists, including computer science, software source code, and information on hardware and software systems.
gnu	Discussions about the GNU (Gnu's Not Unix) project and the Free Software Foundation.
hepnet	Higher Energy Physics network.
humanities	Discussions of humanities and the arts.
info	Creators of Internet mailing lists often place their messages automatically into Usenet. This is where you'll find them.
k12	Topics of interest to teachers of kindergarten through grade 12 (curriculum, language exchanges with native speakers, and classroom-to-classroom projects designed by teachers).
linux	Discussions about Linux, a version of the UNIX operating system that's distributed as freeware for use on personal computers. Linux is a system for the very technical professional—not for casual PC users.
microsoft	Newsgroups devoted to discussions of Microsoft products and services.
misc	A catch-all category for groups that address topics not easily classified anywhere else. Two of the most popular are misc.jobs and misc.forsale.
news	Groups concerned with the Usenet network (not current affairs, as you might think). The newsgroups news.announce.newusers, news.newusers.questions, and news.answers are the places to check for information aimed at first-time Internet and newsgroup users.
rec	Groups focusing on recreational activities and hobbies of all sorts—arts and crafts, games, music, sports, and so on.
schl	Resources for elementary and secondary school teachers (similar to k12).
sci	Discussions of scientific research and applied sciences.
soc	Groups devoted to social issues, often related to a particular culture.
talk	Debates and long-winded discussions without resolution and with very little useful information.
vmsnet	Virtual Memory System Net, a place where people talk about VAX/VMS issues.

USENET NEWSGROUP HIERARCHIES

INDEX

INDEX

INDEX